HBJ TREASURY OF LITERATURE

FEAST YOUR EYES

SENIOR AUTHORS
ROGER C. FARR
DOROTHY S. STRICKLAND

AUTHORS
RICHARD F. ABRAHAMSON
ELLEN BOOTH CHURCH
BARBARA BOWEN COULTER
MARGARET A. GALLEGO
JUDITH L. IRVIN
KAREN KUTIPER
JUNKO YOKOTA LEWIS
DONNA M. OGLE
TIMOTHY SHANAHAN
PATRICIA SMITH

SENIOR CONSULTANTS
BERNICE E. CULLINAN
W. DORSEY HAMMOND
ASA G. HILLIARD III

CONSULTANTS
ALONZO A. CRIM
ROLANDO R. HINOJOSA-SMITH
LEE BENNETT HOPKINS
ROBERT J. STERNBERG

 HARCOURT BRACE JOVANOVICH, INC.
Orlando Austin San Diego Chicago Dallas New York

Requests for permission to make copies of any part of the work should be mailed to: Permissions Department, Harcourt Brace Jovanovich, Publishers, 8th Floor, Orlando, Florida 32887

Printed in the United States of America

ISBN 0-15-300424-X

2 3 4 5 6 7 8 9 10   048   96   95   94   93

Acknowledgments continue on page 590, which constitutes an extension of this copyright page.

Acknowledgments
For permission to reprint copyrighted material, grateful acknowledgment is made to the following sources:
Atheneum Publishers, an imprint of Macmillan Publishing Company: The Gold Coin by Alma Flor Ada, illustrated by Neil Waldman. Text copyright © 1991 by Alma Flor Ada; illustrations copyright © 1991 by Neil Waldman. Cover illustration from *The Big Tree* by Bruce Hiscock. Copyright © 1991 by Bruce Hiscock. Cover illustration by Nancy Oleksa from *The Chickenhouse House* by Ellen Howard. Illustration copyright © 1991 by Nancy Oleksa.
Avon Books: From pp. 9-21 in *The Plant That Ate Dirty Socks* (Retitled: "The Amazing Beans") by Nancy McArthur. Text copyright © 1988 by Nancy McArthur.
Black Butterfly Children's Books: "Grandma's Bones" from *Nathaniel Talking* by Eloise Greenfield. Text copyright © 1988 by Eloise Greenfield; illustrations © 1988 by Jan Spivey Gilchrist.
David Boxley: Illustrations by David Boxley from *Totem Pole* by Diane Hoyt-Goldsmith. Copyright © 1990 by David Boxley.
Bradbury Press, an Affiliate of Macmillan, Inc.: Cover illustration by Clifford Faust from *Windcatcher* by Avi. Illustration copyright © 1991 by Clifford Faust. *Dream Wolf* by Paul Goble. Copyright © 1990 by Paul Goble.
Curtis Brown, Ltd.: "Last Laugh" by Lee Bennett Hopkins. Text copyright © 1974 by Lee Bennett Hopkins.
Curtis Brown Group Ltd., London: "Come on into My Tropical Garden" from *Come on into My Tropical Garden* by Grace Nichols. Text copyright © 1984 by Grace Nichols.
Carolrhoda Books, Inc., Minneapolis, MN: Cover illustration from *A Pianist's Debut* by Barbara Beirne. Copyright © 1990 by Carolrhoda Books, Inc. Cover illustration by Amy Johnson from *What Are You Figuring Now? A Story about Benjamin Banneker* by Jeri Ferris. Illustration copyright © 1988 by Carolrhoda Books, Inc.
Childrens Press: Kwanzaa by Deborah M. Newton Chocolate, illustrated by Melodye Rosales. Copyright © 1990 by Childrens Press®, Inc.
Clarion Books, a Houghton Mifflin Company imprint: Cover photograph by Peter Ziebel from *Greening the City Streets: The Story of Community Gardens* by Barbara H. Huff. Photograph copyright © 1990 by Peter Ziebel.
Cobblehill Books, an affiliate of Dutton Children's Books, a division of Penguin Books USA Inc.: Excerpted from *The Canada Geese Quilt* (Retitled: "The Very Special Gift") by Natalie Kinsey-Warnock. Text copyright © 1989 by Natalie Kinsey-Warnock.
Cobblestone Publishing, Inc., Peterborough, NH 03458: "Happy Vietnamese Holiday" by Tran Phuong Hoa and "Happy Holidays" from *FACES: Happy Holidays*, December 1990. Text © 1990 by Cobblestone Publishing, Inc.
CPP Belwin, Inc.: Lyrics from "Talk To The Animals," music and lyrics by Leslie Bricusse. © 1967 by Twentieth Century Music Corporation. Rights assigned to EMI Catalogue Partnership and controlled and administered by EMI Hastings Catalog Inc. International copyright secured.
Crown Publishers, Inc.: Cover illustration by Robert Andrew Parker from *Grandfather Tang's Story* by Ann Tompert. Illustration copyright © 1990 by Robert Andrew Parker.
Jackie Dedell, on behalf of Richard Williams: Cover illustration by Richard Williams from *Encyclopedia Brown Gets His Man* by Donald J. Sobol.
Dial Books for Young Readers, a division of Penguin Books USA Inc.: Cover illustration by Jerry Pinkney from *Yagua Days* by Cruz Martel. Illustration copyright © 1976 by Jerry Pinkney.
Doubleday, a division of Bantam Doubleday Dell Publishing Group, Inc.: "Sun Dancers" by Patricia Irving from *The Whispering Wind* by Terry Allen. Text copyright © 1972 by the Institute of American Indian Arts.
Farrar, Straus & Giroux, Inc.: Cover illustration from *Kneeknock Rise* by Natalie Babbitt. Copyright © 1970 by Natalie Babbitt. "The Drum" from *Spin a Soft Black Sun* by Nikki Giovanni. Text copyright © 1971, 1985 by Nikki Giovanni.
Sid Fleischman, Inc.: McBroom Tells the Truth by Sid Fleischman. Text copyright © 1966 by Sid Fleischman.
Four Winds Press, an imprint of Macmillan Publishing Company: Cover illustration by Ruth Chew from *Shark Lady: True Adventures of Eugenie Clark* by Ann McGovern. Copyright © 1978 by Ann McGovern.
Greenwillow Books, a division of William Morrow & Company, Inc.: Cover illustration by James Stevenson from *Georgia Music* by Helen V. Griffith. Illustration copyright © 1986 by James Stevenson. *Music, Music for Everyone* by Vera B. Williams. Copyright © 1984 by Vera B. Williams.
Harcourt Brace Jovanovich, Inc.: The Great Kapok Tree by Lynne Cherry. Copyright © 1990 by Lynne Cherry. "The Marmalade Man Makes a Dance to Mend Us" from *A Visit to William Blake's Inn* by Nancy Willard, illustrated by Alice and Martin Provensen. Text copyright © 1981 by Nancy Willard; illustrations copyright © 1981 by Alice and Martin Provensen. Pronunciation Key from *HBJ School Dictionary*, Third Edition. Text copyright © 1990 by Harcourt Brace Jovanovich, Inc.

continued on page 590

HBJ TREASURY OF LITERATURE

Dear Reader,

A character in this book is asked in a dream, "If you destroy the beauty of the rain forest, on what would you feast your eyes?" The literature in this book will challenge you to make decisions as this character must. And you'll feast your eyes on many different kinds of people. As you read, celebrate their beauty—and yours!

Because our country is made up of people from many different places, we are able to enjoy a wide variety of celebrations. Perhaps you've wondered how some of these are alike and different. The literature in this book will transport you to some special times and different cultures. You'll be invited to join an African American family's Kwanzaa celebration. You'll see, hear, and even smell a Vietnamese New Year celebration. You'll share a Polish family's joy as they celebrate their arrival in America. You'll make connections between some of these celebrations and a holiday celebrated by Hispanics both in Mexico and in the United States.

We invite you to make *Feast Your Eyes* an important part of a wonderful school year. We invite you to laugh and cry with the characters, and to explore the wonders of the plant and animal kingdoms. Maybe you'll be moved to change the world for the better. Our invitation may best be stated in these lines by poet Grace Nichols:

> Come on into my tropical garden
> Come on in and have a laugh in
> Taste my sugar cake and my pine drink
> Come on in please come on in

Sincerely,
The Authors

FEAST YOUR EYES

C O N T E N T S

UNIT TWO

ANIMAL·TALES

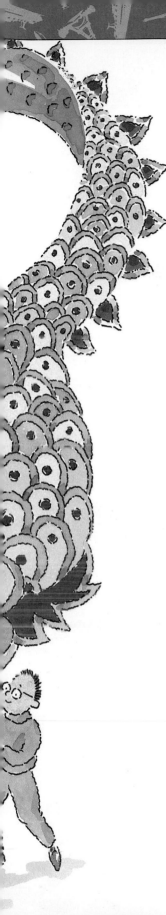

STARGAZERS / 526

UNIT ONE

CELEBRATIONS

How and why do people celebrate important events and holidays? Whether they jump in jubilation for a personal victory or attend a festive cultural celebration such as Kwanzaa or Cinco de Mayo, each event is special. Keep your favorite celebration in mind as you read to appreciate those that are important to others.

BOOKSHELF

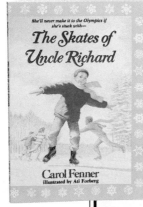

THE SKATES OF UNCLE RICHARD

BY CAROL FENNER

Marsha dreams of performing on the ice in shining white skates, looking like the champion skaters she watches on television. She feels her dream fading when she receives Uncle Richard's old skates for Christmas.

HBJ LIBRARY BOOK

SCHOOL'S OUT

BY JOHANNA HURWITZ

Lucas Cott is looking forward to having the summer off from school. But with the help of Genevieve, the babysitter, he learns a lesson in responsibility.

AWARD-WINNING AUTHOR

A PIANIST'S DEBUT: PREPARING FOR THE CONCERT STAGE

BY BARBARA BEIRNE

Leah dreams of being a concert pianist. She studies and practices hard to be accepted into the famous Juilliard School. Then she prepares for her first New York recital.

GETTING ELECTED: THE DIARY OF A CAMPAIGN

BY JOAN HEWETT

Gloria Molina wants to be elected to the California State Assembly. Read to see whether her hard work and campaigning pay off. AWARD-WINNING AUTHOR

GEORGIA MUSIC

BY HELEN V. GRIFFITH

When a young girl visits her grandfather on his Georgia farm, she learns to appreciate the sounds of the country, especially those of her grandfather's harmonica.
ALA NOTABLE BOOK,
BOSTON GLOBE-HORN BOOK
HONOR, SLJ BEST BOOKS
OF THE YEAR

CONTESTS

Have you ever been involved in a contest or class election that you hoped more than anything to win? Author Johanna Hurwitz's characters find that such events are filled with surprises—and fun!

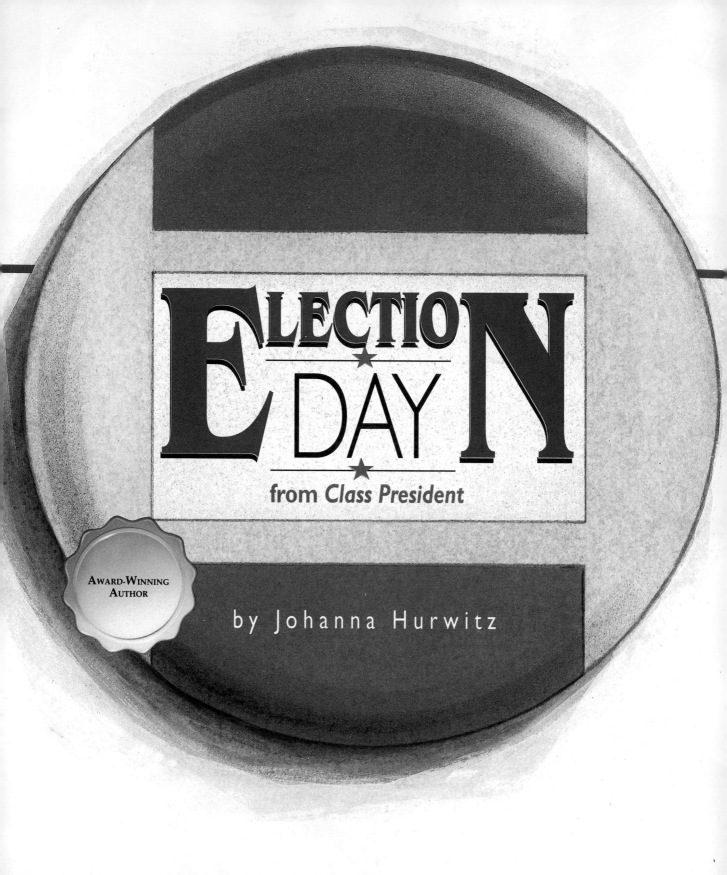

ELECTION DAY

from *Class President*

by Johanna Hurwitz

illustrated by Michael Koelsch

AWARD-WINNING
AUTHOR

Julio's new teacher, Mr. Flores, has announced that there will be an election for class president. At first, it seems like a contest between Cricket Kaufman and Lucas Cott, two of the most popular students. But although Julio has promised to help Lucas campaign, he wonders what qualities a president should have besides popularity.

Before lunch, Mr. Flores read an announcement from the principal. "From now on, there is to be no more soccer playing in the schoolyard at lunchtime."

"No more soccer playing?" Julio called out. "Why not?"

Mr. Flores looked at Julio. "If you give me a moment, I'll explain. Mr. Herbertson is concerned about accidents. Last week, Arthur broke his glasses. Another time, someone might be injured more seriously."

Julio was about to call out again, but he remembered just in time and raised his hand.

"Yes, Julio," said Mr. Flores.

"It's not fair to make us stop playing soccer just because someone *might* get hurt. Someone might fall down walking to school, but we still have to come to school every day."

Julio didn't mean to be funny, but everyone started to laugh. Even Mr. Flores smiled.

"There must be other activities to keep you fellows busy at lunchtime," he said. "Is soccer the only thing you can do?"

Lucas raised his hand. "I don't like jumping rope," he said when the teacher called on him.

All the girls giggled at that.

"You could play jacks," suggested Cricket. Everyone knew it wasn't a serious possibility, though.

"Couldn't we tell Mr. Herbertson that we want to play soccer?" asked Julio.

"You could make an appointment to speak to him, if you'd like," said Mr. Flores. "He might change his decision if you convince him that you are right."

"Lucas and I will talk to him," said Julio. "Right, Lucas?"

"Uh, sure," said Lucas, but he didn't look too sure.

The principal, Mr. Herbertson, spoke in a loud voice and had eyes that seemed to bore right into your head when he looked at you. Julio had been a little bit afraid of Mr. Herbertson since the very first day of kindergarten. Why had he offered to go to his office and talk to him?

Mr. Flores sent Julio and Lucas down to the principal's office with a note, but the principal was out of the office at a meeting.

"You can talk to him at one o'clock," the secretary said.

At lunch, Cricket had chocolate bars. This time, she had pasted labels on them and printed in tiny letters, *Cricket is the ticket*. She must be spending her whole allowance on the campaign, Julio thought.

After a few more days of free chocolate bars, everyone in the class would be voting for Cricket.

At recess, the girls were jumping rope. You could fall jumping rope, too, Julio thought.

Back in the classroom, Julio wished he could think up some good arguments to tell the principal. He looked over at Lucas. Lucas didn't look very good. Maybe he was coming down with the flu.

Just before one o'clock, Julio had a great idea. Cricket was always saying she wanted to be a lawyer. She always knew what to say in class. Julio figured she'd know just what to do in the principal's office, too. He raised his hand.

"Mr. Flores, can Cricket go down to Mr. Herbertson's office with Lucas and me? She's running for president, so she should stick up for our class."

"Me?" Cricket said. "I don't care if we can't play soccer."

"Of course," teased Lucas. "You couldn't kick a ball if it was glued to your foot."

"Cricket," said Mr. Flores, "even if you don't want to play soccer, others in the class do. If you are elected, you will be president of the whole class, not just the girls. I think going to the meeting with Mr. Herbertson will be a good opportunity for you to represent the class."

So that was why at one o'clock Julio, Lucas, and Cricket Kaufman went downstairs to the principal's office.

Mr. Herbertson gestured for them to sit in the chairs facing his desk. Cricket looked as pale as Lucas. Maybe she, too, was coming down with the flu.

Julio waited for the future woman President of the United States to say something, but Cricket didn't say a word. Neither did Lucas. Julio didn't know what to do. They couldn't just sit here and say nothing.

Julio took a deep breath. If Cricket or Lucas wasn't going to talk, he would have to do it. Julio started right in.

"We came to tell you that it isn't fair that no one can play soccer at recess just because Arthur Lewis broke his eyeglasses. Anybody can have an accident. He could have tripped and broken them getting on the school bus." Julio was amazed that so many words had managed to get out of his mouth. No one else said anything, so he went on. "Besides, a girl could fall jumping rope," said Julio. "But you didn't say that they had to stop jumping rope."

"I hadn't thought of that," said Mr. Herbertson.

Cricket looked alarmed. "Can't we jump rope anymore?" she asked.

"I didn't mean that you should make the girls stop jumping rope," Julio went on quickly. He stopped to think of a better example. "Your chair could break while you're sitting on it, Mr. Herbertson," he said.

Mr. Herbertson adjusted himself in his chair. "I certainly hope not," he said, smiling. "What is your name, young man?"

"Julio. Julio Sanchez." He pronounced it in the Spanish way with the *J* having an *H* sound.

"You have a couple of brothers who also attended this school, Julio, don't you?" asked the principal. "Nice fellows. I remember them both."

Julio smiled. He didn't know why he had always been afraid of the principal. He was just like any other person.

"Julio," Mr. Herbertson went on, "you've got a good head on your shoulders, just like your brothers. You made some very good points this afternoon. I think I can arrange things so that there will be more teachers supervising the yard during recess. Then you fellows can play soccer again tomorrow." He turned to Cricket. "You can jump rope if you'd rather do that," he said.

Cricket smiled. She didn't look so pale anymore.

Julio and Lucas and Cricket returned to Mr. Flores's classroom. "It's all arranged," said Cricket as soon as they walked in the door.

The class burst into cheers.

"Good work," said Mr. Flores.

Julio was proud that he had stood up to Mr. Herbertson. However, it wasn't fair that Cricket made it seem as if she had done all the work. She had hardly done a thing. For that matter, Lucas hadn't said anything, either. For a moment Julio wished he hadn't offered to be Lucas's campaign manager. He wished he was the one running for class president. He knew he could be a good leader.

There was bad news on election day. Chris Willard was absent. Since there were twelve girls and twelve boys in Mr. Flores's class, it meant there were more girls than boys to vote in the election. If all the girls voted for Cricket and all the boys voted for Lucas, there would be a tie. Since one boy was absent, Lucas could be in big trouble. Julio hoped it didn't mean that Lucas had lost the election before they even voted.

Then Mr. Flores told the class that the Parent-Teacher Association was going to be holding a book fair in a few weeks. With more than seventeen dollars from the bake sale, the class could buy a good supply of paperbacks for a special classroom library. Cricket seemed to think it was a great idea, but Julio didn't think it was so hot. After all, there was a school library up one flight of stairs. Why did they need extra books, especially books the students had to pay for out of their *own* money?

Julio thought that the class should vote on the way the money was spent. Before he had a chance to say anything, it was time for lunch.

Lunch was chicken nuggets, whipped potatoes, and string beans. Cricket and Zoe didn't even touch their lunches. Julio knew they were talking about the election. Julio clapped Lucas on the back. "You're going to win, pal," he said. "I just know it." He really wasn't so sure, but he felt it was his job to give his candidate confidence. After all, he had convinced Lucas to run for class president in the first place.

Lucas shrugged, trying to act cool. "Maybe yes, maybe no," he said. But Julio could see that he was too excited to eat much lunch, either. Julio polished off his friend's tunafish sandwich and his orange. "I need to keep up my strength to vote for you," he told Lucas.

Cricket had more chocolate bars. "Are you going to vote for me?" she asked everyone.

"Maybe yes, maybe no," said Julio, taking his bar.

When they returned from lunch, Mr. Flores called the class to order. It was time for the election to begin. Mr. Flores reminded them about *Robert's Rules of Order*, which was the way school board and other important meetings were conducted.

"You may nominate anyone you choose," he said, "even if your candidate doesn't have a poster up on the wall. Then you can make a speech in favor of your candidate and try to convince your classmates."

Uh-oh, thought Julio. He was ready to nominate Lucas but he didn't know if he would be able to make a speech. He wasn't good with words, as Cricket and Lucas were.

Zoe Mitchell raised her hand. "I nominate Cricket Kaufman," she said. No surprise there. Julio wondered if Zoe had wanted to run herself.

"Does anyone second the nomination?" Mr. Flores asked.

Julio thought the class election sounded like a TV program, not the way people talked in real life.

Sara Jane seconded the nomination, and Mr. Flores wrote Cricket's name on the chalkboard.

"Are there any other nominations?" he asked.

Sara Jane raised her hand again.

"Do you have a question, Sara Jane?" asked Mr. Flores.

"Now I want to nominate Zoe Mitchell."

"You can't nominate someone when you have already seconded the nomination of someone else," Mr. Flores explained. "That's the way parliamentary procedure works."

Cricket looked relieved. She hadn't been expecting any competition from Zoe.

Julio raised his hand. "I nominate Lucas Cott," he said.

"Does anyone second the nomination?"

"Can I second myself?" asked Lucas.

"I'll second the nomination," said Anne Crosby from the back of the classroom.

"*Ooooh,*" giggled one of the girls. "Anne likes Lucas."

"There is no rule that girls can nominate only girls and boys nominate boys," said Mr. Flores. He wrote Lucas's name on the board. "Are there any other nominations?" he asked.

Arthur Lewis raised his hand. "I want to nominate Julio Sanchez," he said.

"Julio?" Sara Jane giggled. "He's just a big goof-off."

"Just a minute," said Mr. Flores sharply. "You are quite out of order, Sara Jane. Does anyone wish to second the nomination?"

Julio couldn't believe that Arthur had nominated him. Even though Arthur had said that Julio should run for president, Julio hadn't thought he would come right out and say it in front of everyone.

Cricket raised her hand. "Julio can't run for president," she said. "He was born in Puerto Rico. He isn't an American citizen. You have to be an American citizen to be elected President. We learned that last year in social studies."

"Yeah," Lucas called out. "You also have to be thirty-five years old. You must have been left back a lot of times, Cricket."

"Hold on," said Mr. Flores. "Are we electing a President of the United States here, or are we electing a president of this fifth-grade class?"

Cricket looked embarrassed. It wasn't often she was wrong about anything.

Julio stood up without even raising his hand. He didn't care if he was elected president or not, but there was one thing he had to make clear. "I am so an American citizen," he said. "All Puerto Ricans are Americans!"

Julio sat down, and Arthur raised his hand again. Julio figured he was going to say he had changed his mind and didn't want to nominate him after all.

"Arthur?" called Mr. Flores.

Arthur stood up. "It doesn't matter where Julio was born," he said. "He'd make a very good class president. He's fair, and he's always doing nice things for people. When I broke my glasses, he was the one who thought of going to Mr. Herbertson so that we could still play soccer at recess. That shows he would make a good president."

"But Julio is not one of the top students like Zoe or Lucas or me," Cricket said.

"He is tops," said Arthur. "He's tops in my book."

Julio felt his ears getting hot with embarrassment. He had never heard Arthur say so much in all the years that he had known him.

"Thank you, Arthur," said Mr. Flores. "That was a very good speech. We still need someone to second the nomination. Do I hear a second?"

Lucas raised his hand.

"I second the nomination of Julio Sanchez," he said.

Mr. Flores turned to write Julio's name on the board. Lucas was still raising his hand.

Mr. Flores turned from the board and called on Lucas again.

"Do you wish to make a campaign speech?" he asked Lucas.

"Yes. I'm going to vote for Julio, and I think everyone else should, too."

"Aren't you even going to vote for yourself?" asked Cricket.

"No," said Lucas. "I want to take my name off the

board. Julio is a good leader, like Arthur said. When we went to see Mr. Herbertson, Cricket and I were scared stiff, but Julio just stepped in and did all the talking."

"Are you asking to withdraw your name from nomination, Lucas?" asked Mr. Flores.

"Yes, I am. Everyone who was going to vote for me should vote for Julio."

Julio sat in his seat without moving. He couldn't say a word. He could hardly breathe.

"Are there any other nominations?" asked Mr. Flores.

Zoe raised her hand. "I move that the nominations be closed."

"I second it," said Lucas.

Then Mr. Flores asked the two candidates if they wanted to say anything to the class.

Cricket stood up. "As you all know," she said, "I'm going to run for President of the United States some day. Being class president will be good practice for me. Besides, I know I will do a much, much better job than Julio." Cricket sat down.

Julio stood. "I might vote for Cricket when she runs for President of the United States," he said. "But right now, I hope you will all vote for me. I think our class should make decisions together, like how we should spend the money that we earned at the bake sale. We should spend the money in a way that everyone likes. Not just the teacher." Julio stopped and looked at Mr. Flores. "That's how I feel," he said.

"If I'm president," said Cricket, "I think the money should go to the Humane Society."

"*You* shouldn't tell us what to do with the money, either," said Julio. "It should be a class decision. We all helped to earn it."

"Julio has made a good point," said Mr. Flores. "I guess we can vote on that in the future."

Mr. Flores passed out the ballots. Julio was sure he knew the results even before the votes were counted. With one boy absent, Cricket would win, twelve to eleven.

Julio was right, and he was wrong. All the boys voted for him, but so did some of the girls. When the votes were counted, there were fourteen for Julio Sanchez and nine for Cricket Kaufman. Julio Sanchez was elected president of his fifth-grade class.

"I think you have made a good choice," said Mr. Flores. "And I know that Cricket will be a very fine vice-president."

Julio beamed. Suddenly he was filled with all sorts of plans for his class.

Mr. Flores took out his guitar. As he had said, they were going to end each week with some singing. Julio thought he had never felt so much like singing in all his life. However, even as he joined the class in the words to the song, he wished it was already time to go home. He could hardly wait to tell his family the news. Wait till he told them who was the fifth-grade class president. Julio, that's who!

At three o'clock, he ran all the way home.

★ ☆ ★

THINK IT OVER

1. *What qualities did Julio display throughout the story that proved he would make a good class president?*

2. *Why did Julio want Cricket to go with him to the principal's office?*

3. *Why do you think Cricket and Lucas were silent in the principal's office?*

4. *At what point in the story did you know that Julio would be elected class president?*

WRITE

Imagine that you nominated one of your classmates for a club office. Write a list of reasons that tells why others should vote for your candidate.

What would you enjoy most about being a writer? Here is what Johanna Hurwitz shares.

"When you're a writer, you're in charge of the world. If it's a school holiday and it's pouring rain, you might not be able to do what you want. But in my story, if it's raining, I just write, 'It stopped raining,' and it always does. That's a very powerful feeling."

When Johanna Hurwitz first started writing *Class President*, she began writing about Lucas, the class clown who was talked into running for class president. But the more she wrote about Lucas, the more Julio, his best friend and campaign manager, was right there with him. Ms. Hurwitz thought Julio was such a nice kid that she decided to write about him, too. She didn't know when she wrote *Class Clown* that there would be a *Class President*, but Julio just moved in and before she knew it, he had his own book!

IMPORTANT MESSAGE

FOR Johanna

DATE 16-2-93   TIME   A.M. P.M.

David Lloyd

AREA CODE   NUMBER   EXTENSION

CODE   NUMBER   TIME TO CALL

✓ PLEASE CALL

WILL CALL AGAIN

RUSH

As a child, Johanna Hurwitz especially liked to read series of books, such as Maud Hart Lovelace's books about friends Betsy, Tacy, and Tib. She also liked Carolyn Haywood's series about another character named Betsy. In fact, she identified so strongly with that name that she actually wanted to change her own name to Betsy.

Now Ms. Hurwitz writes her own series books about school-children. Read more about Julio, Lucas, and Cricket in *Class Clown*, *Teacher's Pet*, and *School's Out*.

Ms. Hurwitz says, "It's very thrilling to know that something I've written here in my home is being read halfway across the country, or around the world, by children I'll never know but who will know me through my stories and my characters. I got a letter from Papua New Guinea. It's mind-boggling to think that a child there is reading about Aldo."

Words from the Author:

Johanna Hurwitz

MUDDY SNEAKERS

from
Aldo Ice Cream
by Johanna Hurwitz
illustrated by Michael Koelsch

Aldo Sossi wants to buy a special birthday present, an ice-cream freezer, for his sister Karen. To do so, he has borrowed quarters from everyone in his family. Aldo is still far from his goal by the time his best friend DeDe returns from vacation.

On the fifteenth of August, when there were only seventeen more days till Karen's birthday and twenty more days of school vacation, the sun came out. It shone so brightly that Aldo thought it wouldn't rain again for the rest of the month. At last he was able to go off to his swimming lesson. To his relief, he had not forgotten anything.

41

After a good lesson, Aldo went home. He was hoping there might be another letter from DeDe waiting for him. There wasn't, so he started looking through the *Pennysaver*, which had arrived that morning. He had given up looking for a job, but still he looked through the little newspaper out of habit. You never knew when you might find something interesting. Sure enough, midway through the pages, there was a large advertisement for the local shoe store. It read:

Grubby-Sneaker CONTEST

Any Woodside child up to age twelve can enter. Bring your worst-looking, most grubby, absolutely filthy and gross pair of sneakers at 10:30 A.M., August 31. The winner will be announced at noon that day and will be awarded a *free* pair of sneakers.

Aldo looked down at his feet. His sneakers were still caked with bits of dry mud. There was a small hole where he had torn the canvas when he fell off his bike one day. The sneakers were in bad shape, but they could be worse. Aldo decided that he would make them worse.

He showed the advertisement to his mother. "What a great way to save money!" said Mrs. Sossi, laughing. "I think you have a fair chance to win."

Aldo got an idea. "If I won the free pair of sneakers, would you add the money that you save by not having to pay for new sneakers to the ice-cream-freezer fund?"

So far there were only three dollars in his fund. (One dollar had come from two baby molars that had fallen out and for which he had collected fifty cents each.) Sneakers could cost as much as fifteen or even twenty dollars. The total amount would still be a lot less than he needed for the ice-cream freezer, but it was worth trying.

"Sure," agreed Mrs. Sossi. "I've nothing to lose."

Aldo could hardly wait to finish his lunch. He would have a busy afternoon ahead of him. He started thinking of the places in town where the sun wouldn't yet have dried up the puddles. He was determined that he would have the muddiest, grubbiest sneakers in the history of the world, or at least in the history of Woodside, New Jersey.

During the days that followed, Aldo kept his eyes on the ground. Wherever he walked, he was watching to see the effect upon his sneakers. He stepped everywhere and into everything: puddles, mudholes, and on rocks. He never stood still. He never sat still. He was busy wearing out his sneakers. At the same time, he was busy looking at other people's feet. He looked at the sneakers of the other boys and girls at the pool. He saw a pair of sandals that one of the girls was wearing. The straps were broken, and the sole was separating from the bottom of the shoe. Those sandals would have won first prize in an old-sandal contest, but Aldo didn't have to worry about them competing against him.

Another day Aldo saw two boys walking along on the main street of Woodside. One was wearing sneakers that looked much worse than Aldo's. He was a tall boy with red hair, and his sneakers had once upon a time been red too. But now they were an indescribable color. The red-headed boy was walking with Michael Frank, who had been in Aldo's fourth-grade class.

"Hi, Michael," said Aldo.

"Hi, Applesauce," he responded, calling Aldo by his school nickname.

"Applesauce?" asked the redheaded boy.

"Yep!" said Aldo. "Who are you?"

"Trevor," he said. "I'm Mike's cousin."

"He's staying with me this week," Michael explained.

"When are you going home?" asked Aldo.

"Day after tomorrow probably," said Trevor.

"Oh," said Aldo. He almost said "good," but he caught himself in time. Trevor, with his worn-out sneakers, would be out of town before the grubby-sneaker contest.

"Well, see you around," said Aldo, hoping he wouldn't. The sooner Trevor left town, the better Aldo's chances of winning the contest would be.

Trevor's sneakers worried Aldo. He saw that his own were not as bad as they could be. So he started to work harder than ever. He hiked to the park, and he climbed on some jagged rocks there. Then he went home and offered to run any errands his mother might have. Next he walked over to Mr. Puccini's house, instead of taking his bike, even though he had been there the day before. Wearing out his sneakers was an exhausting business. Aldo wasn't sure he could keep up the same level of activity.

One night, when he was getting ready for bed and taking off his sneakers, Aldo thought what a shame it was that the sneakers wouldn't be getting any dirtier during the night. Too bad he couldn't invent some sort of robot that could walk about in his sneakers while he was sleeping. Then Aldo got an idea. He found a corner where nothing was growing in the garden and started to dig with his father's little spade. It wasn't easy to dig in the dark. He kept hitting hard things, which he knew were probably tree roots.

Mrs. Sossi called to him. "Aldo, what are you doing? Aren't you going to bed tonight?"

"I'll be right in," Aldo called back.

He kept digging until the hole was large enough to hold both of his sneakers. Then he covered them with the dirt and stones and walked barefoot into the house.

"How did you get so dirty at this hour?" asked Mrs. Sossi.

"Easy!" said Aldo, wiping the dirt from his hands onto his jeans. "My sneakers are camping out tonight."

"You'd better jump into the shower before you jump into bed," instructed his mother.

Aldo did so. As he stood in the shower with the water dripping down his back, he wondered if perhaps tomorrow night he should wear his sneakers into the shower. The water might add to the aging process. But he wondered how he could wear them into the shower and then bury them outside again.

Wearing out those sneakers was turning out to be hard work.

DeDe returned from her grandparents' six days before the grubby sneakers were to be judged. "I wish

I had known about it," she complained to Aldo, when he brought her up-to-date on the local news. She was wearing a pair of new purple sneakers that her grandparents had bought for her in Michigan. "My grandmother told me to throw my old ones away. She said they smelled."

"Not as bad as mine," said Aldo proudly. He removed his left sneaker and held it up to DeDe's nose.

"Phew," she said, holding her nose. "If they judge by smell, you'll win for sure."

But on the day of the contest Aldo wasn't so sure. About twenty kids were gathered at the Walk Well Shoe Store, and each of them was carrying a pair of old, worn-out, dirty sneakers. Aldo stood wearing his good shoes and carrying his sneakers too. The shoes were practically new because he only wore them to church and on very special occasions. They had gotten too small over the summer, and they hurt his feet badly. His little toes were so squeezed that he could hardly walk.

DeDe had come along to watch the judging. "Yours look the worst," she assured Aldo.

He smiled at her. He was feeling nervous, and it was good to have someone around for moral support.

One of the salesmen handed out tags to each of the children. "Tie your sneakers together," he instructed them, "and then put your name and address on the tag."

None of the boys and girls had a pencil or a pen. The only time Aldo had even touched a pen all summer was when he had written his letter to DeDe. So the name writing took a long time as they all shared the two pencils provided by the store.

Finally all the sneakers were tied together and labeled and set in a long row. All the kids crowded around to look at them. They certainly made a dirty, muddy, smelly collection.

"Ouch." Someone stepped on Aldo's little toe. It hurt terribly, but he didn't care. If he won, it would be worth it.

"Come back at noon," said the salesman. "We'll have picked the winner by then."

The boys and girls started pushing their way out of the store. "Ouch." Someone stepped on Aldo's other toe.

"Do you want to go home, or what?" asked DeDe, when they got outside the store.

"I don't think I can walk anywhere," said Aldo. He sat down on the curb outside the store and removed his shoes. He massaged his little toes. "Let's just sit here," he said.

DeDe sat beside Aldo. He turned to face the shoe store. He wondered how the judging was going. Another girl was walking into the store with a pair of sneakers. He could see that they weren't nearly as worn as his. Now that his shoes were off and he could think about something other than his toes again, Aldo considered his chances of winning. He didn't think any of the sneakers looked as bad as his.

"I sure hope I win," he said to DeDe. "It's my last chance to earn some money this summer."

They saw two more boys coming down the street. The deadline for entering the contest was 10:30 A.M. These sneakers would probably be the last entries. The boys came closer. They were Michael Frank and his cousin Trevor.

"Hi, Frankfurter," DeDe called out.

Aldo didn't say anything. He was too surprised to see Trevor to remember anything else. Hadn't he said that he would be going home in a couple of days? Why was he still here? Trevor was carrying his old sneakers. Even after all the hard work he had put in, Aldo could see that Trevor's sneakers looked worse than his own. Now he would never win the contest.

"I thought you were going home," said Aldo. His voice sounded choked and strange as he spoke. He felt like crying.

"Yeah, I thought so too," said Trevor. "But my little sister just got chicken pox, and my aunt said I should stay on here so I wouldn't catch it from her."

The cousins went inside the shoe store.

Aldo felt awful. "Let's take a walk," he said to DeDe, as he started to put his shoes back on.

"I thought your feet hurt," she said.

"They're OK now," said Aldo. Even though she was his best friend, he didn't want to tell her that the disappointment of losing hurt even worse than his feet.

They walked slowly up the street, looking in the store windows. The stationery store had a big display of notebooks and pencils and other school supplies.

"Only four more days," said DeDe.

They walked on, stopping at each window. The ice-cream store had a sign about a new flavor that had been added to its list, *schoolberry.*

"What do you suppose that really is?" asked DeDe.

"It probably has pieces of homework chopped up inside it," said Aldo in a gloomy voice.

"Hey, don't sound so sad," said DeDe. "Even if school opens, we'll still have fun."

When they reached the hardware store, there was a big sign in that window too: *End-of-Summer-Sale! $10 Off the Price of Any Lawn Mower, Sprinkler Set, Plastic Pool, Ice-Cream Freezer.*

For a moment Aldo felt great. "Hey look! The ice-cream freezer will only cost thirty-nine dollars and ninety-five cents now." But then he remembered that after paying back the borrowed quarters he had only three dollars saved. Now that he wasn't going to win the contest there was no way in the world he could earn thirty-six dollars and ninety-five cents by tomorrow, which was Karen's birthday.

"I guess Karen will have to wait until she's grown up to get the ice-cream freezer," Aldo said, sighing.

"She probably won't want it then," said DeDe. "Grown-ups never want the same things that kids do."

When they came to the bookstore, Aldo suggested that they go inside. "Maybe I can pick out a cookbook for Karen," he said.

Inside it was air-conditioned. DeDe found a cartoon book and sat down on the floor to look at it. Aldo went over to the cookbook section. He figured that he had enough money to buy two paperback cookbooks. The trouble was that there were so many books he didn't know how to pick just two. He began looking through them. "Are you planning to buy something, young man?" asked a salesman.

"I can't decide which is the best for my sister's birthday," said Aldo.

"That's a fine one in your hand," said the salesman. But there was something in his tone that made Aldo suspect he had never cooked a thing in his life. He probably didn't want kids hanging around inside his store.

"I think I'll ask my mother what she thinks I should buy," said Aldo, getting up.

"It's almost noon," said DeDe, when they were outside. "I can tell because I'm getting hungry." The clock in the jeweler's window agreed with DeDe's stomach. It was ten minutes to twelve. They walked back toward the shoe store. Aldo moved slowly, partly because his feet hurt in the too-small shoes and partly because he didn't want to see the sign announcing that Trevor was the winner.

A few boys and girls were already waiting in front of the store. They blocked the window so Aldo couldn't see the display of old sneakers. But he could read the big new sign that said, *If Your Child's Sneakers Look Like This, It's Time for a New Pair.*

Aldo pushed through the crowd to look at the sneakers. He saw Trevor's old red sneakers right in front. He shouldn't have felt disappointed. He had known they would be there. But still he felt tears stinging in his eyes. He blinked quickly so that no one would see. As he stood at the window, the salesman brought Aldo's sneakers and placed them beside Trevor's. I guess I'm a runner-up, thought Aldo. They'll probably give me a pair of shoelaces!

The salesman held a sign that said First Prize, and he placed it next to Trevor's sneakers. He recognized Trevor in the group and said, "Come along, young man. I'll give you any sneaker in the store." Aldo watched as Trevor proudly went inside and sat down to be fitted.

DeDe watched Trevor too. Then she walked over to a contest poster. Aldo watched her reading it. He wondered why she was bothering now. Suddenly DeDe turned and grabbed Aldo. "Come with me," she said, pulling him into the store.

SALE
12.9
IF YOUR CHILD'S SNEAKERS LOOK LIKE THIS, IT'S TIME FOR A NEW PAIR!
FIRST PLACE
1ST

"It says on the sign that any kid who lives in Woodside can enter the contest."

"That's right," agreed the salesman. "But the contest is over now. The deadline for entering was ten-thirty this morning."

"I know that," said DeDe. "But did you know that this boy doesn't live in Woodside?" She pointed her finger accusingly at Trevor. "So I don't think he can be the winner."

"What's your address?" the salesman asked Trevor.

"When I'm at home or when I'm visiting here in Woodside?" Trevor asked.

So that was how the first-prize sign was switched from Trevor's sneakers to Aldo's. Trevor was disqualified because he lived in Delaware, and visiting with his cousin in Woodside for two weeks didn't make him a resident.

Trevor's face turned as red as his hair. "I didn't mean to cheat," he said.

"That's OK," said the salesman, and to show that there were no hard feelings, he gave Trevor a pair of green shoelaces as a consolation prize. Every boy and girl who entered the contest got a pair of shoelaces too, but thanks to DeDe's quick thinking Aldo didn't get any. He got a brand-new pair of sneakers.

The last time Aldo had been shopping in the shoe store, he had selected a pair of blue suede sneakers. Mrs. Sossi quickly vetoed them because they were much too expensive. Now Aldo could have any pair in the store for free. The salesman measured his foot. It had grown another half size during the summer, and the price of the blue suede sneakers had grown too. They cost three dollars more than they had in the spring.

The salesman put the new sneakers in their box and presented them to Aldo. DeDe stood nearby, smiling proudly.

"I can't wait to show them to my mother," said Aldo, when they finally left the store.

"I can't wait to eat," said DeDe. "It's way past lunchtime."

So Aldo and DeDe rushed back to Aldo's house, running most of the way, even though it was very hot and Aldo's shoes were still pinching his toes.

THINK IT OVER

1. *Why was having grubby sneakers so important to Aldo?*

2. *What are some of the things Aldo did to make his sneakers grubbier for the contest?*

3. *Do you think DeDe should have told the salesman that Trevor was from another town? Explain why you think as you do.*

4. *If DeDe had not returned from visiting her grandparents until after the contest, how would the story have been different?*

WRITE

Think of an idea for a different kind of contest. Make a poster that displays the contest rules, the time and place of the judging, and a description of the prize.

CONTESTS

Johanna Hurwitz wrote about a couple of winners. Do you think Aldo would have stood up to the principal if he had been in Julio's class? Explain why you think as you do.

. . . .

Which contest in the selections do you think was the more challenging one to win? Explain why you think as you do.

. . . .

WRITER'S WORKSHOP Think about a time when you competed for something. Did you win or lose? How did you feel during and after the contest? List in order the things you remember about that experience. Then write a paragraph describing the contest and how you felt.

HOLIDAYS

Holidays are shared celebrations. What is your favorite holiday? How do you celebrate it? Many holidays are held to remember famous people or historic events. In the following selections, you will read about some uncommon holidays celebrated around the world.

C O N T E N T S

59

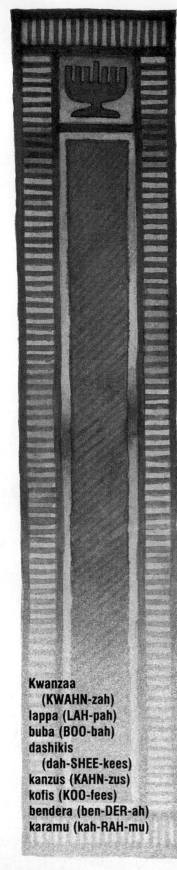

Kwanzaa
   (KWAHN-zah)
lappa (LAH-pah)
buba (BOO-bah)
dashikis
   (dah-SHEE-kees)
kanzus (KAHN-zus)
kofis (KOO-fees)
bendera (ben-DER-ah)
karamu (kah-RAH-mu)

KWANZAA

by Deborah M. Newton Chocolate
illustrated by Melodye Rosales

Every year, from the day after Christmas until the first day of the new year, our family celebrates Kwanzaa!

Kwanzaa is an African-American celebration. The name comes from the East African Swahili word *kwanza*, meaning "the first." Kwanzaa is a gathering time, just like Thanksgiving or a family reunion.

Many of our ancestors were farmers. The seven principles of Kwanzaa celebrate African harvesttime and a way of life handed down to us by our ancestors and parents.

In keeping with the spirit of Kwanzaa, Mama wears a *lappa* or *buba*, which is an African dress. She braids her hair into beautiful cornrows.

Daddy and Allen and I wear *dashikis* or *kanzus*. This is traditional dress for African men. We wear *kofis* on our heads and beads around our necks.

We decorate our home in the black, red, and green colors of Kwanzaa. We fly our *bendera*, or flag. Black is for the color of our people. Red is for our continuing struggle. And green is for the lush, rolling hills of our beautiful motherland, Africa. Green also is the color of hope, represented by African-American children. Together we prepare a table for the Kwanzaa *karamu*, or feast.

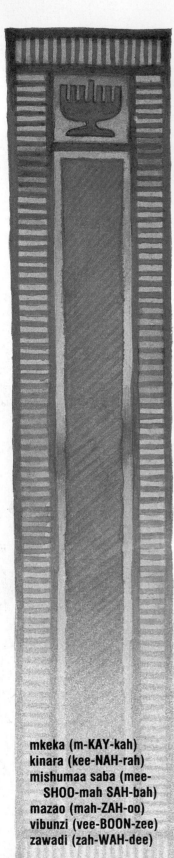

Mama puts a *mkeka*, or straw mat, on the table. Aunt Ife wove it for the celebration. In Africa it is an old custom to make things by hand. The hand-woven mkeka stands for our past.

On top of the mkeka, Daddy puts a *kinara*, or candle holder. The kinara is the holder of the flame. It stands for all black people, both past and present. The *mishumaa saba*, or seven candles in the kinara, stand for the seven Kwanzaa principles that teach us how to live.

Allen places a basket filled with *mazao*, or crops, on the table. It is a symbol of the African harvest and thanksgiving. We gather with our relatives to give thanks just as our ancestors did.

I put *vibunzi*, or ears of corn, on the table. The ears of corn stand for the number of children in the home. Our table has two ears of corn.

We show our love for our family through the *zawadi*, or gifts, we make. On the night before the last day of Kwanzaa, we give our parents gifts that remind us of Africa and our African-American ancestors. Allen and I earn our gifts by keeping the promises we made in the past year.

Each day, from sunrise to sunset, we do not eat. In the evening we gather in a circle around the karamu table. We share our home and food with family and friends, just as our ancestors shared the fruits of the hunt and the harvest.

Each night a candle is lit and one of the seven Kwanzaa principles is recited. On the first day of Kwanzaa, Daddy lights the black candle in the center of the kinara.

mkeka (m-KAY-kah)
kinara (kee-NAH-rah)
mishumaa saba (mee-
    SHOO-mah SAH-bah)
mazao (mah-ZAH-oo)
vibunzi (vee-BOON-zee)
zawadi (zah-WAH-dee)

"Harambee!" he says.

"Harambee!" we answer. He recites the first principle of the *nguzo saba*, the seven principles of Kwanzaa. *"Umoja* means unity," says Daddy. "On this first day of Kwanzaa, let us remember the importance of unity in the family. Let us love one another and stand up for one another. Let us honor our ancestors by celebrating our past."

We pass the *kikombe cha umoja*, or unity cup. We pour a libation, an offering to the memory of our ancestors, in the direction of the four winds—north, south, east, and west. And then, to honor our ancestors and in the spirit of unity, each person takes a sip.

The delicious aromas of collard greens simmering in sweet meat, black-eyed peas, and buttermilk cornbread mean it is time for the first karamu, or feast. We eat black-eyed peas for good luck and greens for

harambee
(hah-RAHM-bee)
nguzo saba (n-GOO-
zoo SAH-bah)
umoja (oo-MO-jah)
kikombe cha umoja
(kee-KOOM-bay CHA
oo-MO-jah)

prosperity. There are platters of fried chicken and baked catfish. For dessert, there is sweet potato pie, peach cobbler, rice pudding, and carrot cake.

Mufaro, a cousin, and Allen and I play congas. The rhythm is a heartbeat that brings everyone to their feet. Everyone dances to the music we make.

On the second day of Kwanzaa, Uncle Buddy lights a red candle in the kinara. "Always do the right thing," says Uncle Buddy. "Always stand up for what is right. This is what *kujichagulia*, or self-determination, means."

Uncle Buddy passes the *kikombe*, or cup. He recalls the days when he was a boy living on a share-cropping farm down south. He tells us stories about our grandfathers. He remembers the name of the village in Africa where his great-great grandmother was born.

■ ■ ■

"Habari gani?" ("What's the news?") greets Mama.
"Ujima!" everyone answers.

"Today I light the third candle of Kwanzaa for ujima!"

The glow from the flame dances across Mama's dark face. Shadows fill the room. Mama takes an ear of corn from the basket. "Ujima stands for collective work and responsibility. Our corn," she explains, "reminds us of the harvest that comes from ujima. Without work, there is no reward, no harvest for our people."

A family photo album, a cane-bottomed basket, a flatiron, and a set of wedding rings are some of the things that have been handed down in our family from generation to generation. We hear the story that goes with each of them. There is a top hat that belonged to my great-great grandfather, and a feathered headband that belonged to my great-great grandmother. Our great-great grandparents once sang and danced in traveling stage shows across the South.

■ ■ ■

kujichagulia (koo-jee-cha-goo-LEE-ah)
kikombe (kee-KOOM-bay)
habari gani (hah-BAH-ree GAH-nee)
ujima (oo-JEE-mah)

Mufaro stands behind the kinara and lights the candle for the fourth celebration day, a red one, for *ujamma*. "Ujamma means 'cooperative economics.' My family honors ujamma by helping me finish school. When I become a doctor, I'll come back to the community and help out."

■ ■ ■

Nia means "purpose." On the fifth day, I light a green candle. I greet everyone with, "Harambee!"

"Harambee!" they answer.

"I have a purpose, no matter how small. My purpose is to keep promises and to honor my ancestors and parents." Both Mama and Daddy give me a great big hug after the kikombe cha umoja is passed around.

ujamma (oo-JAH-mah)
nia (NEE-ah)
kuumba (koo-OOM-bah)

■ ■ ■

On New Year's Eve we celebrate the sixth principle of Kwanzaa, which is *kuumba*, or creativity. We work on the gifts we will exchange. There is more music and song and dance. Some of the music is African and some of it is African-American. Cousin Ebon plays a thumb piano. Uncle Will dances a cakewalk to it.

Later that evening, we present our gifts. Allen and I give Mama a tie-dyed red, black, and green *gele*, or head wrap, made in art class. For Daddy we have a hand-carved flute.

Mama and Daddy surprise us with pocket watches that once belonged to our grandfathers.

After midnight, in the early morning of New Year's Day, Grandma Lela lights the last candle in honor of Kwanzaa. She recites the principle of *imani*, which means "faith." "It is up to us to keep the faith of our ancestors. We must always stand together and be strong." She talks about Sojourner Truth and Dr. Martin Luther King, Jr. "Let imani burn as a flame in our hearts in the coming year," Grandma says. "Let it light our way until we gather to celebrate this time next year."

gele (GAY-lay)
imani (ee-MAH-nee)

THINK IT OVER

1. *How does the family in the selection celebrate Kwanzaa?*

2. *What part of the Kwanzaa celebration would you enjoy most? Explain why you would enjoy some parts more than others.*

3. *What are the colors of Kwanzaa? What does each color represent?*

4. *Why do family members exchange gifts during Kwanzaa?*

WRITE

Imagine that you and your family have just finished celebrating one of the nights of Kwanzaa. Write a journal entry telling about what you have just observed or learned.

HAPPY *Holidays*

by the Editors of *FACES* and Tran Phuong Hoa
illustrated by Cristoph Blumrich

When your birthday comes, your family and friends often celebrate with a party, a cake, and gifts—with you as the star. That kind of celebration is private: The people who know you want to say they're glad you were born and wish you well in the coming year.

A birthday celebration also can be public, and then it becomes a holiday. Our national holidays celebrating the birthdays of George Washington, Abraham Lincoln, and Martin Luther King, Jr., honor them as heroes of American life. Holidays like the Fourth of July and Columbus Day also celebrate birthdays—the birthdays of historic events. People in other countries have similar holidays that mark important people and events in their past, and people all over the world celebrate the birth of the new year.

Our New Year's celebration, set by a calendar linked to the sun, always falls on the same date and lasts for a night and a day. In Indonesia, the Ngaju people on the island of Borneo link their new year to the spring planting of rice, their staple food. Their big celebration is the two-month Harvest Festival that gives thanks for the rice crop and encourages another year to begin. The Asante people in Ghana, West Africa, celebrate with parades and festivities when they harvest the first ripe yams.

Some of the Africans from Ghana and other places who have immigrated to the United States now celebrate Kwanzaa, a new holiday that keeps their native traditions alive. In Japan, children are honored on May 5, Children's Day. You can participate in that celebration by making a flying fish to display in your yard. And Carnival is the holiday when Caribbean peoples dress in exotic costumes and march in colorful parades. Carnival often is linked with Christmas or the beginning of Lent in the Christian calendar.

The Vietnamese follow the lunar calendar when fixing the dates of their festivals. The most important Vietnamese holiday, Tet, marks the lunar New Year. Tet is a joyous time filled with wonderful sounds, colors, and scents.

In Hanoi, the capital city, families prepare for Tet by buying flowers, decorations, firecrackers, new clothes, and gifts and cooking Banh Chung cakes, the special Tet food. No family's Tet would be complete without having a peach tree in blossom or a mandarin orange tree in fruit in a corner of the living room. This is no easy feat, since Tet comes in the middle of winter. But the special effort pays off, as the flowers decorating every market, street, and home help the people to forget momentarily the gray winter skies over Hanoi.

Each family makes a Banh Chung cake from sticky rice, pork, and beans, all wrapped in large green arrowroot leaves and boiled in a drum for 12 hours. Family members sit around the fire, keeping it going and exchanging stories about the past year and their hopes for the coming one. A "Tet air" brightens conversations and adds a touch of spring to everyone's heart.

HOLIDAYS

Holidays can be celebrated in many ways. How is the celebration of Kwanzaa similar to the celebration of Tet? How are they different?

. . . .

What holiday that you and your family celebrate is most like Kwanzaa? Describe the similarities and differences in the way your holiday and Kwanzaa are celebrated.

. . . .

WRITER'S WORKSHOP   Think about a time of year that you enjoy. Invent a holiday you would like to celebrate then. Your holiday may be in honor of a person or a special happening in your family or school. You may want to combine parts of three or four holidays that you celebrate. Write a story about a celebration of your invented holiday.

PERFORMANCES

Do you play a musical instrument or like to listen to music? Do you like to draw or paint? Artists celebrate their talents through their music and art. Read the following selections and poem to find out how each artist uses his or her gift.

C O N T E N T S

· ·

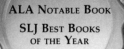

76

MUSIC, MUSIC FOR EVERYONE
VERA B. WILLIAMS

Our big chair often sits in our living room empty now.

When I first got my accordion, Grandma and Mama used to sit in that chair together to listen to me practice. And every day after school while Mama was at her job at the diner, Grandma would be sitting in the chair by the window. Even if it was snowing big flakes down on her hair, she would lean way out to call, "Hurry up, Pussycat. I've got something nice for you."

But now Grandma is sick. She has to stay upstairs in the big bed in Aunt Ida and Uncle Sandy's extra room. Mama and Aunt Ida and Uncle Sandy and I take turns taking care of her. When I come home from school, I run right upstairs to ask Grandma if she wants anything. I carry up the soup Mama has left for her. I water her plants and report if the Christmas cactus has any flowers yet. Then I sit on her bed and tell her about everything.

77

Grandma likes it when my friends Leora, Jenny, and Mae come home with me because we play music for her. Leora plays the drums. Mae plays the flute. Jenny plays fiddle and I play my accordion. One time we played a dance for Grandma that we learned in the music club at school.

Grandma clapped until it made her too tired. She told us it was like the music in the village where she lived when she was a girl. It made her want to dance right down the street. We had to keep her from trying to hop out of bed to go to the kitchen to fix us a treat.

Leora and Jenny and Mae and I left Grandma to rest and went down to get our own treat. We squeezed together into our big chair to eat it.

"It feels sad down here without your grandma," Leora said. "Even your big money jar up there looks sad and empty."

"Remember how it was full to the top and I couldn't even lift it when we bought the chair for my mother?" I said.

"And remember how it was more than half full when you got your accordion?" Jenny said.

"I bet it's empty now because your mother has to spend all her money to take care of your grandma till she gets better. That's how it was when my father had his accident and couldn't go to work for a long time," Mae said.

Mae had a dime in her pocket and she dropped it into the jar. "That will make it look a little fuller anyway," she said as she went home.

But after Jenny and Leora and Mae went home, our jar looked even emptier to me. I wondered how we would ever be able to fill it up again while Grandma was sick. I wondered when Grandma would be able to come downstairs again. Even our beautiful chair with roses all over it seemed empty with just me in the corner of it. The whole house seemed so empty and so quiet.

I got out my accordion and I started to play. The notes sounded beautiful in the empty room. One song that is an old tune sounded so pretty I played it over and over. I remembered what my mother had told me about my other grandma and how she used to play the accordion. Even when she was a girl not much bigger than I, she would get up and play at a party or a wedding so the company could dance and sing. Then people would stamp their feet and yell, "More, more!" When they went home, they would leave money on the table for her.

That's how I got my idea for how I could help fill up the jar again. I ran right upstairs. "Grandma," I whispered. "Grandma?"

"Is that you, Pussycat?" she answered in a sleepy voice. "I was just having such a nice dream about you. Then I woke up and heard you playing that beautiful old song. Come. Sit here and brush my hair."

I brushed Grandma's hair and told her my whole idea. She thought it was a great idea. "But tell the truth, Grandma," I begged her. "Do you think kids could really do that?"

"I think you and Jenny and Leora and Mae could do it. No question. No question at all," she answered. "Only don't wait a minute to talk to them about it. Go call and ask them now."

And that was how the Oak Street Band got started.

Our music teachers helped us pick out pieces we could all play together. Aunt Ida, who plays guitar, helped us practice. We practiced on our back porch. One day our neighbor leaned out his window in his pajamas and yelled, "Listen, kids, you sound great but give me a break. I work at night. I've got to get some sleep in the daytime." After that we practiced inside. Grandma said it was helping her get better faster than anything.

At last my accordion teacher said we sounded very good. Uncle Sandy said so too. Aunt Ida and Grandma said we were terrific. Mama said she thought anyone would be glad to have us play for them.

It was Leora's mother who gave us our first job. She asked us to come and play at a party for Leora's great-grandmother and great-grandfather. It was going to be a special anniversary for them. It was fifty years ago on that day they first opened their market on our corner. Now Leora's mother takes care of the market. She always plays the radio loud while she works. But for the party she said there just had to be live music.

All of Leora's aunts and uncles and cousins came to the party. Lots of people from our block came too. Mama and Aunt Ida and Uncle Sandy walked down from our house very slowly with Grandma. It was Grandma's first big day out.

There was a long table in the backyard made from little tables all pushed together. It was covered with so many big dishes of food you could hardly see the tablecloth. But I was too excited to eat anything.

Leora and Jenny and Mae and I waited over by the rosebush. Each of us had her instrument all ready. But everyone else went on eating and talking and eating some more. We didn't see how they would ever get around to listening to us. And we didn't see how we could be brave enough to begin.

At last Leora's mother pulled us right up in front of everybody. She banged on a pitcher with a spoon to get attention.

Then she introduced each one of us. "And *now* we're going to have music," she said. "Music and dancing for everyone."

It was quiet as school assembly. Every single person there was looking right at Leora and Jenny and Mae and me. But we just stood there and stared right back. Then I heard my grandma whisper, "Play, Pussycat. Play anything. Just like you used to play for me."

I put my fingers on the keys and buttons of my accordion. Jenny tucked her fiddle under her chin. Mae put her flute to her mouth. Leora held up her drums. After that we played and played. We made mistakes, but we played like a real band. The little lanterns came on. Everyone danced.

Mama and Aunt Ida and Uncle Sandy smiled at us every time they danced by. Grandma kept time nodding her head and tapping with the cane she uses now. Leora and Jenny and Mae and I forgot about being scared. We loved the sound of the Oak Street Band.

And afterward everybody clapped and shouted. Leora's great-grandfather and great-grandmother thanked us. They said we had made their party something they would always remember. Leora's father piled up plates of food for us. My mama arranged for Leora, Jenny, and Mae to stay over at our house. And when we finally all went out the gate together, late at night, Leora's mother tucked an envelope with our money into Leora's pocket.

As soon as we got home, we piled into my bed to divide the money. We made four equal shares. Leora said she was going to save up for a bigger drum. Mae wasn't sure what she would do with her share. Jenny fell asleep before she could tell us. But I couldn't even lie down until I climbed up and put mine right into our big jar on the shelf near our chair.

THINK IT OVER

- *Think about the part of the story you enjoyed the most. Use your own words to retell your favorite part of the story to a friend.*

- *Which instrument featured in the girls' band would you enjoy playing most? Tell why you would choose that instrument.*

- *Did you think the girls would be successful when they first formed the band? Tell how you felt about the girls' band after you read the story.*

WRITE

Suppose that you asked the girls' band to play music for a party that you were having. Write an advertisement for the Oak Street Band that you could include in the party invitations.

Dear Readers and Lookers,

I'm glad you've had a chance to read my story in this collection. The complete story is printed here just as I wrote it. But it wasn't possible to put in all the pictures and borders and backgrounds.

I'd like you to see my whole book in a library or bookstore sometime because I planned *Music, Music for Everyone* from the very front cover to the back cover. I painted all the borders and the watercolored backgrounds. I even picked out the kind of alphabet letters to use from the hundreds of kinds that the printing company has.

First I wrote the story. It took about a month till I got it just right. After that I made a sample book of the right size and glued in copies of the paragraphs and sketches. I tried different arrangements for the pages. When I made the paintings I had to imagine how everyone should look and all the rooms and all the food. Everything. That's the most exciting part for me.

While I worked I had the radio on. I listened to all kinds of music, and I think that music is in the colors and wave shapes of the borders now for everyone to see.

Vera B Williams

AWARD-WINNING
AUTHOR

Philippe

Philippe AND THE BLUE Parrot

by Nancy White Carlstrom
illustrated by Lambert Davis

When Philippe was a young boy, his mother told him a story about a beautiful blue parrot who stole a golden earring from the sun.

"Watch for it, Philippe, my boy," she said. "And when you find that golden earring, we will never go hungry again."

And so Philippe kept his head down as he walked to school through the streets of Port-au-Prince, always looking for a glint of gold.

Years passed. Philippe did well in his studies. He was especially good at art. When Philippe was thirteen, he decided to make a birthday gift for his mother.

He took his art supplies to the park, and there, leaning the canvas against a bench, he painted *Blue Parrot and the Sun*. As he waited for the paint to dry, he studied the blue smudges between his fingers and a drop of yellow shining on his black wrist.

"Is that for sale?"

Philippe was startled by the question. He had not heard the tourist walk up to him. The woman squinted her eyes at the bright colors and asked again.

"Is that for sale?" Before Philippe could answer, she added, "I'll pay twenty-five dollars for it."

Twenty-five dollars! That was more than Philippe had earned in his whole life. It would take a long time to make that much money, even if he could get a job. What wonderful things he could buy his mother.

And so Philippe sold *Blue Parrot and the Sun*.

Years passed. Philippe's paintings were sold in a Port-au-Prince gallery. Many tourists liked his work and bought the canvases.

Every time Philippe painted a *Blue Parrot and the Sun* for his mother, the gallery owner had a buyer. The price went up and Philippe could not resist. But every time he sold a *Blue Parrot,* he put aside some money for his mother.

Many years passed. Now Philippe's paintings could not be afforded by most tourists. His work hung in galleries and museums in Europe and the United States.

One day, he sat in his fine studio, ready to begin work on another *Blue Parrot and the Sun*. A journalist who had come to interview him stood nearby.

"Monsieur, your *Blue Parrot and the Sun* paintings are now very famous. Some critics say that they have a life and power that your other works lack. Why is that? Do you know?"

"Oh yes, I know," Philippe replied slowly. "It is because I paint each *Blue Parrot* for my mother."

"And how much will this new one sell for?" the journalist asked. "Thousands, I suppose?"

"Oh, this painting will not be for sale," Philippe answered. He knew he had said that before, but this time, he really meant it.

And he added: "I found the golden earring many years ago. Now it's time to give it back."

There is a story the art collectors tell about a famous painting called *Blue Parrot and the Sun*. Oh, there are many, but the one to hunt for has a small golden earring hidden in the picture. Yes, that is the one worth a fortune. Some say it hangs on the wall of a simple house in the Haitian countryside. Others are not so sure. It could be anywhere.

THINK IT OVER

1. *Why does Philippe paint the same picture again and again for so many years?*

2. *Why do you think Philippe decides not to sell the newest* Blue Parrot and the Sun *painting?*

WRITE

Imagine that you are the journalist in the story. Write a short interview in which Philippe tells about his painting.

SUN DANCERS

by Patricia Irving
illustrated by Cary Henrie

Sun dancers
Whirling, twirling madly—
Feet churning Mother Earth
Until clouds weep.

Sun dancers
Bringing song to life
With forlorn drumbeat,
With feathers bright.

Sun dancers'
Feathers bowing to four winds,
Feathers dampened by the rain;
Corn feathering on the stalk.

Sun dancers
Throw humble gratitude to sky
In thundering beat
From whirling, churning feet.

PERFORMANCES

Think about a time when you performed in some way for an audience. Did you sing, play a musical instrument, dance, or show a drawing or painting? How was your performance similar to or different from that of the girls' band or Philippe?

· ·

How did the girls in the Oak Street Band and how did Philippe give of themselves through their music and art?

· ·

WRITER'S WORKSHOP   Think about a favorite painting you have observed or a musical composition you have heard. Write a descriptive paragraph of that painting or song. Use vivid details in your description so that your readers will feel as though they've also seen the painting or heard the music.

95

CONNECTIONS

Benito Juárez

MEXICAN NATIONAL HOLIDAY

Mexicans are proud that they, like North Americans, fought hard for their independence. That's why *Cinco de Mayo* (fifth of May) is a national holiday in Mexico. On this day in 1862, invading French troops were defeated by a great Mexican leader, Benito Juárez.

Cinco de Mayo is celebrated with parades, plays, and fairs in Mexico and also in parts of the United States. This holiday is just one of many traditions preserved by Mexican immigrants.

■ *If you have ever celebrated Cinco de Mayo, share with your classmates how you and your family celebrated the holiday. As a class, put on a Mexican-heritage festival. Learn about and share folktales, poetry, music, dances, art, recipes, costumes, language, and customs from Mexico that now enrich other cultures.*

Cinco de Mayo celebration

SING OUT, AMERICA!

Music plays an important part in cultural celebrations. Ask family members, older friends, or a librarian to help you find a traditional song of your cultural group or another in your area. Before sharing the song with your classmates, tell something about its history and meaning.

CELEBRATE YOUR CULTURE

Find out more about a special day your family celebrates or another interesting cultural holiday. Write about the holiday in a story, a friendly letter, a magazine article, or a poem. Read aloud what you wrote to your classmates.

You might use a web like the one shown to help you organize your thoughts.

Who celebrates it? — Name of Holiday — Where?

When? — How?

Why?

ANIMAL·TALES

All cultures tell stories about animals. Some of these stories are true, and others are make-believe. Some are about wolves that roam the plains of North America, and others are about graceful cats that rule the forests and plains of Africa. Each culture's tales can help you understand and appreciate the animals of your world. As you read about the animals in this unit, think about what a remarkable creature each one is.

TURTLE IN JULY
BY MARILYN SINGER

The changing of the seasons affects not only trees and flowers but also animals. Each poem, beautifully illustrated by Jerry Pinkney, focuses on an animal in one season or month of the year.

AWARD-WINNING ILLUSTRATOR

HBJ LIBRARY BOOK

RAISING GORDY GORILLA AT THE SAN DIEGO ZOO
BY GEORGEANNE IRVINE

Gordy Gorilla is cared for at the San Diego Zoo during the first year of his life. Then he must adjust to life in a wild animal park.

URBAN ROOSTS:
WHERE BIRDS NEST IN THE CITY
BY BARBARA BASH

Many kinds of birds can be found in any city. Sometimes they make their homes in interesting places. AWARD-WINNING AUTHOR

I'LL MEET YOU
AT THE CUCUMBERS
BY LILIAN MOORE

Adam Mouse visits the city for the birthday party of his pen friend, Amanda. While there, he makes some interesting discoveries! SLJ BEST BOOKS OF THE YEAR

SHARK LADY
BY ANN McGOVERN

Follow the adventures of Dr. Eugenie Clark to find out how her childhood interest in marine life led to her career. She became an ichthyologist—a person who studies and works with fish.

ANIMAL TALK

Did you ever wish that you could talk to a puppy at home or a tiger at the zoo? The animals in the following selections communicate with people in special ways.

CONTENTS

MIRACLE

from *Charlotte's Web*

by E. B. White
illustrated by Garth Williams

Fern sold her favorite pig, Wilbur, to her uncle, Homer Zuckerman. Fern knew that her uncle and his hired hand, Lurvy, would take good care of Wilbur. They did their best to keep Wilbur well fed.

When the other animals in Zuckerman's barnyard informed Wilbur that he was to be the main course at the Christmas feast, only Charlotte, the beautiful spider, had a plan to save Wilbur.

On foggy mornings, Charlotte's web was truly a thing of beauty. This morning each thin strand was decorated with dozens of tiny beads of water. The web glistened in the light and made a pattern of loveliness and mystery, like a delicate veil. Even Lurvy, who wasn't particularly interested in beauty, noticed the web when he came with the pig's breakfast. He noted how clearly it showed up and he noted how big and carefully built it was. And then he took another look and he saw something that made him set his pail down. There, in the center of the web, neatly woven in block letters, was a message. It said:

SOME PIG!

Lurvy felt weak. He brushed his hand across his eyes and stared harder at Charlotte's web.

"I'm seeing things," he whispered. He dropped to his knees and uttered a short prayer. Then, forgetting all about Wilbur's breakfast, he walked back to the house and called Mr. Zuckerman.

"I think you'd better come down to the pigpen," he said.

"What's the trouble?" asked Mr. Zuckerman. "Anything wrong with the pig?"

"N-not exactly," said Lurvy. "Come and see for yourself."

The two men walked silently down to Wilbur's yard. Lurvy pointed to the spider's web. "Do you see what I see?" he asked.

Zuckerman stared at the writing on the web. Then he murmured the words "Some Pig." Then he looked at Lurvy. Then they both began to tremble. Charlotte, sleepy after her night's exertions, smiled as she watched. Wilbur came and stood directly under the web.

"Some pig!" muttered Lurvy in a low voice.

"Some pig!" whispered Mr. Zuckerman. They stared and stared for a long time at Wilbur. Then they stared at Charlotte.

"You don't suppose that that spider . . ." began Mr. Zuckerman—but he shook his head and didn't finish the sentence. Instead, he walked solemnly back up to the house and spoke to his wife. "Edith, something has happened," he said, in a weak voice. He went into the living room and sat down, and Mrs. Zuckerman followed.

"I've got something to tell you, Edith," he said. "You better sit down."

Mrs. Zuckerman sank into a chair. She looked pale and frightened.

"Edith," he said, trying to keep his voice steady, "I think you had best be told that we have a very unusual pig."

A look of complete bewilderment came over Mrs. Zuckerman's face. "Homer Zuckerman, what in the world are you talking about?" she said.

"This is a very serious thing, Edith," he replied. "Our pig is completely out of the ordinary."

"What's unusual about the pig?" asked Mrs. Zuckerman, who was beginning to recover from her scare.

"Well, I don't really know yet," said Mr. Zuckerman. "But we have received a sign, Edith—a mysterious sign. A miracle has happened on this farm. There is a large spider's web in the doorway of the barn cellar, right over the pigpen, and when Lurvy went to feed the pig this morning, he noticed the web because it was foggy, and you know how a spider's web looks very distinct in a fog. And right spang in the middle of the web there were the words 'Some Pig.' The words were woven right into the web. They were actually part of the web, Edith. I know, because I have been down there and seen them. It says, 'Some Pig,' just as clear as clear can be. There can be no mistake about it. A miracle has happened and a sign has occurred here on earth, right on our farm, and we have no ordinary pig."

"Well," said Mrs. Zuckerman, "it seems to me you're a little off. It seems to me we have no ordinary *spider*."

"Oh, no," said Zuckerman. "It's the pig that's unusual. It says so, right there in the middle of the web."

"Maybe so," said Mrs. Zuckerman. "Just the same, I intend to have a look at that spider."

"It's just a common grey spider," said Zuckerman. They got up, and together they walked down to Wilbur's yard. "You see, Edith? It's just a common grey spider."

Wilbur was pleased to receive so much attention. Lurvy was still standing there, and Mr. and Mrs. Zuckerman, all three, stood for about an hour, reading the words on the web over and over, and watching Wilbur.

Charlotte was delighted with the way her trick was working. She sat without moving a muscle, and listened to the conversation of the people. When a small fly blundered into the web, just beyond the word "pig," Charlotte dropped quickly down, rolled the fly up, and carried it out of the way.

After a while the fog lifted. The web dried off and the words didn't show up so plainly. The Zuckermans and Lurvy walked back to the house. Just before they left the pigpen, Mr. Zuckerman took one last look at Wilbur.

"You know," he said, in an important voice, "I've thought all along that that pig of ours was an extra good one. He's a solid pig. That pig is as solid as they come. You notice how solid he is around the shoulders, Lurvy?"

"Sure. Sure I do," said Lurvy. "I've always noticed that pig. He's quite a pig."

"He's long, and he's smooth," said Zuckerman.

"That's right," agreed Lurvy. "He's as smooth as they come. He's some pig."

When Mr. Zuckerman got back to the house, he took off his work clothes and put on his best suit. Then he got into his car and drove to the minister's house. He stayed for an hour and explained to the minister that a miracle had happened on the farm.

"So far," said Zuckerman, "only four people on earth know about this miracle—myself, my wife Edith, my hired man Lurvy, and you."

"Don't tell anybody else," said the minister. "We don't know what it means yet, but perhaps if I give thought to it, I can explain it in my sermon next Sunday. There can be no doubt that you have a most unusual pig. I intend to speak about it in my sermon and point out the fact that this community has been visited with a wondrous animal. By the way, does the pig have a name?"

"Why, yes," said Mr. Zuckerman. "My little niece calls him Wilbur. She's a rather queer child—full of notions. She raised the pig on a bottle and I bought him from her when he was a month old."

He shook hands with the minister, and left.

Secrets are hard to keep. Long before Sunday came, the news spread all over the county.

Everybody knew that a sign had appeared in a spider's web on the Zuckerman place. Everybody knew that the Zuckermans had a wondrous pig. People came from miles around to look at Wilbur and to read the words on Charlotte's web. The Zuckermans' driveway was full of cars and trucks from morning till night. The news of the wonderful pig spread clear up into the hills, and farmers came rattling down in buggies and buckboards, to stand hour after hour at Wilbur's pen admiring the miraculous animal. All said they had never seen such a pig before in their lives.

In the days that followed, Mr. Zuckerman was so busy entertaining visitors that he neglected his farm work. He wore his good clothes all the time now—got right into them when he got up in the morning. Mrs. Zuckerman prepared special meals for Wilbur. Lurvy shaved and got a haircut; and his principal farm duty was to feed the pig while people looked on.

Mr. Zuckerman ordered Lurvy to increase Wilbur's feedings from three meals a day to four meals a day. The Zuckermans were so busy with visitors they forgot about other things on the farm. The blackberries got ripe, and Mrs. Zuckerman failed to put up any blackberry jam. The corn needed hoeing, and Lurvy didn't find time to hoe it.

On Sunday the church was full. The minister explained the miracle. He said that the words on the spider's web proved that human beings must always be on the watch for the coming of wonders.

All in all, the Zuckerman's pigpen was the center of attraction. Fern was happy, for she felt that Charlotte's trick was working and that Wilbur's life would be saved. But she found that the barn was not nearly as pleasant—too many people. She liked it better when she could be all alone with her friends the animals.

One evening, a few days after the writing had appeared in Charlotte's web, the spider called a meeting of all the animals in the barn cellar.

"I shall begin by calling the roll. Wilbur?"

"Here!" said the pig.

"Gander?"

"Here, here, here!" said the gander.

"You sound like three ganders," muttered Charlotte. "Why can't you just say 'here'? Why do you have to repeat everything?"

"It's my idio-idio-idiosyncrasy," replied the gander.

"Goose?" said Charlotte.

"Here, here, here!" said the goose. Charlotte glared at her.

"Goslings, one through seven?"

"Bee-bee-bee!" "Bee-bee-bee!" "Bee-bee-bee!" "Bee-bee-bee!" "Bee-bee-bee!" "Bee-bee-bee!" "Bee-bee-bee!" said the goslings.

"This is getting to be quite a meeting," said Charlotte. "Anybody would think we had three ganders, three geese, and twenty-one goslings. Sheep?"

"He-aa-aa!" answered the sheep all together.

"Lambs?"

"He-aa-aa!" answered the lambs all together.

"Templeton?"

No answer.

"Templeton?"

No answer.

"Well, we are all here except the rat," said Charlotte. "I guess we can proceed without him. Now, all of you must have noticed what's been going on around here the last few days. The message I wrote in my web, praising Wilbur, has been received. The Zuckermans have fallen for it, and so has everybody else. Zuckerman thinks Wilbur is an unusual pig, and therefore he won't want to kill him and eat him. I dare say my trick will work and Wilbur's life can be saved."

"Hurray!" cried everybody.

"Thank you very much," said Charlotte. "Now I called this meeting in order to get suggestions. I need new ideas for the web. People are already getting sick of reading the words 'Some Pig!' If anybody can think of another message, or remark, I'll be glad to weave it into the web. Any suggestions for a new slogan?"

"How about 'Pig Supreme'?" asked one of the lambs.

"No good," said Charlotte. "It sounds like a rich dessert."

"How about 'Terrific, terrific, terrific'?" asked the goose.

"Cut that down to one 'terrific' and it will do very nicely," said Charlotte. "I think 'terrific' might impress Zuckerman."

"But Charlotte," said Wilbur, "I'm *not* terrific."

"That doesn't make a particle of difference," replied Charlotte. "Not a particle. People believe almost anything they see in print. Does anybody here know how to spell 'terrific'?"

"I think," said the gander, "it's tee double ee double rr double rr double eye double ff double eye double see see see see see."

"What kind of an acrobat do you think I am?" said Charlotte in disgust. "I would have to have St. Vitus's Dance to weave a word like that into my web."

"Sorry, sorry, sorry," said the gander.

Then the oldest sheep spoke up. "I agree that there should be something new written in the web if Wilbur's life is to be saved. And if Charlotte needs help in finding words, I think she can get it from our friend Templeton. The rat visits the dump regularly and has access to old magazines. He can tear out bits of advertisements and bring them up here to the barn cellar, so that Charlotte can have something to copy."

"Good idea," said Charlotte. "But I'm not sure Templeton will be willing to help. You know how he is—always looking out for himself, never thinking of the other fellow."

"I bet I can get him to help," said the old sheep. "I'll appeal to his baser instincts, of which he has plenty. Here he comes now. Everybody keep quiet while I put the matter up to him!"

The rat entered the barn the way he always did—creeping along close to the wall.

"What's up?" he asked, seeing the animals assembled.

"We're holding a directors' meeting," replied the old sheep.

"Well, break it up!" said Templeton. "Meetings bore me." And the rat began to climb a rope that hung against the wall.

"Look," said the old sheep, "next time you go to the dump, Templeton, bring back a clipping from a magazine. Charlotte needs new ideas so she can write messages in her web and save Wilbur's life."

"Let him die," said the rat. "I should worry."

"You'll worry all right when next winter comes," said the sheep. "You'll worry all right on a zero morning next January when Wilbur is dead and nobody comes down here with a nice pail of warm slops to pour into the trough. Wilbur's leftover food is your chief source of supply, Templeton. *You* know that. Wilbur's food is your food; therefore Wilbur's destiny and your destiny are closely linked. If Wilbur is killed and his trough stands empty day after day, you'll grow so thin we can look right through your stomach and see objects on the other side."

Templeton's whiskers quivered.

"Maybe you're right," he said gruffly. "I'm making a trip to the dump tomorrow afternoon. I'll bring back a magazine clipping if I can find one."

"Thanks," said Charlotte. "The meeting is now adjourned. I have a busy evening ahead of me. I've got to tear my web apart and write 'Terrific.'"

Wilbur blushed. "But I'm *not* terrific, Charlotte. I'm just about average for a pig."

"You're terrific as far as *I'm* concerned," replied Charlotte, sweetly, "and that's what counts. You're my best friend, and *I* think you're sensational. Now stop arguing and go get some sleep!"

THINK IT OVER

1. *Why are the barnyard animals trying to help Wilbur?*

2. *Which creature does Edith Zuckerman think is out of the ordinary?*

3. *How does the message in Charlotte's web change daily activities in the barnyard?*

4. *Why is it important that Mr. Zuckerman believe Charlotte's messages?*

5. *Charlotte says that people believe almost anything they see in print. Do you agree? Explain your answer.*

WRITE

Wilbur is Charlotte's best friend. Write a postcard to your best friend, telling why his or her friendship makes you happy.

WORDS About the ILLUSTRATOR:
Garth Williams

Garth Williams's most famous illustrations can be seen in the *Little House* books by Laura Ingalls Wilder. Mr. Williams has also drawn pictures for many other classic books, such as E. B. White's *Charlotte's Web.*

After Garth Williams went to school in England to study painting and sculpting, he moved to New York and worked for the *New Yorker* magazine. Soon he began illustrating children's books. *Stuart Little,* also by E. B. White, was his first children's book. In over fifty years, Mr. Williams has illustrated more than fifty books.

Mr. Williams doesn't just draw things the way they look. He tries to draw the way things feel, too. He wants to see things the way the writer does. When Garth Williams was beginning to draw pictures for the *Little House* books, he visited with Laura Ingalls Wilder and took a trip to the same places that the Ingalls family had traveled to in their covered wagon. He worked on the illustrations for that series of books for almost ten years. Mr. Williams says his work is not "just making pictures." He wants his pictures to have a special feeling that goes with the story.

Turn to the illustrations in "Runaway" on page 380 to see more examples of Garth Williams's drawings.

Talk To The Animals

by Leslie Bricusse

illustrated by Sylvie Daigneault

If we could Talk To The Animals, just imagine it,
Chatting to a chimp in chimpanzee,
Imagine talking to a tiger,
chatting to a cheetah,
What a neat achievement it would be.

If we could Talk To The Animals,
learn their languages,
Maybe take an animal degree,
We'd study elephant and eagle,
buffalo and beagle,
Alligator, guinea pig and flea.
We would converse in polar bear and python,
And we would curse in fluent kangaroo.
If people asked us, "Can you speak rhinoceros?"
We'd say, "Of courseros! Can't you?"

If we conferred with our furry friends,
man to animal,
Think of all the things we could discuss.
If we could walk with the animals,
talk with the animals,
Grunt and squeak and squawk with the animals,
And they could talk to us.
If we consulted with quadrupeds, think what fun
    we'd have,
Asking over crocodiles for tea,
Or maybe lunch with two or three lions,
walruses and sea lions,
What a lovely place the world would be.

If we spoke slang to orangutangs,
the advantages
Any fool on earth can plainly see.
Discussing eastern art and dramas
with intellectual llamas,
That's a big step forward, you'll agree.
We'd learn to speak in antelope and turtle,
Our Pekinese would be extremely good.
If we were asked to sing in hippopotamus,
We'd say, "Why notamus?" And would!

And we are sure ev'ry octopus,
Plaice and platypus
certainly would see it as a plus.
If we could walk with the animals,
talk with the animals,
Grunt and squeak and squawk with the animals,
And they could talk to us.

119

WITH LOVE FROM KOKO

by Faith McNulty

Photos by Ronald H. Cohn

AWARD-WINNING
AUTHOR

Koko is a gorilla. Like other gorillas, she is dark and hairy, agile and strong. Like them, she holds within her— somewhere beneath her black cap of bristly hair— the secrets of what gorillas think and feel. But Koko is different from other gorillas in one respect. She is the first gorilla ever to learn to "talk."

Since she was six months old, Koko has lived among humans, almost as though she were a human child. At one year, Koko began to learn to "speak" by making signs with her hands. At five, she knew the signs for two hundred words and was learning new words every day.

Koko lives in California with a woman named Penny Patterson, who has cared for her since she was a baby. Penny is a scientist. By studying Koko, she hopes to learn more about the mystery of the gorilla mind.

I love animals and I love to write about them. I heard about Koko in 1976 when she was five years old. I wanted to meet her very much. I had seen gorillas only in cages, looking bored and sad. What is a happy gorilla like? I wondered. How would it feel to meet a gorilla who could talk?

I telephoned Penny at Stanford University, where Koko was living in a trailer especially fitted to house a young gorilla. Penny answered the telephone in a friendly voice, but soon broke off our conversation to say, "No, Koko! Please! Penny is talking!" A breathy voice came on the phone, and I heard a soft "whooooo" sound. "I'm sorry," Penny said, laughing. "Koko loves to talk on the phone." I laughed, too, delighted at having had my first phone contact with a gorilla, no matter how brief.

I was able to arrange a special trip to see Penny and Koko. A few weeks later I arrived at the campus. I found their trailer in an open space among large brick buildings. As I walked across dry, withered grass, I thought how different this was from the leafy jungles in which most gorillas live. I felt a shiver of excitement, too. Gorillas are peaceful and hardly ever hurt people, but they are large and powerful. Their mysterious faces often seem to scowl. The idea of meeting a gorilla face to face made my heart beat a little faster.

I went up steps at the side of the trailer and walked through the doorway. Inside I found a wall of wire mesh creating a large cage. Its floor was covered with toys: a big ball, a doll, a rumpled blanket, a rubber tub.

Inside the cage, a woman in blue jeans, Penny Patterson, was bending over and being held by two furry black arms.

Koko, sitting on the floor, stared at me intently. I was relieved to see that she wasn't as big as I'd imagined. She was about the size of a child of six or seven, but obviously much stronger. As Penny greeted me, Koko leaped over to the wire separating us and squatted down. I said, "Hi, Koko," and knelt down so that my face was on her level. We looked into each other's eyes. Hers were brown and brimming with intelligence.

When humans meet politely, they shake hands. Animals often sniff each other. Anxious to be polite, I held my hand against the wire so Koko could smell it. She sniffed, then poked a finger through the mesh to touch my hand very gently, as a human might. Her fingers looked thick and clumsy next to mine.

Koko moved her face near the wire. She pursed her lips and gently blew. Her breath smelled fresh. This is because, like all gorillas, she eats lots of crunchy vegetables that keep her teeth clean and fresh.

"She is greeting you," Penny said.

Koko picked up a spoon from among her toys and pushed it through the wire to me.

"Thank you, Koko," I said, taking her gift. I was truly pleased by this sign that she wanted to be friends. Koko handed me a rubber dog bone. I saw that she was watching my face, so I smiled and tried to look very, very grateful.

Penny and I began to talk. She told me how she had begun her work with Koko four years before. Penny was then a student at Stanford University, studying psychology—the science of the mind. She was fascinated by the idea of "talking" with apes.

For many years, scientists wondered why apes, though clearly very intelligent, cannot learn to speak like humans. Efforts to teach them always failed. Gradually it became clear that apes lack the muscles that we humans use to control our voices, and the tongues of apes are very long and not shaped to form words.

However, scientists knew that apes naturally communicate with each other by gestures. This

suggested the possibility that they could learn
American Sign Language, a system many deaf people
use. In this language, gestures and facial expressions
communicate ideas.

Penny wondered if a gorilla could learn to "speak"
in the same way. At the San Francisco Zoo, she
discovered a baby gorilla in the nursery whose mother
couldn't care for her. Penny got permission to work
with the baby, then one year old. As Penny "mothered"
Koko, the two became strongly attached. Koko learned
sign language. Her first words were "drink," "food,"
and "more." When Koko was three, Penny brought her
to live in the trailer. That was two years before my visit.
Koko was now a happy, healthy five-year-old. Her use
of language, Penny said, was like that of a human child
of two.

While we talked, Koko began noisily leaping around. Penny explained that she didn't like being left out of our conversation. "Koko! Stop that noise!" Penny ordered when the din became unbearable. Koko, satisfied that she had regained Penny's attention, quieted down and sat by the wire mesh, watching me write notes.

After a time, Koko picked up a small toy car and pushed it to me through the wire. She didn't want to lose my attention either.

Penny said, "Koko, would you like a sandwich?"

Koko made a sign that Penny said meant yes. Penny went to a counter in the kitchen. Koko leaped onto the counter and sat beside her, watching closely as Penny spread peanut butter on bread. She took the sandwich eagerly, put it between her teeth, and jumped down. Walking upright, she picked up a stool and dragged it

to the corner farthest from me. Penny smiled. "She's afraid you might ask her to share," she explained.

When Koko finished, she returned and stood before Penny, looking up and signing "more" by putting her fingertips together. With her hands raised and her face trustingly uplifted, she was a touching figure.

"All right, Koko, more what?" Penny asked. Koko quickly moved her hands in a series of gestures.

"What did she say?" I asked.

"'More eat sandwich nut,'" Penny translated, and explained that lessons in signing are part of Koko's daily life.

When Koko had finished the sandwich, she made signs that meant "Juice, please." Penny handed Koko a plastic cup. Koko drank from it, sitting on a stool, one leg crossed over the other. As she sipped, sitting like a human, it was hard to think of her as an animal. She looked like a child in a gorilla suit.

Suddenly Penny noticed that Koko was letting her juice spill. "Watch it, Koko," she warned. "Don't spill. Mess! Dirty!"

Koko looked down at the wet floor and hung her head.

Penny handed her a sponge. "All right, young lady," she said. "You may clean it up."

Koko jumped up and busily rubbed the floor.

"She loves to clean," Penny said.

Cheerful again, Koko picked up the empty cup and pushed it through the wire. I took the crumpled gift. Penny laughed. "Koko is generous with empty cups and apple cores," she said, "and once in a while she will share something really good."

Koko sat down on the floor and began turning the pages of a tattered picture book—the story of Cinderella. Penny said that Koko likes to look at pictures and "reads" to herself.

I asked Penny what she had found out about Koko's inner feelings. She said that Koko seemed to feel many of the things a child feels. She could be sad or happy, playful, peaceful, anxious, frightened, or angry. She might be "good" or "naughty" according to her mood.

Koko is very sensitive to Penny's moods. "If I'm hurt, she hugs me," Penny said. "Once when I cried, she licked the tears away. When I cheered up, she was very happy. She loves to see me laugh."

I asked Penny if she was ever afraid Koko might hurt her. "Never on purpose," Penny said, "but I know I have to be careful because she is so strong. She is stronger than she knows, and gorillas are tough, too. The power of a blow that would knock me down would hardly hurt her at all. I'm not sure she knows how breakable people are. I never, never slap her. I don't want to teach her to slap."

Fortunately scolding is usually all it takes to make Koko behave, Penny went on to explain. When scolding doesn't work, Penny goes away and leaves Koko alone for a few minutes. This upsets her, and she immediately becomes "good."

Penny said that Koko seems to know she is a gorilla. When Penny gave her a toy gorilla, Koko signed, "Me!"

Koko likes to look in a mirror. She seems to know that she is looking at herself. Even such intelligent animals as dogs and monkeys do not recognize

themselves. A child recognizes his or her own face in a mirror at about eighteen months of age. Koko did so at three-and-a-half years.

I asked Penny in what other ways Koko was like a human child. Penny said that, like a child, Koko invents new names. Once, by mistake, Penny gave her a stale roll. Koko signed, "Cookie rock!" When Penny gave her a mask, she called it an "eye hat." As small children do, Koko talks to herself when she is alone. Spreading out her blanket she may sign, "This pink," or pick up a doll and sign, "Baby."

Koko decided it was time to rejoin us. She dropped the book and picked up a rubber duck. She kissed it, then shoved it at me to be kissed. Next Koko put the duck in her mouth and crossed her arms on her breast. Penny said this was the sign for love.

"Koko love what?" Penny asked.

"Love baby," Koko signed.

"That's a duck," Penny replied. "Is that your baby?"

Koko looked about and picked up another plaything—a large rubber tub. She turned it over and squeezed most of herself underneath. Her feet stuck out a bit, and I could see her laughing face peeking out from under the rim.

Penny picked up the game. "Where is Koko?" Penny looked around wildly. "Where can she be?"

Penny looked under the blanket and in the toy box. "No Koko!" she cried. Then she lifted the edge of the tub just a bit. Koko's hands appeared, making signs.

"Oh, Koko, you funny kid," Penny said, laughing. She explained that Koko had signed, "Go-away! (I'm) hiding!"

Suddenly Koko sprang out from under the tub and jumped into Penny's arms. Penny hugged her. They sank to the floor and rolled around, wrestling and tickling. Koko joined in Penny's laughter with soft grunts of delight.

When Koko was quiet, Penny got up. "It's time for Koko's walk," she said. "Do you want to go with us?"

"Oh, yes. Of course," I said, inwardly preparing myself to meet Koko without the wire between us.

Pointing to her neck, Koko signed, "On necklace." Penny put a red collar around her neck. A long rope served as a leash. Koko is probably strong enough to break it, Penny explained, but she doesn't try.

Penny decided Koko should sit on the toilet before she went out. There was a small potty chair in a corner. Penny said Koko had learned to use it, though she sometimes forgets. In the jungle, gorillas don't bother to use any special place.

Koko sat on the potty and then quickly signed, "Time off." Penny said, "All right, but if you do it outside we'll need to come back."

Koko hustled to the door. Her eyes were fastened on me as she waited impatiently for Penny to undo the latch.

I felt a flutter of uncertainty. The door opened and Koko bounded forward. She stopped just in front of me. For a moment, while we looked at each other, I wondered what to do. Then Koko signed "up," raising her arms to me like a small child who wants to be lifted. Instinctively I bent down. Koko clasped her arms around my neck. She pulled me to her with gentle strength, sniffed my cheek, and abruptly let me go. As I straightened up, I laughed with relief and joy.

Koko and Penny went into the yard. I followed. Koko turned back and grabbed my wrist. Walking on two legs and one arm, she pulled me along. I followed willingly, happy that she wanted me with her.

Koko led us to an outdoor water faucet with a hose attached. She turned the handle, and we took turns drinking from the hose. While I drank, Koko put her face close to mine and watched each swallow go down.

I, in turn, looked deep into Koko's clear, eager eyes, which seemed to drink in experience as I drank water. I remembered something a zookeeper had once said to me about the eyes of animals. "Other animals," he said, "have eyes that don't let you see in, but if you look a primate in the eye, you feel you can look into their minds."

We strolled about in the sunshine. Koko's enjoyment was evident. She made a purr that Penny said meant happy excitement. She searched the ground and picked up small things that interested her—an empty matchbox, a plastic spoon. She plucked leaves. When a bird flew over, she excitedly watched its flight and gestured, "Bird! Please come-here!"

We wandered back to the trailer. I squatted down beside Koko to say good-bye, but Koko had a different idea. Hooking a finger in the neck of my shirt, she peered inside. Her curiosity satisfied, she raised her face to mine, purring softly.

I held out my arms, and Koko's long arms went around me in a gentle hug. My face was buried in the soft hair on her chest. Her smell was light and clean. It reminded me of a teddy bear I had as a child.

Koko let me go. She stood up and thumped her chest. Penny said, "She is saying good-bye. That's a gorilla greeting, but it also means good-bye." She took Koko's hand and together they went up the steps. The door closed behind them.

As I turned away, I thought: "Thank you, Koko, for being so gentle and friendly and kind. I only wish that humans could learn to treat animals in the same way."

If you are interested in knowing more about the work done with gorillas such as Koko, please write to

The Gorilla Foundation
Box 620-530
Woodside, CA 94062

THINK IT OVER

1. *How is Koko different from other gorillas?*

2. *Why does the author visit Koko?*

3. *How does Penny understand what Koko says?*

4. *How does Koko act during the author's visit?*

WRITE

Koko is a kind and gentle animal. Write a letter to the editor of your local newspaper, explaining why people should treat all animals gently and kindly.

ANIMAL TALK

You read about a spider that weaves messages to help a friend and a gorilla that uses sign language to talk to her teacher. How are Charlotte and Koko alike? How are they different?

· ·

Which animal do you think communicates more successfully— Charlotte or Koko? Share your reasons for your opinion.

· ·

WRITER'S WORKSHOP Choose one of the animals mentioned in the selections or song. Find out how that animal really communicates in its natural environment. You may want to read books, magazine or encyclopedia articles, or ask someone who works with animals. Write a paragraph of information using the facts you gather. Share your paragraph with a friend.

CREATURE CARE

Think about a time when you had to make a decision. Was it easy to make? Did you have many choices? The following selection and poems tell about making decisions concerning animals and their treatment.

CONTENTS

ALA Notable
Book

138

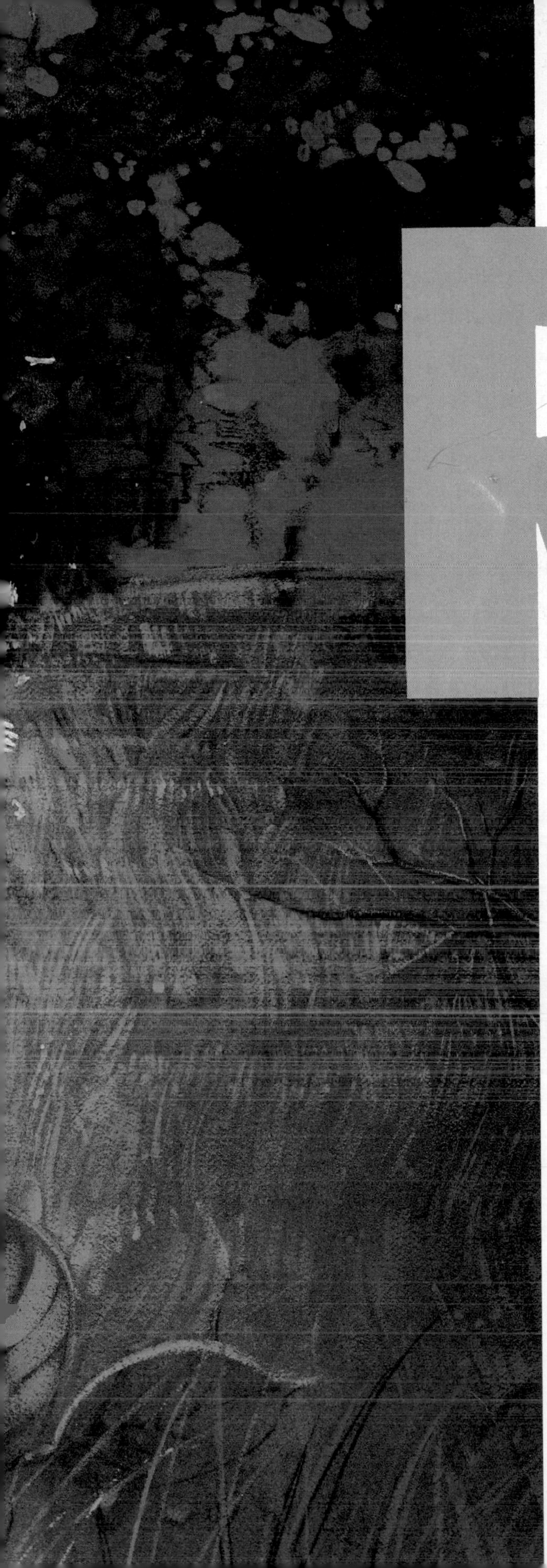

THE *Stormy* RESCUE

FROM
THE MIDNIGHT FOX

by Betsy Byars
illustrated by
Jeffrey Terreson

TOM NEVER EXPECTED THAT
BORING SUMMER ON HIS AUNT
AND UNCLE'S FARM TO TURN INTO
AN EXCITING GAME OF CHANCE. IT
STARTED WHEN TOM BECAME
ENTRANCED AT THE FIRST SIGHT
OF THE BEAUTIFUL MIDNIGHT
FOX. HE QUICKLY DEVELOPED A
STRONG ATTACHMENT TO THE
GRACEFUL BLACK FOX AND HER
PLAYFUL CUB. BUT WHEN AUNT
MILLIE'S CHICKENS STARTED
DISAPPEARING, UNCLE FRED
DECIDED IT WAS TIME TO TRAP
THE FOX. TOM RELUCTANTLY
WENT WITH HIM TO FIND THE FOX.

139

By this time we were only a hundred feet from the entrance to the fox's den. Uncle Fred had crossed the creek again and moved up toward the thicket of trees. From where he was standing, he could have thrown a rock over the trees and it would have landed in the little clearing where I had seen the baby fox play.

He walked past the thicket to a lone tree in the center of the field and stood there for a moment. Then he knocked the creek mud on his shoe off on one of the roots and walked back to me. He turned and walked the length of the thicket. It was like that old game Hot and Cold, where you hide something and when the person gets close to it you say, "You're getting warmer—you're warmer—now you're hot—you're red-hot—you're on fire, you're burning up!" Inside right then I was scream- ing, "You're burning up."

"Look at that," he said. He pointed with his gun to a pile of earth that had been banked up within the last two months. "Sometimes when a fox makes a den she'll bring the earth out one hole, seal it up, and then use the other hole for the entrance. It'll be around here somewhere."

He moved through the trees toward the den, walking sideways. I could not move at all. I just stood with the sun beating down on my head like a fist and my nose running.

I heard the sound of Happ's barking coming closer. He had lost the fox in the woods but now he had a new scent, older, but still hot. He came crashing through the bushes, bellowing every few feet, his head to the ground. He flashed past me, not even seeing me in his intensity, his red eyes on the ground. Like a charging bull, he entered the thicket and he and Uncle Fred stepped into the small grassy clearing at the same moment.

"Here it is," Uncle Fred called. "Come here."

I wanted to turn and run. I did not want to see Uncle Fred and Happ standing in that lovely secluded clearing, but instead I walked through the trees and looked at the place I had avoided so carefully for weeks. There were the bones, some whitened by the sun, a dried turkey wing, feathers, and behind, the partially sheltered hole. Of course Uncle Fred had already seen that, and as I stepped from the trees he pointed to it with his gun.

"There's the den."

I nodded.

"The baby foxes will be in there."

This was the first time he had been wrong. There was only one baby fox in there, and I imagined him crouching now against the far wall of the den.

"Go back to the house and get me a shovel and sack," Uncle Fred said.

Without speaking, I turned and walked back to the house. Behind me the black fox barked again. It was a desperate high series of barks that seemed to last a long time, and Happ lunged after the fox for the third time. It was too late now for tricks, for Uncle Fred remained, leaning on his gun, waiting for the shovel and sack.

I went up the back steps and knocked. Usually I just went in the house like I did at my own home, but I waited there till Aunt Millie came and I said, "Uncle Fred wants me to bring him a sack and a shovel."

"Did you get the fox?"

"Uncle Fred found the den."

"If it's in the woods, he'll find it," she said, coming out the door, "but you ought to see that man try to find a pair of socks in his own drawer. Hazeline," she called up to her window, "you want to go see your dad dig out the baby foxes?"

"No."

"I declare that girl is in the worst mood." She walked with me to the shed, put the shovel in my hand, and then pressed a dusty grain sack against me. "Now, you don't be too late."

"I don't think it will take long."

"Are you all right? Your face is beet red."

"I'm all right."

"Because I can make Hazeline take that shovel to her dad."

"I feel fine."

I started toward the orchard with the shovel and sack and I felt like some fairy tale character who has been sent on an impossible mission, like proving my worth by catching a thousand golden eagles in the sack and making a silver mountain for them with my shovel. Even that did not seem as difficult as what I was really doing.

It must have taken me longer to get back than I thought, for Uncle Fred said, "I thought you'd gotten lost."

"No, I wasn't lost. I've been here before."

I handed him the shovel and let the sack drop to the ground. As he began to dig, I closed my eyes and pressed my hands against my eyelids, and I saw a large golden sunburst, and in this sunburst the black fox came running toward me.

I opened my eyes and watched Uncle Fred. He dug as he did everything else—powerfully, slowly, and without stopping. His shovel hit a rock and he moved the shovel until he could bring the rock out with the dirt. At my feet the gravelly pile of earth was growing.

I turned away and looked across the creek, and I saw for the fifteenth and last time the black fox. She moved anxiously toward the bushes and there was a tension to her steps, as if she were ready to spring or make some other quick, forceful movement. She barked. She had lost the dog again, and this bark was a high clear call for Uncle Fred and me to follow her.

There was a grunt of satisfaction from Uncle Fred and I turned to see him lift out, on the shovel, covered with sand and gravel, the baby fox.

He turned it onto the sack and the baby fox lay without moving.

"He's dead," I said.

Uncle Fred shook his head. "He's not dead. He's just play-acting. His ma taught him to do that."

We both looked down at the little fox without speaking. I knew that if I lived to be a hundred, I would never see anything that would make me feel any worse than the sight of that little fox pretending to be dead when his heart was beating so hard it looked like it was going to burst out of his chest.

I looked over my shoulder and the black fox was gone. I knew she was still watching us, but I could not see her. Uncle Fred was probing the den with his shovel. I said, "I don't think there are any more. She just had one."

He dug again, piled more earth on the pile, then said, "You're right. Usually a fox has five or six cubs."

"I think something happened to the others."

He bent, folded the ends of the sack, and lifted the baby fox. I took the shovel, he the gun, and we started home, the baby fox swinging between us. Happ joined us as we crossed the creek and began to leap excitedly at the sack until Uncle Fred had to hold it shoulder-high to keep it from him.

We walked back to the house without speaking. Uncle Fred went directly to some old rabbit hutches beside the garage. Uncle Fred opened one, shook the baby fox out of the sack, and then closed the wire door.

The baby fox moved to the back of the hutch and looked at us. His fur was soft and woolly, but his eyes were sharp. Nervously he went to one corner.

Aunt Millie came out and looked. "Just like a baby lamb," she said. "It's a sweet little thing, isn't it?"

"That's not the way you were talking yesterday," Uncle Fred said.

"Well, I'm not going to have anything after my chickens," she said. "Not *anything!* I'd be after you with the broom if you bothered my chickens." They laughed. Her spirits seemed greatly improved now that the fox was doomed, and she called, "Hazeline, come on out here and look at this cute little baby fox."

"No."

Uncle Fred went into the shed, returned, and snapped a lock over the cage latch.

"You think somebody's going to steal your fox?" Aunt Millie laughed.

"I wouldn't put it past a fox to open up an unlocked cage to get her baby."

Aunt Millie shook her head in amazement, then said, "Well, you men have got to get washed up for supper."

We went into the house and I said to Uncle Fred, "What are you going to do with the baby fox?"

"That's my bait. Every hunter alive's got some way to get a fox. They got some special trap or something. Mr. Baynes down at the store makes up a special mixture that he says foxes can't resist. My way is to set up a trap, using the baby fox for bait. I'll sit out on the back porch tonight and watch for her."

"Oh."

"It never fails. That is one bait a fox can't resist."

"Are you getting sick?" Aunt Millie asked at supper that night.

"I guess I'm a little tired."

"Well, I should think so! Helping with the pump out in the broiling sun all morning and then tracking that fox all afternoon. It's a wonder you don't have heat stroke. You eat something though, hear? You have to keep up your strength."

"I'm just not hungry."

"It's the heat. But, listen, you drink your tea. You *will* have heat stroke sure enough if you let your body get dried out."

I finished my tea and went up to my room. I did not even look out the window, because I knew I could see the rabbit hutch by the garage and I never again wanted to see that baby fox cowering against the wall.

Hazeline came out of her room and looked in at me on the bed. "You feeling better?"

I nodded.

"Hazeline?"

"What?"

"You know that fox I was telling you about? The black one?"

"Sure."

"Well, your dad has her baby out in the rabbit hutch and he's going to shoot her."

"I know it. I heard. But, listen, don't let it upset you, hear?"

"Hazeline, I don't want anything to happen to that fox."

"Tommy, listen, all wild animals die in some violent way. It's their life. Wild animals just don't die of old age. They get killed by an enemy or by the weather or they have an accident or they get rabies or some other disease or they get shot. That's the way nature is."

"I know that," I said quickly, because I did not want to hear any more.

"You just forget the fox. Tomorrow maybe we can go to the picture show in Clinton or something."

"All right."

She went down the steps then and out onto the porch, and I could hear the swing begin to creak.

I got up and went down the steps and walked to the tree in front of the rabbit hutch. I could not explain why I did this. I didn't want to see the baby fox again, and yet here I was.

He did not see me. He was busy biting the wires of his cage with great fury and determination. I could hear the clicking of his sharp tiny teeth against the wire, but he was making no progress. Then he stopped. He still had not seen me, but he had heard or smelled something and he raised his head and let out a short cry. He waited, then after a moment he began biting the wires again.

I remained by the tree watching him, listening for the quavering cry that he uttered from time to time.

"Don't get your fingers in the cage," Uncle Fred warned behind me. "He may not be able to cut wire yet, but he sure could hurt a finger."

"All right."

"In a bit, when it starts getting dark, you can sit up here with me and watch for the fox."

I went into the kitchen where Aunt Millie was standing in front of the electric fan.

I heard the cry of the baby fox again, and I thought I would be hearing that sound forever. One time Petie Burkis fell down and broke his leg on the school playground and he said, "Oh!" in this real terrible, painful way, and I never could forget it. Later I tried to make him say it again that same way, and one whole afternoon Petie did nothing but say the word *Oh* over and over—a thousand times maybe, and in all those thousand tries, he never sounded that same way again. I still remember it though, exactly, like I will always remember the way that baby fox sounded when he cried.

It seemed to get dark quickly that night. Uncle Fred was already out on the back porch. He had brought out a chair and was sitting with his gun beside him, pointing to the floor. I never saw anyone sit quieter. You wouldn't have noticed him at all he was so still.

I stood behind him inside the screen door. Through the screen I could see the tiny fox lift his black nose and cry again. Now, for the first time, there was an answer— the bark of his mother.

I looked toward the garden, because that's where the sound had come from, but Uncle Fred did not even turn his head. In a frenzy now that he had heard his mother, the baby fox moved about the cage, pulling at the wire and crying again and again.

Just then there was the sound of thunder from the west, a long rolling sound, and Aunt Millie came to the door beside me and said, "Bless me, is that thunder?" She looked out at the sky. "Was that thunder, Fred?"

"Could be," he said without moving.

"Look!" Aunt Millie said. "I swear I see black clouds. You see, Tom?"

"Yes'm."

"And feel that breeze. Honestly, when you think you have reached absolutely the end of your endurance, then the breeze comes. I could not have drawn one more breath of hot air, and now we are going to have a storm."

We stood in the doorway, feeling the breeze, forgetting for a moment the baby fox.

Then I saw Uncle Fred's gun rise ever so slightly in the direction of the fence behind the garage. I could not see any sign of the fox, but I knew that she must be there. Uncle Fred would not be wrong.

The breeze quickened, and abruptly the dishpan which Aunt Millie had left on the porch railing clattered to the floor. For the first time Uncle Fred turned his head and looked in annoyance at the pan and then at Aunt Millie.

"Did it scare your fox off?" she asked.

He nodded, then shifted in the chair and said, "She'll be back."

In just this short time the sky to the west had gotten black as ink. Low on the horizon forks of lightning streaked the sky.

"Now, Fred, don't you sit out here while it's thundering and lightning. I mean it. No fox is worth getting struck by lightning for."

He nodded and she turned to me and said, "You come on and help me shut the windows. Some of those upstairs are stuck wide open. Just hit them with the heel of your hand on the side till you can get them down."

I started up the stairs and she said again, "Fred, come on in when it starts storming. That fox'll be back tomorrow night too."

I went upstairs and started hitting the sides of the windows. I had just gotten one window to jerk down about two inches when I heard the gunshot. I had never heard any worse sound in my life. It was a very final sound, like the most enormous period in the world. Bam. Period. The end.

I ran out of my room and down the steps so fast I could not even tell you how many times my feet touched the stairs, none maybe. I went out the back door, opening it so fast I hit the back of Uncle Fred's chair. I looked toward the rabbit hutch, said, "Where?" then looked at the back fence. Then I looked down at Uncle Fred, who was doing something with his gun.

"Missed," he said.

Suddenly I felt weak. My legs were like two pieces of rope, like that trick that Hindu magicians do when they make rope come straight up out of a basket and then say a magic word and make the rope collapse. My legs felt like they were going to collapse at any second. I managed

to force these two pieces of rope to carry me up the stairs and into the room.

I closed two windows, and the third one, in sympathy perhaps, just banged down all by itself. Then I sank to the bed.

■■■■■■■■■

I had no intention of going to sleep when I lay down on the bed; I did not think I would ever be able to sleep again, but that is what I did. I fell right asleep and did not even move until four hours later when I awoke. It was one o'clock in the morning.

The storm was in full force, or perhaps it was a second storm, but the house was quiet. I got up and went out into the hall. I could not hear anything but the sound of the rain and Hazeline's transistor radio, which was sputtering with static beside her on the pillow.

I went down the stairs, one by one. I did not make a sound. I stepped on the part of the steps near the wall because Petie had told me that was how burglars got up stairs unheard. I was just stepping into the hall when without warning the hall light went on. Aunt Millie was standing there in her bathrobe squinting at me.

"What's wrong?" she asked.

"Nothing. I just didn't know what time it was."

"Well"—she looked closely at her watch—"it's just past one o'clock."

"I went to sleep in my clothes."

"Well, you get on your pajamas and get back to bed. This is the first good sleeping night we've had, and you mustn't let it go to waste."

"Sure."

"Well, go on back up the steps." She watched me go up two steps and then she said, "Goodness, we've gotten on so well all summer, I'd hate for anything to happen now right before your parents get home."

"Aunt Millie, did Uncle Fred get the fox?"

"No."

"Is he still out on the porch?"

"In this rain? No, he is fast asleep in his bed like you ought to be."

She waited until I was up the stairs and then she turned out the light. I went into my room and she called, "Are you getting in bed?"

I lay down. "Yes."

"And go to sleep."

I lay in bed for a long time, still in my clothes, and then I got up very carefully. I walked over to the window and looked out at the tree. I opened the window, pushed out the screen, reached out into the rain, and felt for the smooth spot Aunt Millie had told me was worn into the bark of the tree.

I took off my shoes and knelt on the window sill. There was an enormous flash of lightning that turned the whole world white for a moment, and then I climbed out onto the nearest branch and circled the trunk round with my arms.

I thought that I could never get one step farther. I thought that I could never move even one muscle or I would fall. I thought that in the morning when Aunt Millie came up to see why I wasn't at breakfast she would find me here, pressed into the tree, still frozen with fear.

The rain was hard and slanting directly into my face. Finally I got up just enough courage to turn my face out of the rain. Then the lightning flashed again and I saw the ground about a million miles below. I held the tree so tightly the bark was cutting into my cheek.

I don't know how long I stayed that way. If I had tried to look at my watch, just that little movement would have thrown me off balance. After a while, though, I began to sort of slip down the tree. I never let go of the main trunk for a second. I just moved my arms downward in very small movements. Then slowly, when I was practically kneeling on the first limb, I let my foot reach down for the next one.

If there were smooth spots on those branches, my feet never found them. They only touched one rough limb after another as, slowly, I kept inching down the tree, feeling my way, never looking down at the ground until, finally, my foot reached out for another limb and felt the cold wet grass. It shocked me for a moment and then I jumped down, landing on my hands and knees.

I got up and ran to the rabbit hutch. The baby fox was huddled in one corner of the pen where there was some shelter from the rain. The lightning flashed and I saw him watching me.

"I'm going to get you out," I said.

He crouched back farther in the hutch. In the next flash of lightning I looked on the ground for a rock and I saw at my feet a small dead frog. I knew that the black fox in all this rain had brought that frog here to her baby. She was right now watching me somewhere.

There were bricks stacked in a neat pile under the hutch and I took one and began to bang it against the lock. I was prepared to do this all night if necessary, but the lock was an old one and it opened right away.

The noise had scared the baby fox and he was now making a whimpering sound. I unhooked the broken lock, opened the cage, and stepped back against the tree.

The baby fox did not move for a moment. I could barely see him, a small dark ball in the back of the cage. He waited, alert and suspicious, and then, after a moment he moved in a crouch to the door of the cage. He cried sharply. From the bushes there was an answering bark.

He crouched lower. The lightning flashed again and in that second he jumped and ran in the direction of the bushes. He barked as he ran. There was an immediate answer, and then only the sound of the rain. I waited against the tree, thinking about them, and then I heard the black fox bark one more time as she ran through the orchard with her baby.

And I thought, Someday I will be in a famous museum, walking along on the marble floors, looking at paintings. There will be one called "Blue Flowers" and I will look at that for a while, and the next one will be "Woman on the Beach" and I will look at that for a while, and then I will glance at the name of the next painting and it will be "Fox with Baby at Midnight," and I will look up and my heart will stop beating because there it will be, just the way it was this night, the black fox and her baby running beneath the wet ghostly apple trees toward a patch of light in the distance. And I thought, leaning against that tree in the rain, if there is a picture like that, I hope sometime I will get to see it.

Suddenly the rain began to slacken and I walked around the house. I had never been so wet in my life and now that it was over I was cold too. And I was tired. I looked up at the tree and there didn't seem to be any point in climbing back up when in just a few hours everyone would know what I had done anyway. I went up on the porch and rang the doorbell.

In all my life I have never felt so dumb and foolish as I did barefooted, soaking wet on that slick porch at two o'clock in the morning, waiting for someone to come and answer the door.

It was Aunt Millie in her cotton robe who turned on the porch light and peered out through the side windows at me.

I must have been an awful sight, like the poor little match girl, for she flung open the door at once and drew me in.

"What are you doing out there? What are you doing?"

"Who is it?" Uncle Fred asked as he came into the hall. He was pulling his pants up over his pajamas.

"It's Tom," Aunt Millie said.

"I meant who's at the door."

"Tom," she said again.

"Tom?"

"Yes, he was just standing out there on the porch."

They both turned and looked at me, waiting for an explanation, and I cleared my throat and said, "Uncle Fred and Aunt Millie, I am awfully sorry but I have let the baby fox out of the rabbit hutch." I sounded very stiff and formal, and I thought the voice was a terrible thing to have to depend on, because I really did want them to know that I *was* sorry, and I didn't sound it the least bit. I knew how much Uncle Fred had looked forward to the hunt and how important getting rid of the fox was to Aunt Millie, and I hated for them to be disappointed now.

There was a moment of silence. Then Aunt Millie said, "Why, that's perfectly all right, isn't it, Fred? Don't you think another thing about that. You just come on to bed. You're going to get pneumonia standing there in that puddle." She started for the linen closet. "I'll get you some towels."

158

Uncle Fred and I were left in the hall alone and I looked up at him and he looked like an enormous blue-eyed Indian.

"I'm sorry," I said again.

He looked at me and I knew he was seeing through all the very casual questions I had been asking all summer about foxes, and seeing through the long days I had spent in the woods. He was remembering the sorry way I had tried to keep him from finding the fox's den and the way I had looked when we did find it. I think all those pieces just snapped into place right then in Uncle Fred's mind and I knew that if there was one person in the world who understood me it was this man who had seemed such a stranger.

He cleared his throat. "I never liked to see wild things in a pen myself," he said.

Think It Over

1. *Did Tom have a boring summer on his uncle's farm? Explain your answer.*

2. *What did Uncle Fred first decide to do with the baby fox?*

3. *Even though he knew Uncle Fred might be angry, Tom released the baby fox. What did Tom believe that made him do that?*

4. *Do you think Tom did the right thing? Explain your answer.*

Write

Visualize the painting, "Fox with Baby at Midnight," that Tom imagined. Then write a poem with the same title.

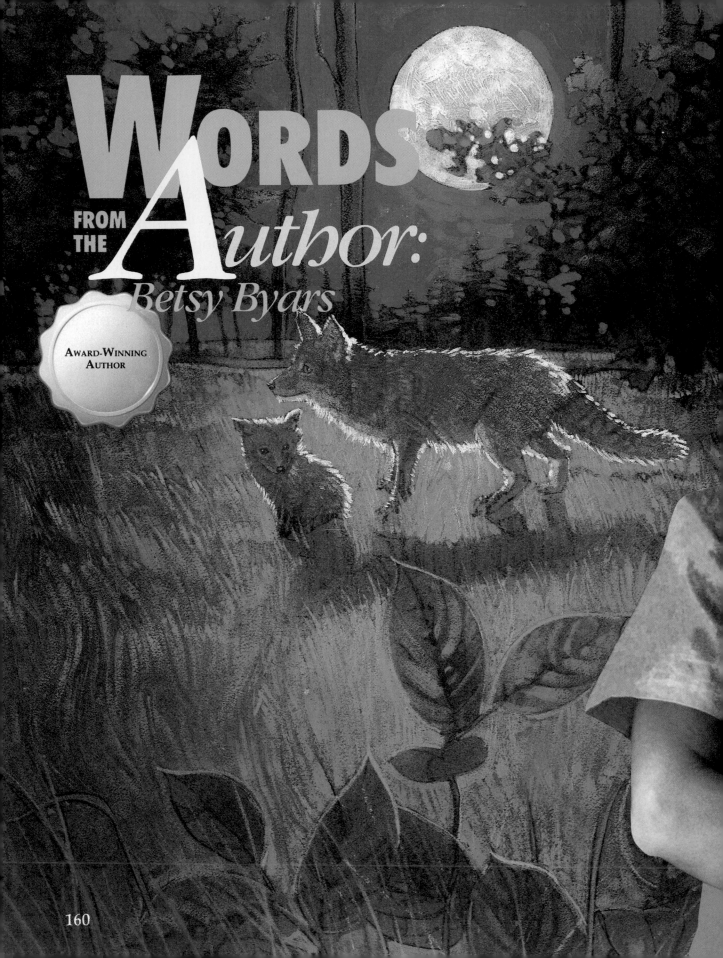

WORDS FROM THE AUTHOR: Betsy Byars

AWARD-WINNING AUTHOR

When I started to write children's books, my own children were very helpful. They were never very excited about reading my manuscripts, but when they did, they would tell me, "No one talks like this," or "this would never happen." I also got many of my ideas from my children's lives. Sometimes I think I've used every single thing that ever happened to them. Now they're beginning to write their own books, and they say they've got nothing left to write about!

The Midnight Fox is my favorite book. It is one of the first ones I wrote that actually came out the way I thought it would. There can be such a gap between what you see in your mind's eye and what actually comes out on the page. The idea for *The Midnight Fox* came from a personal experience. We had a small cabin in West Virginia. We saw deer, raccoons, snakes, and beavers all the time, but I had never seen a fox. One day, I did. It was a stunning moment, and that's when the story came to me. Sometimes when I'm visiting schools, I read the beginning or the end of the book, and I like it more each time. I keep thinking I'm going to write something I like better, but I haven't yet.

THE MARMALADE MAN

from *A Visit to William Blake's Inn*

by Nancy Willard
illustrated by Alice and Martin Provensen

Tiger, Sunflowers, King of Cats,
Cow and Rabbit, mend your ways.
I the needle, you the thread—
follow me through mist and maze.

Fox and hound, go paw in paw.
Cat and rat, be best of friends.
Lamb and tiger, walk together.
Dancing starts where fighting ends.

MAKES A DANCE TO MEND US

HURT NO LIVING THING

by Christina G. Rossetti

Hurt no living thing;
Ladybird, nor butterfly,
Nor moth with dusty wing,
Nor cricket chirping cheerily,
Nor grasshopper so light of leap,
Nor dancing gnat, nor beetle fat,
Nor harmless worms that creep.

ILLUSTRATED BY DUGALD STERMER

CREATURE CARE

Everyone has a responsibility to take care of the creatures on our earth. How do you think people should treat animals? Tell how reading the selection and poems helped you come to your conclusion.

Which poem would you most like to share with other people? What do you want others to learn by reading it?

WRITER'S WORKSHOP Think about an animal that you know is endangered. Write a letter to a friend. Ask your friend to join you in a campaign to try to save the animal from extinction. Include details that tell why you feel as you do about saving the animal. Mail or give the letter to your friend.

WILD WONDERS

Imagine what it would be like to be a leopard or a wolf. Do you think you would like to change places with one of these animals for a day? The animals in the following selections face humorous, exciting, and dangerous problems.

C O N T E N T S

How Many Spots Does A Leopard Have?

from
*How Many Spots Does A Leopard Have?
And Other Tales*

by Julius Lester

illustrated by
David Shannon

ALA NOTABLE
BOOK

One morning Leopard was doing what he enjoyed doing most. He was looking at his reflection in the lake. How handsome he was! How magnificent was his coat! And, ah! The spots on his coat! Was there anything in creation more superb?

Leopard's rapture was broken when the water in the lake began moving. Suddenly Crocodile's ugly head appeared above the surface.

Leopard jumped back. Not that he was afraid. Crocodile would not bother him. But then again, one could never be too sure about Crocodile.

"Good morning, Leopard," Crocodile said. "Looking at yourself again, I see. You are the most vain creature in all of creation."

Leopard was not embarrassed. "If you were as handsome as I am, if you had such beautiful spots, you, too, would be vain."

"Spots! Who needs spots? You're probably so in love with your spots that you spend all your time counting them."

169

Now there was an idea that had not occurred to Leopard. "What a wonderful idea!" he exclaimed. "I would very much like to know how many spots I have." He stopped. "But there are far too many for me to count myself."

The truth was that Leopard didn't know how to count. "Perhaps you will count them for me, Crocodile?"

"Not on your life!" answered Crocodile. "I have better things to do than count spots." He slapped his tail angrily and dove beneath the water.

Leopard chuckled. "Crocodile doesn't know how to count, either."

Leopard walked along the lakeshore until he met Weasel. "Good morning, Weasel. Would you count my spots for me?"

"Who? Me? Count? Sure. One-two-three-four."

"Great!" exclaimed Leopard. "You can count."

Weasel shook his head. "But I can't. What made you think that I could?"

"But you just did. You said, 'One-two-three-four.' That's counting."

Weasel shook his head again. "Counting is much more difficult than that. There is something that comes after four, but I don't know what it is."

"Oh," said Leopard. "I wonder who knows what comes after four."

"Well, if you ask at the lake when all the animals come to drink, you will find someone who can count."

"You are right, Weasel! And I will give a grand prize to the one who tells me how many spots I have."

"What a great idea!" Weasel agreed.

That afternoon all the animals were gathered at the lake to drink. Leopard announced that he would give a magnificent prize to the one who could count his spots.

Elephant said he should be first since he was the biggest and the oldest.

"One-two-three-four-five-six-seven-eight-nine-ten," Elephant said very loudly and with great speed. He took a deep breath and began again. "One-two-three-four-five-si—"

"No! No! No!" the other animals interrupted. "You've already counted to ten once."

Elephant looked down his long trunk at the other animals. "I beg your pardon. I would appreciate it if you would not interrupt me when I am counting. You made me forget where I was. Now, where was I? I know I was somewhere in the second ten."

"The second ten?" asked Antelope. "What's that?"

"The numbers that come after the first ten, of course. I don't much care for those 'teen' things, thirteen, fourteen, and what have you. It is eminently more sensible to count ten twice and that makes twenty. That is multiplication."

None of the other animals knew what Elephant was talking about.

"Why don't you start over again?" suggested Cow.

Elephant began again and he counted ten twice and stopped. He frowned and looked very confused. Finally he said, "Leopard has more than twenty spots."

"How many more than twenty?" Leopard wanted to know.

Elephant frowned more. "A lot." Then he brightened. "In fact, you have so many more spots than twenty that I simply don't have time to count them now. I have an important engagement I mustn't be late for." Elephant started to walk away.

"Ha! Ha! Ha!" laughed Mule. "I bet Elephant doesn't know how to count higher than twenty."

Mule was right.

"Can *you* count above twenty?" Leopard asked Mule.

"Who? Me? I can only count to four because that's how many legs I have."

Leopard sighed. "Can *anyone* count above twenty?" he asked plaintively.

Bear said, "Well, once I counted up to fifty. Is that high enough?"

Leopard shrugged. "I don't know. It might be. Why don't you try and we will see."

Bear agreed. "I'll start at your tail. One-two-three-four-five-six. . . . Hm. Is that one spot or two spots?"

All the animals crowded around to get a close look. They argued for some time and finally agreed that it should only count as one.

"So, where was I?" asked Bear.

"Five," answered Turkey.

"It was six, you turkey," said Chicken.

"Better start again," suggested Crow.

Bear started again and got as far as eleven. "Eleven. That's a beautiful spot right there, Leopard."

"Which one?" Leopard wanted to know.

"Right there. Oh, dear. Or was it that spot there? They're both exquisite. My, my. I don't know where I left off counting. I must start again."

Bear counted as far as twenty-nine this time and then stopped suddenly. "Now, what comes after twenty-nine?"

"I believe thirty does," offered Turtle.

"That's right!" exclaimed Bear. "Now, where did I leave off?"

"You were still on the tail," offered Lion.

"Yes, but was that the twenty-ninth spot, or was it this one here?"

The animals started arguing again.

"You'd better start again," suggested Cow.

"Start what again?" asked Rabbit, who had just arrived.

The animals explained to Rabbit about the difficulty they were having in counting Leopard's spots.

"Is that all?" Rabbit said. "I know the answer to that."

"You do?" all the animals, including Leopard, exclaimed at once.

"Certainly. It's really quite simple." Rabbit pointed to one of Leopard's spots. "This one is dark." He pointed to another. "This one is light. Dark, light, dark, light, dark, light." Rabbit continued in this way until he had touched all of Leopard's spots.

"It's simple," he concluded. "Leopard has only two spots—dark ones and light ones."

All the animals remarked on how smart Rabbit was, all of them, that is, except Leopard. He knew something was wrong with how Rabbit counted, but unless he learned to count for himself, he would never know what it was.

Leopard had no choice but to give Rabbit the magnificent prize.

What was it?

What else except a picture of Leopard himself!

THINK IT OVER

1. *What happens when Leopard tries to have his spots counted?*

2. *How does Leopard fool the other animals?*

WRITE

Imagine that you are Leopard. Write a speech for your classmates, explaining why it is important to know how to count.

Dream Wolf

by Paul Goble

TEACHERS'
CHOICE

Paul Goble

DREAM WOLF

Bradbury Press

Indian people have wonderful stories of wolves (and other animals) who helped women and children when they were lost or in danger; stories of men who were wounded, far from home and help, whom the wolves fed until they recovered.

For centuries Indian people relied upon their dogs to help them. This close relationship extended to the wolves. We, too, love our dogs, and yet we seem unable to see the same expressions in the faces of wolves. We have driven them from nearly every part of North America, and where they still live they are fearful of us. Where the wolf no longer roams he is missed by everything in nature. We feel his loss; Creation is incomplete.

In the old days the people travelled over the plains. They followed the great herds of buffalo.

Every year when the berries were ripe, they would leave the plains and go up into the hills. They made camp in a valley where the berry bushes grow. Everyone picked great quantities. They mashed the berries into little cakes which they dried in the sun. These they stored in painted bags for the winter.

Tiblo (tee-blow) was too young to play with the older boys. He and his little sister, Tanksi (tawnk-she), had to go berry-picking with their mother and the other women and children.

Tiblo was soon tired of picking, and too full to eat any more. When nobody was looking he slipped away with Tanksi to climb the hills.

They climbed up and up among the rocks and cedar trees where bighorn sheep and bears live. Soon they could hardly hear the berry-pickers laughing and calling to each other far below. Tiblo wanted to reach the top. They climbed on.

They never noticed the sun starting to go down behind the hills.

It was getting dark when Tiblo knew they had to go back home. In the twilight every hill and valley looked the same. He did not know which way to go. He called out. . . . Only the echoes answered him.

They wandered on. Tiblo was lost. Darkness closed around them. It grew colder. They were tired and hungry, and Tanksi began to cry.

Speaking of happy things, Tiblo found a small cave among the rocks. They crawled inside to shelter for the night.

The children were tired, and in a little while they fell asleep. Tiblo had a dream.

He dreamed that a wolf with shining eyes entered the cave. In his dream he felt the wolf's hot breath and its rough tongue licking his face. The wolf lay down beside him. His shaggy fur was like a blanket which kept Tiblo and Tanksi warm.

The sun was already shining into the mouth of the cave when Tiblo opened his eyes again.

Tiblo woke up his sister. They crawled out of the cave into the warm sunshine. He took Tanksi by the hand, and they set off walking down the hill.

When the children came to a stream, they stopped to drink. Suddenly Tiblo saw that a wolf was sitting on some rocks close by, watching them. At once he remembered his dream.

"O Wolf," Tiblo said, "we are lost. Mother will be crying. Help us to find our way home again."

The wolf panted and smiled. "My children, do not worry. I will help you. Last night you slept in my den. Follow me now, and I will take you home."

The wolf trotted off. He looked back to see that the children were following. From time to time he trotted ahead out of sight, but he always returned.

At last the wolf led them to a hilltop. The children were filled with joy to see their home in the valley below. The wolf sat back on his haunches and smiled. And then he trotted off back toward the hills. The children begged him to come and live with them.

"No," the wolf called back, "I like to wander from place to place with my friends. Listen for me in the evenings! You will hear me calling, and you will know that I never forget you."

People in the camp saw the children coming down the hill. The men jumped onto their horses, and galloped out to bring them home. Everyone was happy that the children were safe.

Tiblo told how the wolf had brought them home. Everyone walked into the hills to thank the wolf. They spread a blanket for him to sit on. They gave him necklaces and other beautiful gifts.

There has been close kinship with the Wolf People for as long as anyone can remember. That is what they say.

The wolves are no longer heard calling in the evenings at berry-picking time. Hunters have killed and driven them away with guns and traps and poisons. People say that the wolves will return when we, like Tiblo and Tanksi, have the wolves in our hearts and dreams again.

THINK IT OVER

1. *How did the wolf help Tiblo and Tanksi?*

2. *Why do you think Tiblo dreamed about a wolf?*

3. *How did the people in the camp thank the wolf after the children returned?*

WRITE

Wolves need to be protected. Choose another animal, and make a poster that tells what a person can do to help protect that animal.

Running with the

BY SHARON L. BARRY

PHOTOS BY
JIM BRANDENBURG
AND L. DAVID MECH

In a well-known fairy tale, the Big Bad Wolf tries to eat up Little Red Riding Hood. This story is one of many that have caused people to misunderstand and fear wolves. The truth is that healthy wolves do not attack people. Scientists say wolves tend to be intelligent and shy. They live in groups called packs, and cooperate to survive.

Wolves are the largest wild members of the dog family. Gray wolves, shown on these pages, live in parts of North America, Europe, and Asia—usually in packs with no more than eight members. A pack includes a head male and female, their young, and sometimes other adults. The head male usually decides when and what to hunt, and he settles fights. The head female leads the other females, the young, and sometimes the weaker males. The leaders and other pack members communicate by using facial expressions, body postures, and sounds. For example, by standing tall with its ears erect and tail held high, a leader says: "I'm boss." By crouching and lowering its ears and tail, a follower replies: "I know."

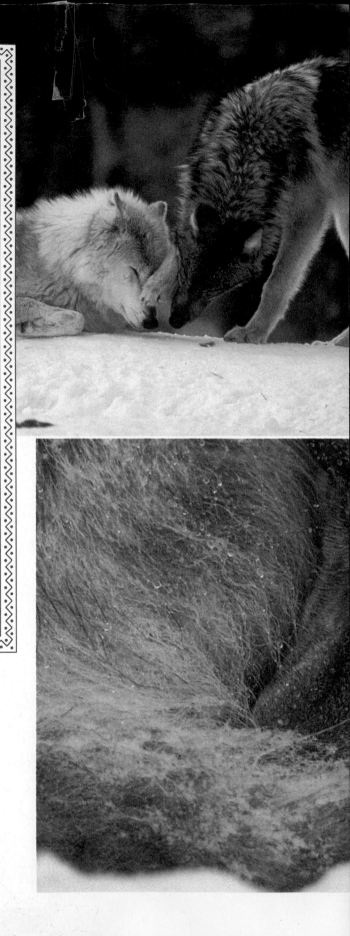

Usually only the head male and female have pups. But all pack members help raise the young. The mother gives birth to about six pups in a den underground, in a rock crevice, or under a fallen tree. She feeds them milk from her body. As the pups grow older, all the adults help feed them by bringing up meat they have swallowed. The whole pack plays with the pups and guards them against bears and other enemies.

Wolves will eat small mammals, lizards, and fruit, but they feed mainly on animals larger than themselves, such as deer and moose. Hunting large prey usually requires group efforts for success. However, even a group hunt may fail, and the wolves may have to go days without eating.

KEEPING IN TOUCH. A youngster nudges its mother's nose. Wolves show affection for other pack members by touching, nuzzling, and licking each other—and by wagging their tails. These gestures help keep the pack close together.

ASLEEP IN THE SNOW, a gray wolf lies curled in a ball with its nose tucked under its bushy tail. By pulling its legs, tail, and head close to its body, the wolf keeps warm. The animal's thick coat helps hold in body heat. Wolves spend most of their time in the open. They even sleep outside on winter days as cold as −50°F (−46°C). Wolves dig dens or use other sheltered areas only when they have young.

188

Wolves once roamed most of North America. But as people settled the land the wolves occupied, many wolves were killed. Today, gray wolves still occupy much of Canada, but they are considered endangered in most of the United States. They can be found in Alaska, Minnesota, Michigan, Montana, and Wisconsin. Because wolves are shy, you probably won't see them if you visit these areas. But you may hear their howls echoing through the wilderness.

TIME-OUT. A pack of gray wolves rests on a snowy hillside in Minnesota. Most gray wolves live in northern areas. In winter, a pack may travel 40 miles (64 km) a day across snow to find food.

THINK IT OVER

1. *Describe how wolves cooperate to survive.*

2. *What areas do wolves occupy today?*

3. *Wolves have been misunderstood for a long time. How has this affected them?*

4. *How do the photographs help you understand wolves?*

WRITE

If you were a writer for a nature magazine, which animal would you choose to study before writing an article? Write the first paragraph for your article, describing that animal.

WILD WONDERS

Animals face many problems just as people do. Decide which animal or animals in the selections face the most serious problems. Why do you feel that these problems are serious?

. . . .

Wolves are fascinating creatures. Think about what you learned about wolves from reading "Dream Wolf" and "Running With the Pack." Which selection did you enjoy more? What did you like about the way the information was presented in that selection? Tell why you feel as you do.

. . . .

WRITER'S WORKSHOP Of the animals' problems that you read about, which could you help solve? Choose one problem and brainstorm some solutions. Then choose one idea and write a how-to paragraph telling step by step how you would help solve that animal's problem.

CONNECTIONS

Augusta Baker

AFRICAN STORYTELLERS

Long ago, African children listened to "why" tales, stories that explained such things as why a certain animal came to look or act as it does.

The art of storytelling is still alive today. Augusta Baker is known as one of America's greatest storytellers and teachers of the art of storytelling. Many other African Americans travel across the United States sharing stories, including "why" tales, that celebrate their culture.

■ *Work with a group to find animal "why" stories from various cultures, and compare the tales. Select one to present as a play or a Readers Theatre production. Create masks for the actors and readers.*

Children from a village in Africa listen to a storyteller.

192

SAVE THE SPECIES

In our country, early Native Americans told "why" stories about many animals that are in danger today. Choose a region of the United States, and find out what animals are endangered there and what is being done to save them. Share your findings in an oral report.

Endangered American bald eagle

FANTASY CREATURE

"Why" tales tell about animals that exist, but there are other tales that describe imaginary animals. Read a story about a fantasy animal, and make a clay or papier-mâché sculpture or a painting to show how you visualize it. Share the story through your art.

To help you visualize your fantasy animal, take notes on a chart like the one shown as you read.

Head	
Body	
Legs/Feet	
Wings	
Tail	
Body covering	

193

NATURE'S·GIFTS

Come forth into the light of things,
Let Nature be your teacher.
William Wordsworth

Native Americans shared nature's gifts with the early European settlers. Since then, Americans have begun to understand that nature provides food and other materials that are necessary for life. When we look at the beauty of different plants found around the world, we begin to see why we should save the rain forests of Brazil and take care of the plants around our homes. Think about ways in which you appreciate nature's gifts as you read the selections in this unit.

MAIN COURSE
. . . .
198

GARDEN VARIETY
. . . .
236

HARVEST HUMOR
. . . .
264

BOOKSHELF

YAGUA DAYS
BY CRUZ MARTEL

Adan thinks rainy summer days are boring until he visits family in Puerto Rico. There he learns that rainy days are special because they are "yagua days." NOTABLE CHILDREN'S TRADE BOOK IN THE FIELD OF SOCIAL STUDIES

HBJ LIBRARY BOOK

GREENING THE CITY STREETS: THE STORY OF COMMUNITY GARDENS
BY BARBARA A. HUFF

Children and adults have fun growing food to eat and flowers to enjoy. At the same time, their gardens make their communities more beautiful. NOTABLE CHILDREN'S TRADE BOOK IN THE FIELD OF SOCIAL STUDIES

THE PEOPLE WHO HUGGED THE TREES

BY DEBORAH LEE ROSE

As a young girl in India, Amrita loved the trees. Her love grew and inspired the people of her village to hug the trees in order to save them from being chopped down.

THIS PLACE IS WET

BY VICKI COBB

Much can be learned from the native Indian tribes of Brazil. For years they have used their imagination to live in harmony with the creatures and the plants of the rain forest. AWARD-WINNING AUTHOR

THE BIG TREE

BY BRUCE HISCOCK

A seed sprouted in 1775, and from it a tree still grows today. For more than 200 years, the big tree has lived through seasons of change.

MAIN COURSE

Did you ever plant a seed, water it, and wait for it to sprout? What did you feed your plant? The plants in the following selections grow and grow because they eat well!

C O N T E N T S

The Amazing BEANS

Michael was the world's messiest kid. He shared a room with his brother, Norman, who was a neatness nut. To keep Norman from complaining about their messy room, Michael gave him an "Amazing Bean." Michael ordered the beans weeks before, and the package just arrived. Both boys planted the beans, but Michael accidentally lost the instructions.

from The Plant That Ate Dirty Socks

by Nancy McArthur

Both plants were growing fast. The sprouts turned into strange vines and began crawling up the window.

As the days passed, little leaves spread out into long pointed shapes. Then they curled up like dark-green ice cream cones.

Norman said, "These plants look weird."

"You're right about something for once," Michael agreed.

Michael's friend Jason, who lived on the other side of town, had his mother drop him off one Saturday to see the plants. "You're right," he said. "These ARE weird."

illustrated by Albert Co

Norman was using bottled plant food, measuring carefully.

Michael sloshed some of that on his plant once in a while. He also slipped it a little dessert—a dab of peanut butter, chocolate chip cookie crumbs, a spoonful of pumpkin pie, and bits of Muncho Cruncho.

His vines got thicker than Norman's. Were they getting fat from all the goodies? He switched to bits of vegetables to see what would happen.

"Can I have a little broccoli, please?" he asked at dinner.

"Why this sudden urge for broccoli?" said Mom, passing it to him. "I usually have to tell you to eat it or else."

"I want to feed some to my plant."

"Aha!" said Norman. "No fair feeding your plant extra stuff!"

"I'm just experimenting."

Dad said, "Those plants are getting too big too fast. If they keep on like this, they'll fill up the whole room. So no more feeding them plant food. Not even broccoli. Just sun and water."

"But that will wreck my experiment," protested Michael.

"No, you've seen how it grows with feeding. Now see how it grows without it."

"But what if it collapses from no food?"

Dad smiled. "That plant looks as if it can take care of itself."

Mom added, "It looks as if it could take over the whole house. Now eat your broccoli or else."

"Or else what?" asked Michael with his mouth full of broccoli.

"Or else tomorrow we'll have those plants for dinner," joked Mom.

Both plants slowed down. Then Norman's seemed to stop growing while Michael's kept getting bigger.

"Are you sneaking food to yours," asked Norman, "when I'm asleep?"

"No, honest, I'm not," replied Michael. He was puzzled, too.

"Then why is yours still growing when mine isn't?"

"Maybe my messy growing methods work better than your neat ones."

Mom came in with a laundry basket. They handed over their dirty clothes. But Michael could find only five escaped socks.

"There must be more here somewhere," he said.

"They'll turn up," said Mom, "the next time you clean up."

But they didn't. The next time he found only three.

This mystery, he decided, was easy to solve.

"Norman, you're swiping my socks and hiding them when I'm asleep!"

"Nope, honest, I'm not. I wouldn't touch your yukky old socks!"

"OK, you guys," said Mom. "We're all going to look until we find them. Norman, why are you putting on your football helmet?"

"Because I'm going to look in the closet." He yanked the door open.

"Avalanche!" he yelled, but not much fell out. He was only up to his knees in junk. Norman looked disappointed. He high-stepped out of the pile and dived into the back of the closet.

Michael found one sock in his acorn collection box.

Mom found another one in a bulging book called *The Glob That Ate Outer Space*.

"Don't lose my place," said Michael, putting a blue jay feather between the pages where the sock had been.

"Aha!" exclaimed Norman from the closet. A rolled-up sock came flying out and bounced off Michael's head.

"Aha! Aha!" shouted Norman. Two more zoomed through the air and bonked Michael.

"Stop throwing socks!" yelled Michael.

"I can't stop throwing them."

"Why not?"

"Because I'm kicking them!" Another sock sailed overhead.

"If you don't stop that," Michael warned, "I'm going to drop-kick your football helmet with you in it."

"No fighting," said Mom. "And no more sock kicking."

Norman came out holding a sock with one hand and his nose with the other.

"Give me that," Mom said. "Now we're missing at least ten more."

They looked into and under everything. No more socks.

"Strange," said Mom, "that there were more in the closet than out here."

"Yeah," said Michael. "Mostly I drop my socks right around here by my bed."

That night when he took off his socks, he put them on top of his acorn box right next to the bed. That way they could not get lost among his junk.

In the morning they were gone.

"OK, Norman, very funny. Where are the socks I put right here last night?"

"I didn't touch your smelly old socks."

"Well, they couldn't walk away by themselves."

"Why not? Socks have feet in them."

"Come on, where did you hide them?"

"Maybe the monster in the closet took them."

"The only monster that's been in that closet is you."

"Honest, I didn't take them. Something very weird is going on."

They looked all over. They even used the magnifying glass from Norman's detective kit to search for clues.

But the socks had disappeared without a trace.

At bedtime Michael told Norman, "We're going to solve this mystery tonight."

"Good, I love to detect," said Norman.

Michael dug around in his stuff and found some black string he had known would come in handy some day.

He took off his socks, tied the strings to them, and put them where the others had vanished. Then he got into bed, lay there with his arms straight out, and told Norman to tie the strings to his wrists.

Norman got his Super Splasher Water Blaster and favorite disguise from his detective kit and climbed into bed.

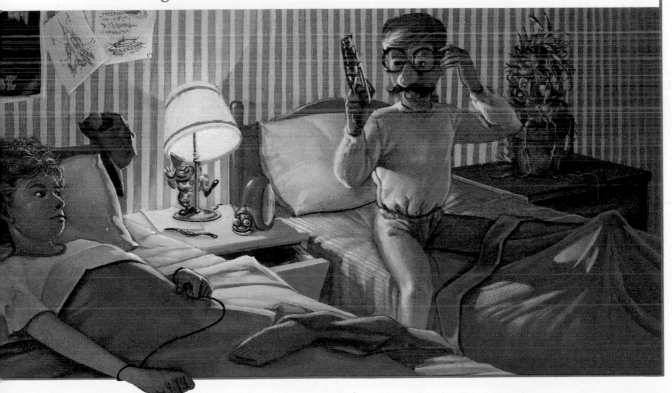

"You don't need a disguise in the dark," said Michael.

"I always detect better when I'm wearing one," replied Norman. He turned out the light and put on his disguise.

"Ready?" asked Michael.

"Ready," said Norman.

They had left the door ajar so a little light came in from the hall. They could barely see the white socks on the floor.

They lay there in the dark waiting. Nothing happened. They waited some more. Norman was lying on his side staring at the socks.

Suddenly one moved!

"It's moving!" he shouted and began squirting wildly with his Water Blaster.

"Oh, no!" yelled Michael.

"I saw it!" Norman insisted excitedly. "It was creeping fast across the floor! Then it jumped up in the air and fell down! There it goes again!" he yelled, bouncing up and down on his bed and squirting more water in every direction.

"No," said Michael. "My nose started to itch. I forgot and reached up to scratch it."

Their parents ran in and turned on the light.

There was Michael with strings and socks dangling. Water was dripping off his hair and the end of his nose.

Norman was waving a giant water pistol and wearing glasses with an attached rubber nose and moustache.

Water was dripping off the plants, soaking into the rug and beds, and running down the walls.

"I know," said Mom, "that there has to be a logical explanation for all this, but it better be a good one, or else."

As they wiped up with towels, Michael explained.

Mom took the socks for safekeeping. Norman refilled his Water Blaster, but Dad took it away from him.

"But I need that," wailed Norman, "to water my plant!"

"No," said Dad. "Everything in this room has been watered enough already. I'll keep it next to my bed so there won't be any more midnight underwater adventures in here."

Since the beds were damp, Michael and Norman had to spend the rest of the night on the living room couch, one at each end with their feet kicking each other in the middle.

As they were falling asleep, Michael whispered, "Tomorrow I'll think of a new master plan."

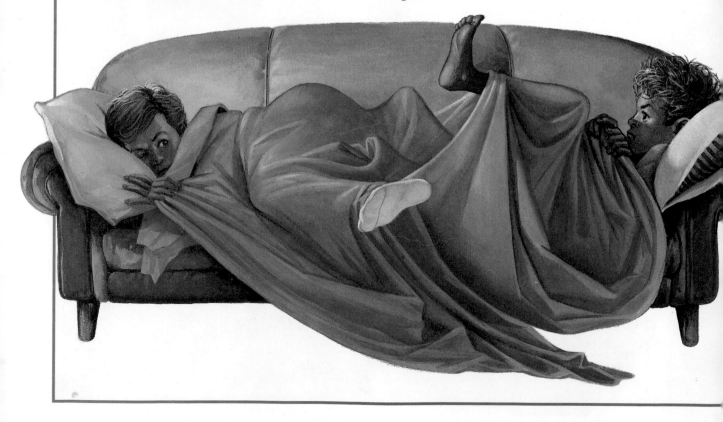

But the next day he decided to try his original master plan once more. It might have worked if his nose hadn't itched.

"But what if your nose itches again?" asked Norman.

"I'm only going to use one sock so I'll have one hand to scratch."

Norman said, "I don't have my Water Blaster, so I'll use my bow and rubber suction cup arrows."

"Your aim with that," said Michael, "would be worse than the water pistol. We'd end up with rubber arrows stuck all over me and the ceiling."

"Then I'll just wear a disguise so if something is stealing your socks I can scare it off. My robot helmet looks pretty scary. See, if something sneaks in here, it'll expect to see kids in our beds. Not a robot. You should wear a disguise, too. Then it will get really scared."

Michael thought Norman's idea was dumb but wouldn't hurt. He dug around in his stacks and pulled out a rubber gorilla head.

"Where did you get that?" asked Norman, his eyes lighting up.

"I traded Jason Greensmith a lot of stuff for it. He terrified everybody in his neighborhood with it."

"It doesn't look very scary," said Norman.

"It does when you have it on," replied Michael.

"Oh, good! Can I wear it? Please!"

Michael could see this would be the perfect thing to make a deal with the next time he wanted something big from Norman.

"No, maybe we can make a deal later," he said. "I'm going to wear it tonight. You get your robot helmet."

After they went to bed they whispered back and forth in the dark until they heard their parents close their bedroom door.

Then they got their flashlights from under the blankets where they had hidden them. Norman tied the string to Michael's wrist. Michael tied the other end to the sock. Then they turned off the flashlights, got back into bed, and put on their disguises.

"Ready?" asked Michael.

"Ready," said Norman.

They waited a long time.

Suddenly Norman whispered, "If your nose itches, remember, don't use the wrong hand."

"OK, OK."

They waited some more.

Norman whispered, "How will you scratch your nose with that mask on?"

"My nose is probably not going to itch. It hardly ever does."

"But what if it does?"

"The mask has big holes under the nose to breathe. I can scratch through there."

"Be sure not to use the wrong hand."

"Will you stop worrying about my nose!"

"I just want to be sure after what happened the last time."

"Norman, if we're going to find out what makes these socks disappear, we have to keep quiet. It only happens when we're asleep, so we have to pretend we are."

Norman was quiet for a long time. Nothing happened. Then he whispered, "I hope it's a raccoon."

"Why?"

"I like raccoons."

"Norman, stop it!"

"OK, OK."

Then Michael whispered, "Now don't get excited. I'm just going to scratch my nose."

"I knew this would happen," said Norman. "Are you using the wrong hand?"

"No!"

It was getting late. Lying there in the dark, pretending to be asleep, they could not stay awake.

Michael woke suddenly. Something was tugging on the string!

He whispered, "It's moving," to Norman and switched on his flashlight.

He saw something green curling around the white sock. A long vine from his plant was dragging it along the floor.

He yelled at Norman to wake up.

"Smurg," mumbled Norman, still completely konked out.

The vine lifted the sock up to one of the big curled leaves. The ice-cream cone shape slowly began sucking it in.

"Schlurrrrrp," said the plant as the sock disappeared.

"Wake up!" shouted Michael as he cut the string from his wrist.

Norman, who had fallen asleep holding his flashlight, turned it on.

Seeing a gorilla looming up in the dark, he gave a bloodcurdling "EEEEEEK," leaped from his bed, and zoomed out the door.

His parents, awakened by the horrible noises, were getting out of bed to come to the rescue. Suddenly they saw a ghostly robot hurtle into their room.

Dad, still half-asleep, grabbed Norman's Super Splasher Water Blaster from the bedside table. He let the robot have it right in the snoot.

At the first cold wet squirt, Norman ducked and disappeared.

Michael, running in right behind him, got the rest of the water.

Mom turned on the light. A short gorilla in wet pajamas stood at the end of the bed.

"You're not going to believe this," he said, "but my plant just ate my sock."

"You're right," said the gorilla's mother. "I don't believe any of this."

Dad looked around. "I saw something in the dark that looked like a robot. Where's Norman?"

"Down here," said a familiar voice from under the bed. "I thought a gorilla was after me."

Mom grabbed his feet and pulled him out.

"Remember," she asked, "when nights used to be normal around here? When everybody went to bed and just stayed there? What's next? Frankenstein and Wolfman?"

"My friend Bob's got a good Frankenstein mask I could borrow," Norman suggested helpfully.

"No way," said Dad. "Now Michael, what about this dream you had about your plant?"

"It wasn't a dream. I woke up and saw it suck up my sock!"

Dad said soothingly, "Everybody has amazing dreams once in a while that seem real."

Michael turned to Norman. "You woke up while it was happening. Tell Dad what you saw."

"All I saw was a gorilla coming at me in the dark. But I'm not going back in there. That plant might get me!" He clutched his throat and made a horrible noise.

"Nothing is going to get you," said Mom. "I think you've both been reading too many books like *The Glob That Ate Outer Space*. Let's find you some dry pajamas. Then we'll check out that plant. You'll see it was only a dream and there's nothing to be afraid of."

Michael explained, "It won't come after us. It only eats socks."

Dad led the way to the boys' room and turned on the light.

"See?" said Mom. "Your plant is just sitting there doing nothing as usual."

Michael walked up to it. "But I saw it eat the sock." He picked a black string off the floor. "This was tied to the sock. Here's the end I cut. The other end looks sort of chewed."

His parents looked closely.

"There must be some logical explanation for this," said Mom, "but I have no idea what it is."

Michael replied, "The logical explanation is that the plant ate my sock. Especially since I saw it."

"There is a Venus-flytrap plant that eats insects," said Dad, "but this is ridiculous."

"This must be a Sock Trap plant," said Norman.

"The way it's been growing," said Mom, "and with all the socks we're missing, I wouldn't be surprised."

"I'll prove it to you with an experiment," said Michael. He took a pair of socks from his dresser drawer and put one in front of his plant and the other in front of Norman's. He tied black string around them and fastened the other ends to the bedposts.

"Now Norman and I will sleep on the couch. We'll lock this door. In the morning you'll see what happened."

He turned out the lights, locked the door, and gave the key to Mom.

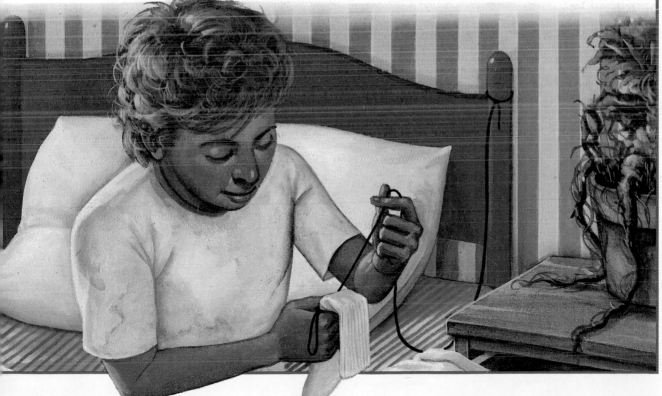

A moment after the door closed, Michael's plant rustled its leaves as if a little breeze were passing by. Then it made a funny noise that sounded like a contented burp after a good meal.

Michael woke up early and awakened everyone else. Mom handed over the key. Michael slowly opened the door.

They stared in amazement.

The sock in front of Michael's plant was still there. But the one in front of Norman's had vanished!

Michael was baffled.

Norman was upset. "Your plant reached over on my side of the room! It's not supposed to do that!"

"I don't think it did," said Michael. He pointed to the string still tied to Norman's bedpost. The other end was hanging from Norman's plant.

"My plant wouldn't eat your yukky old dirty socks," Norman protested.

"That's it!" exclaimed Michael. "Those socks weren't dirty. I got them out of the drawer. The ones that disappeared before were dirty. That's the only kind I leave on the floor. So my plant only likes dirty socks. It didn't want a clean one."

THINK IT OVER

1. What did Michael and Norman do to solve the missing-sock mystery?

2. What foods did Michael feed to his plant?

3. How was each boy's plant like him?

4. Would you rather be Michael's or Norman's friend? Explain why.

WRITE

Imagine that you planted some amazing beans. Write seven journal entries recording how you cared for your plant and how it reacted.

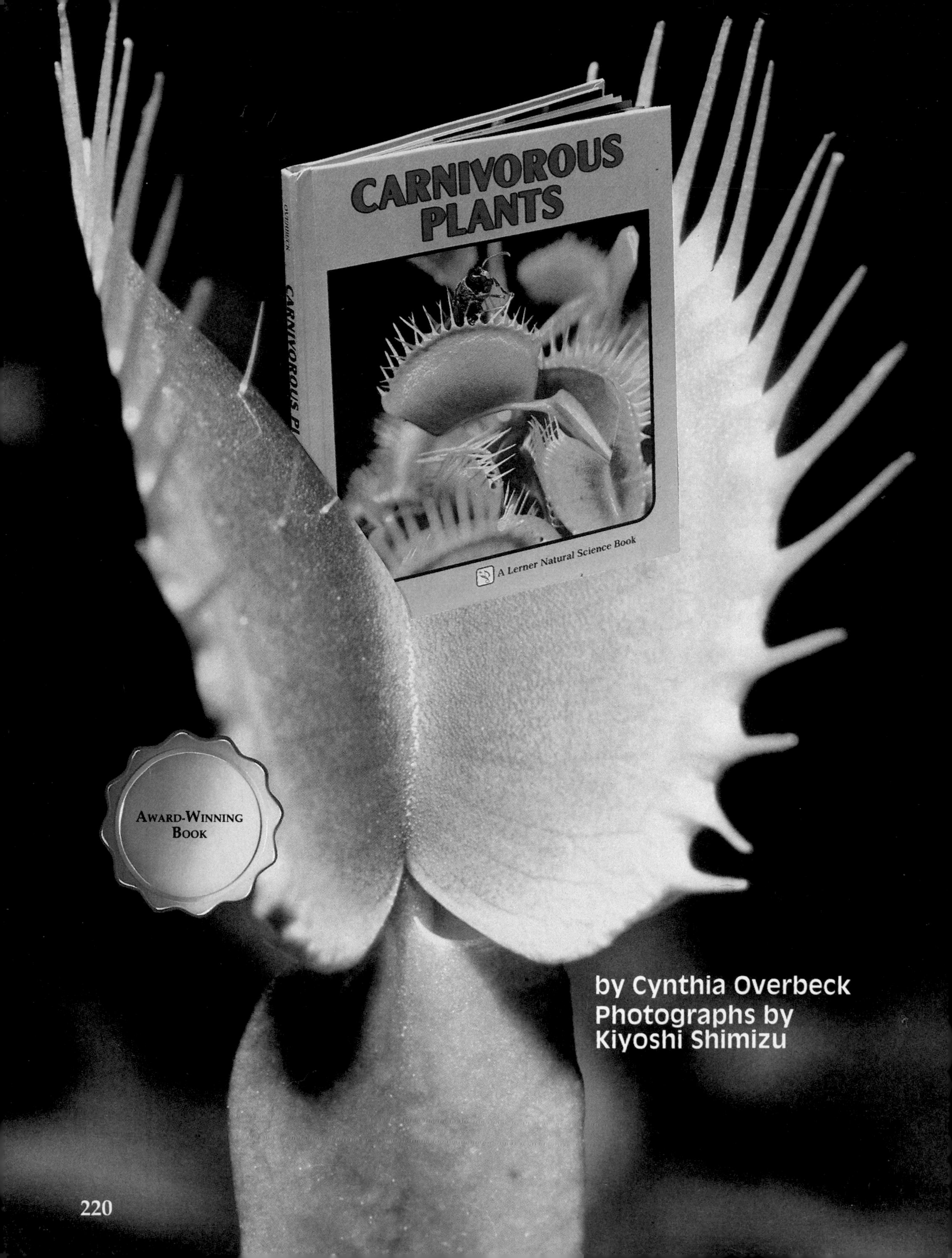
CARNIVOROUS PLANTS
OVERBECK
CARNIVOROUS PL
A Lerner Natural Science Book
AWARD-WINNING BOOK

by Cynthia Overbeck
Photographs by
Kiyoshi Shimizu

xotic Plants

A black fly hovers in the air over a strange-looking plant. Attracted by a sweet smell, the fly lands on the flat, reddish surface of one of the plant's leaves. It begins to crawl across. Suddenly, the leaf moves! Before the fly can get away, the two halves of the leaf close around it. Two rows of "teeth" clamp together. All escape is cut off. The fly struggles to free itself, but the trap only closes more tightly. Soon, the fly is dead. In a few days, there is nothing left but the hard parts of its body.

This unlucky insect has become food for one of the world's most exotic plants—the Venus flytrap. The flytrap is one of about 450 species, or kinds, of carnivorous plants. **Carnivorous** (kar-NIH-vor-us) means "meat-eating." A plant that is carnivorous actually traps and eats insects, spiders, and, in some cases, tiny animals like frogs and mice. Carnivorous plants have developed this special way of feeding themselves in order to live and grow in a particular kind of environment.

In order to survive, most plants must take in water and minerals from the soil. These elements are combined with carbon dioxide and energy from sunlight to make the food that plants need to grow. Nitrogen is one of the most important minerals needed for plant growth. For this reason, most plants grow best in places where the soil is rich in nitrogen.

But carnivorous plants grow in wet, low-lying swamps and marshes. Here the damp soil is nitrogen-poor. Plants that take in nitrogen through their roots cannot live in such soil. Carnivorous plants stay alive by getting nitrogen and other minerals from another source. These plants get minerals from the bodies of the creatures that they trap and kill. The special leaves of carnivorous plants allow them to catch and use this handy source of food.

How do these unusual plants work? First, they must lure, or attract, animals. Unlike a frog or a bird, a carnivorous plant cannot reach out and grab an insect. It must wait until the insect comes to it. For this reason, carnivorous plants have special ways of attracting insects and other animals.

Some carnivorous plants give off a sweet smell like that of nectar, which attracts insects such as flies, bees, and ants. Others give off a smell of decay, to which flies and some other insects are equally attracted. Many carnivorous plants have bright colors and patterns that serve as lures. And a whole group has leaves covered with sparkling droplets that attract insects with bright color and light, as well as with a sweet smell.

Once an animal has been lured to the plant, it must be trapped. Generally, carnivorous plants have two main kinds of traps: **active,** or moving, traps and **passive,** or still, traps. Plants with active traps, like those of the Venus flytrap and the waterwheel, have parts that move quickly to trap any insect that lands on them. The moving parts may clamp together like jaws. Or they may swing shut like a trapdoor.

Passive traps do not depend on movement of their parts to trap animals. Some passive traps, like those of

A waterwheel plant

the sundews, are sticky traps. Although some of them may move after they have caught an insect, the actual trapping is done by a sticky substance on their leaves. This substance catches and holds insects without the need for movement.

Other passive traps are the "pitfall" type. They are found in the pitcher plants. Inside the leaves of these plants are cleverly made one-way tunnels into which insects are lured by sweet nectar. Once they are inside, the insects cannot get back out.

One type of pitcher plant

All of these traps help to feed the plants on which they grow. Usually, many traps grow on one plant. They all work together to catch, digest, and absorb the nutrition that the plant needs to survive.

Active Traps

Perhaps the most familiar of the carnivorous plants is the Venus flytrap. This plant is found only in the United States, in the swamps of North Carolina. The entire plant grows about a foot (30 centimeters) tall. In spring it has pretty white flowers blooming on top of tall stalks. But the most interesting parts of this plant are its leaves.

The flytrap's narrow green leaves grow in a circle around the plant's base. Each leaf blade opens into two halves, almost like a clamshell. The two halves, or **lobes,** are attached to a center rib. Each lobe averages about an inch (2.5 centimeters) in length. The inside surfaces of the lobes are usually a reddish color. Around the curved outer edge of each lobe is a row of stiff, pointed bristles, called **cilia** (SIL-ee-uh). On the inside surface of each lobe are three "trigger" hairs.

The Venus flytrap

These strange leaves are the plant's traps. When the lobes are in an open position, the traps are set, ready for a meal. In the pictures, a spider has been attracted by a leaf's red color and by the sweet smell of a nectar-like substance produced on its edges. As the spider crawls onto the leaf's surface, it disturbs the trigger hairs. This is the signal for the lobes to move. But the trap must receive two signals in order to close. It will react only if one hair is touched twice or if two hairs are touched. This is the plant's way of making sure that it has caught a live, moving creature and not a piece of grass or a leaf.

Once the double signal has been given, the lobes close quickly around the spider. The cilia lock together to prevent escape. At this point, a very small spider or insect could still crawl out from between the cilia. The plant rejects such tiny animals because it would use more of its energy to digest them than it would gain from their bodies in food value.

As the trap closes, a fluid begins to ooze out of the inner surfaces of the lobes, and the spider is drowned. The fluid contains **digestive enzymes** (EN-zimes), substances that change the spider's body material into a form that the plant can absorb as nourishment. As more and more enzymes flow into the trap, the spider's soft body parts gradually dissolve.

In 8 to 10 days, the body parts of the animal have become a nitrogen-rich liquid that is absorbed into the plant. The trap opens, and out fall the hard body parts that the plant could not digest. The trap is now set again. One trap will usually catch and digest an average of three meals before it withers and dies.

Left: **The pictures show the leaf of a Venus flytrap capturing a spider.**

Right: **Another Venus flytrap catches an insect.**

A waterwheel plant with its leaves open

Another carnivorous plant that uses an active trap much like that of the Venus flytrap is known as the waterwheel plant. It is found in Europe, Australia, India, Japan, and Africa. This small, rootless plant floats just under the surface of quiet ponds and swamps. The whole plant is only about 4 to 12 inches (10 to 30 centimeters) long. Its little white flowers, which bloom in the spring, show above the water's surface. The traps are underwater.

Each plant has a slender stem with leaves that are almost transparent. Groups of eight leaves are arranged around the stem like the spokes of a wheel. This is why the plant is called the waterwheel.

The waterwheel's leaves are its traps. Each leaf is very tiny—less than $\frac{1}{4}$ inch (6 millimeters) long. Such tiny traps can catch only very small creatures. The waterwheel feeds on water fleas, on **plankton,** or microscopic water animals, and on tiny **larvae** (LAR-vee)—insects in an early stage of development.

This waterwheel leaf has caught an insect larva.

The waterwheel's leaves act just like underwater Venus flytraps. They have two lobes, rows of bristles, and trigger hairs inside their lobes. When an insect enters a trap, the halves snap shut in a fraction of a second. The waterwheel then digests its meal and reopens to catch the next one.

Both the Venus flytrap and the waterwheel plant use a clamping movement to trap animals. But another type of carnivorous plant with an active trap—the bladderwort—moves in a different way. The bladderwort has a kind of trapdoor for catching its meals.

Bladderworts are found in many parts of the world. Although some bladderworts grow on land, most grow in quiet ponds and swamps. Like the waterwheel plants, they do not have roots. They float in strands or clumps just below the water's surface. In summer, their tiny yellow or purple flowers bloom above the water.

Growing all along the bladderwort's thin stems are its leaves. Each leaf is actually a little air bag, or **bladder.** The bladders are very small; the biggest is only about $\frac{1}{5}$ inch (5 millimeters) long. These tiny, balloon-like leaves are the traps the bladderwort uses to catch water fleas, insect larvae, and sometimes small tadpoles.

At one end of each bladder are feathery hairs that serve as triggers. These hairs are arranged around an opening, across which is a tiny "trapdoor." This door swings open only one way—inward.

To trap insects, the bladder uses suction. When the door is closed and the bladder is empty, its walls are limp and collapsed. Then an insect swims by and brushes against the trigger hairs. Suddenly the bladder walls expand. This forces the trapdoor open and creates a sucking action. As the walls expand, water rushes in, pulling the insect with it. Then the trapdoor slams shut, and the insect is caught inside the bladder.

Immediately the digestive enzymes inside the bladder go to work. If the insect is tiny, the bladder takes only 15 to 30 minutes to absorb the nitrogen and other minerals from its body. If the insect is larger, digestion may take up to 2 hours. Sometimes, a bladder gets hold of an insect or larva that is too large to fit inside it. Then it digests the meal bit by bit. A single bladder can catch and digest about 15 small creatures before it dies.

This photograph, taken through a microscope, shows the many tiny bladders that grow on a single plant.

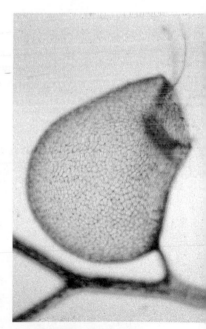

An enlarged picture of a single bladder

Above: **Sundews growing among other marsh plants**

Passive Traps

Flytraps, waterwheels, and bladderworts all use active traps to catch their food. But other carnivorous plants use passive traps—traps that do not depend on movement to capture insects. One group of plants, the sundews, uses a sticky trap.

Left: **A closeup view of the surface of a sundew leaf**

229

The small roundleaf sundew provides a good example of the way a sticky trap works. This plant grows in many swampy areas of the world, including parts of the United States. The plant is small—about $3\frac{1}{2}$ inches (8 centimeters) across. It is often partly hidden among taller weeds and plants that grow around it.

In summer the roundleaf's tall center stems carry white flowers. The leaves of the sundew look bright red. They seem to be covered with sparkling drops of dew. But what looks like a pretty red, dewdrop-covered leaf is really a deadly trap for flies and other insects.

The sundew's leaves are covered with many little stalks of different heights. At the top of each stalk is a tiny **gland,** or organ, that produces a clear, sticky liquid. This liquid forms a droplet on the tip of the stalk. Usually the gland is a reddish color, so the liquid on it appears to be red, too.

Flies and other insects are drawn to the sundew by the color and sparkling light, as well as by an attractive scent that the plant gives off. But when a fly lands on a sundew leaf, it is in trouble.

Immediately its feet are caught in the sticky liquid on top of the taller stalks. As the fly struggles to escape, more sticky liquid flows out of the glands. Now the fly is trapped for good. The stalks around the fly bend toward its body, giving off more liquid. The whole leaf curls slightly to cup the body. Digestive enzymes work until the soft parts of the fly have dissolved and become absorbed into the leaf. After four or five days, the leaf and stalks uncurl.

The pictures on these two pages show a fly being trapped and digested by a sundew leaf.

Of all the carnivorous plants with passive traps, perhaps none are more exotic-looking than the pitcher plants. These plants have special leaves that are hollow and can hold water, almost like a real jug or pitcher. The leaves are the plant's traps. Their structure and appearance are so unusual that people have given them many fanciful nicknames, such as huntsman's cup and Indian dipper.

There are about 80 kinds of pitcher plants growing in the wetlands of the world. Many, like the North American pitcher plant, grow close to the ground in a circle around a center base. All of the leaves of these plants are traps for catching insects.

Other pitcher plants are found in the tropical wetlands of Malaysia, Madagascar, and Sri Lanka. These plants have many brightly colored pitcher leaves growing on vines.

These tropical pitcher plants have ordinary green leaves as well as brightly colored pitcher leaves. The pictures show how their pitchers grow from a **tendril,** or threadlike stem. As the leaf grows, it swells to form a colorful "jug." The top opens to form a leafy hood. In some pitcher plants this hood is just a kind of frill around the pitcher's edges. In others it forms a flat "roof" above the whole opening.

The leaves of various kinds of pitcher plants may differ in size as well as in color, pattern, and shape. They can be from 2 inches (5 centimeters) to more than 2 feet (60 centimeters) tall. Small pitcher plants trap insects such as flies, beetles, and ants. The largest pitchers can also

Three stages in the development of a pitcher leaf

trap small frogs or mice. But whatever their size or outer appearance, all pitchers trap animals in basically the same way.

A pitcher trap is passive; it does not need to move in order to trap an insect. Instead, its clever design becomes a prison for almost any insect that crawls into it.

The leaf forms a kind of tube. At the top is an opening, usually brightly colored. The bottom part of the tube is shaped like a cup. Rainwater collects in this cup. (In the pitchers that grow close to the ground, water is also drawn up from the soil to fill the cup.) In most types of plants, the hood above the opening helps to keep too much rainwater from coming in. This hood always stays open. It never snaps shut to trap an insect, as some people believe.

A sweet nectar is produced around the lip of the pitcher opening. Attracted by the nectar and the bright colors of the pitcher, an insect flies or crawls onto the convenient lip. It begins to sip the nectar and soon crawls further into the opening, searching for more.

When the insect moves into the tube of the pitcher plant, it is in trouble. The inside walls of the tube are slick and slippery as ice. The insect slips further down. There it finds its footing along hairs that line the lower part of the tube. But the hairs all face downward, toward the pool of water below. Once the insect has crawled past them, it is impossible for it to get back up. The insect struggles but finally becomes exhausted and falls into the water below. There it drowns.

This x-ray picture shows a pitcher partly filled with water.

Now digestive enzymes flow into the pool. As in other carnivorous plants, the soft parts of the insect's body are digested and absorbed into the plant. The hard parts of the body collect in the bottom of the pitcher.

Pitcher plants, like all the carnivorous plants in this article, have found ways to thrive in places where most plants could not live. With the help of their strange and often beautiful leaves, they feed on the creatures that share their marsh environment.

Plant Preservation

But as hardy as carnivorous plants are, today the lives of many of them may be in danger. As people drain more and more marshland to make way for buildings and roads, the plants have fewer places to grow. They are becoming increasingly rare.

Today people are trying to grow some carnivorous plants in indoor greenhouses. In this way, they hope to preserve these fascinating and unusual plants and to make sure that they do not disappear from our world.

THINK IT OVER

1. *How are carnivorous plants different from most other plants?*

2. *Where do carnivorous plants grow?*

3. *What is the difference between a passive trap and an active trap?*

4. *How are all carnivorous plants alike?*

5. *Which carnivorous plant would be most helpful in your house? Explain why you think as you do.*

A cross-section view of a pitcher plant leaf. The fly is about to become a prisoner inside the pitcher tube.

WRITE

Draw an imaginary carnivorous plant. Then list the steps it takes to trap insects.

MAIN COURSE

Some plants have very unusual eating habits. In what ways are the plants in the two selections you read alike? How are they different?

Which plant that you read about would you give as a gift? To whom would you give it? Why would it make a good gift for that person?

WRITER'S WORKSHOP Choose one of the plants described in "Carnivorous Plants" that you would like to have for your own. Suppose you fed your plant an unusual diet, something that it does not normally eat. Think about how it might grow. Write a descriptive paragraph that tells about the plant's food and how the plant reacts to its diet.

236

GARDEN VARIETY

Picture yourself exploring a jungle or wandering through a beautiful garden as you read the following selections and poems.

C O N T E N T S

THE GREAT KAPOK TREE

A TALE OF THE AMAZON RAIN FOREST

by Lynne Cherry

In the Amazon rain forest it is always hot, and in that heat everything grows, and grows, and grows. The tops of the trees in the rain forest are called the canopy. The canopy is a sunny place that touches the sky. The animals that live there like lots of light. Colorful parrots fly from tree to tree. Monkeys leap from branch to branch. The bottom of the rain forest is called the understory. The animals that live in the understory like darkness. There, silent snakes curl around hanging vines. Graceful jaguars watch and wait.

And in this steamy environment the great Kapok tree shoots up through the forest and emerges above the canopy.

This is the story of a community of animals that live in one such tree in the rain forest.

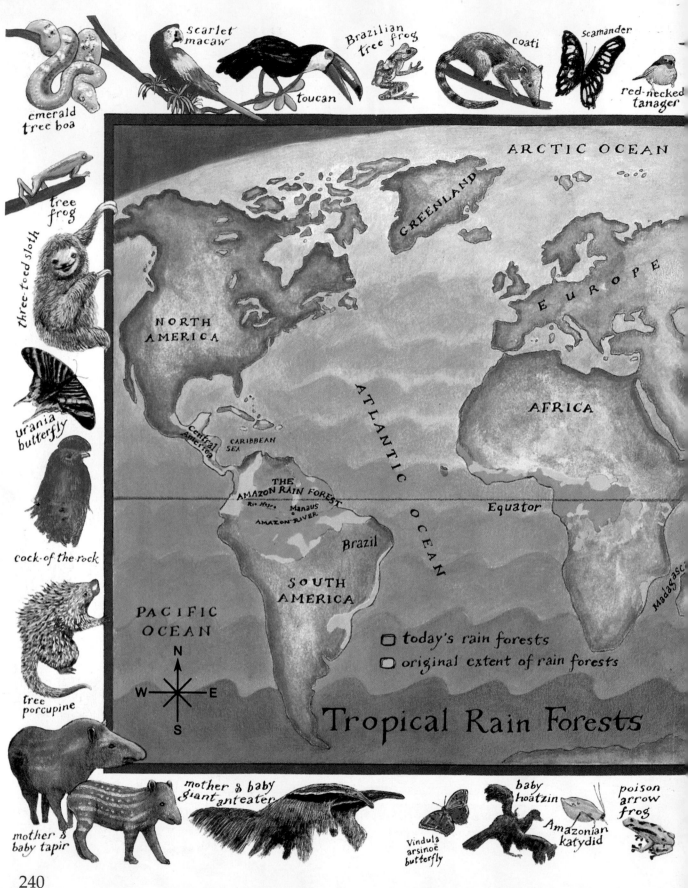

emerald
tree boa

scarlet
macaw

toucan

Brazilian
tree frog

coati

scamander

red-necked
tanager

tree
frog

three-toed sloth

urania
butterfly

cock-of-the-rock

tree
porcupine

mother &
baby tapir

mother & baby
giant anteater

Vindula
arsinoë
butterfly

baby
hoatzin

Amazonian
katydid

poison
arrow
frog

ARCTIC OCEAN

GREENLAND

EUROPE

NORTH
AMERICA

AFRICA

ATLANTIC OCEAN

Central
America

CARIBBEAN
SEA

THE
AMAZON RAIN FOREST

Rio Negro

Manaus

AMAZON RIVER

Brazil

Equator

Madagascar

SOUTH
AMERICA

PACIFIC
OCEAN

☐ today's rain forests
☐ original extent of rain forests

N
W   E
S

Tropical Rain Forests

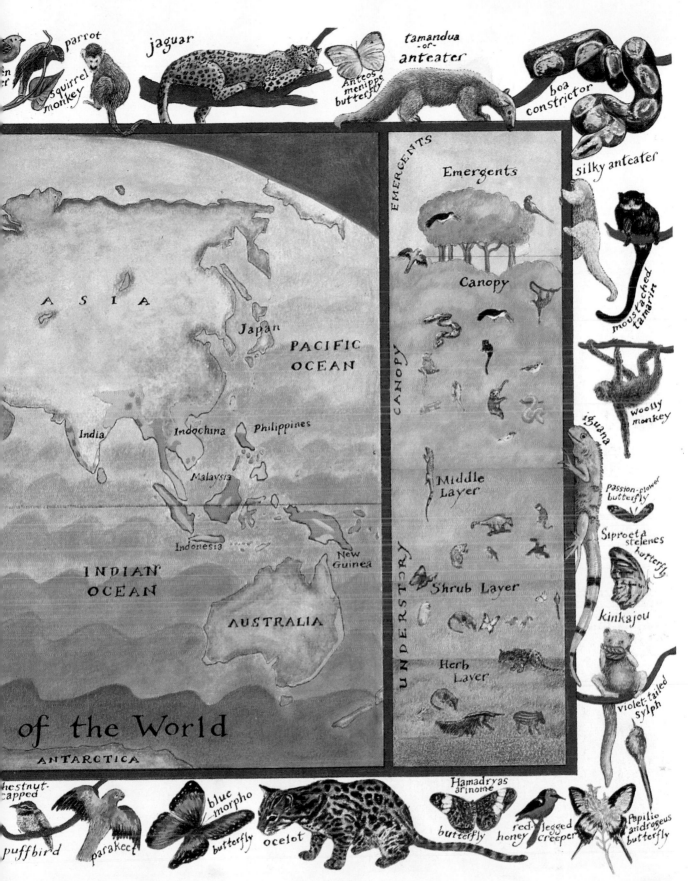

parrot

squirrel monkey

jaguar

Anteos menippe butterfly

tamandua -or- anteater

boa constrictor

silky anteater

moustached tamarin

woolly monkey

iguana

Passion-flower butterfly

Siproeta stelenes butterfly

kinkajou

violet-tailed sylph

EMERGENTS

Emergents

CANOPY

Canopy

UNDERSTORY

Middle Layer

Shrub Layer

Herb Layer

ASIA

Japan

PACIFIC OCEAN

India

Indochina

Philippines

Malaysia

Indonesia

New Guinea

INDIAN OCEAN

AUSTRALIA

of the World

ANTARCTICA

chestnut-capped puffbird

parakeet

blue morpho butterfly

ocelot

Hamadryas arinome butterfly

red-legged honey creeper

Papilio androgeus butterfly

241

Two men walked into the rain forest. Moments before, the forest had been alive with the sounds of squawking birds and howling monkeys. Now all was quiet as the creatures watched the two men and wondered why they had come.

The larger man stopped and pointed to a great Kapok tree. Then he left.

The smaller man took the ax he carried and struck the trunk of the tree. Whack! Whack! Whack! The sounds of the blows rang through the forest. The wood of the tree was very hard. Chop! Chop! Chop! The man wiped off the sweat that ran down his face and neck. Whack! Chop! Whack! Chop!

Soon the man grew tired. He sat down to rest at the foot of the great Kapok tree. Before he knew it, the heat and hum of the forest had lulled him to sleep.

A boa constrictor lived in the Kapok tree. He slithered down its trunk to where the man was sleeping. He looked at the gash the ax had made in the tree. Then the huge snake slid very close to the man and hissed in his ear: "Senhor, this tree is a tree of miracles. It is my home, where generations of my ancestors have lived. Do not chop it down."

A bee buzzed in the sleeping man's ear: "Senhor, my hive is in this Kapok tree, and I fly from tree to tree and flower to flower collecting pollen. In this way I pollinate the trees and flowers throughout the rain forest. You see, all living things depend on one another."

A troupe of monkeys scampered down from the canopy of the Kapok tree. They chattered to the sleeping man: "Senhor, we have seen the ways of man. You chop down one tree, then come back for another and another. The roots of these great trees will wither and die, and there will be nothing left to hold the earth in place. When the heavy rains come, the soil will be washed away and the forest will become a desert."

A toucan, a macaw, and a cock-of-the-rock flew down from the canopy. "Senhor," squawked the toucan, "you must not cut down this tree. We have flown over the rain forest and seen what happens once you begin to chop down the trees. Many people settle on the land. They set fires to clear the underbrush, and soon the forest disappears. Where once there was life and beauty only black and smoldering ruins remain."

A bright and small tree frog crawled along the edge of a leaf. In a squeaky voice he piped in the man's ear: "Senhor, a ruined rain forest means ruined lives . . . many ruined lives. You will leave many of us homeless if you chop down this great Kapok tree."

A jaguar had been sleeping along a branch in the middle of the tree. Because his spotted coat blended into the dappled light and shadows of the understory, no one had noticed him. Now he leapt down and padded silently over to the sleeping man. He growled in his ear: "Senhor, the Kapok tree is home to many birds and animals. If you cut it down, where will I find my dinner?"

Four tree porcupines swung down from branch to branch and whispered to the man: "Senhor, do you know what we animals and humans need in order to live? Oxygen. And, Senhor, do you know what trees produce? Oxygen! If you cut down the forests you will destroy that which gives us all life."

Several anteaters climbed down the Kapok tree with their young clinging to their backs. The unstriped anteater said to the sleeping man: "Senhor, you are chopping down this tree with no thought for the future. And surely you know that what happens tomorrow depends upon what you do today. The big man tells you to chop down a beautiful tree. He does not think of his own children, who tomorrow must live in a world without trees."

A three-toed sloth had begun climbing down from the canopy when the men first appeared. Only now did she reach the ground. Plodding ever so slowly over to the sleeping man, she spoke in her deep and lazy voice: "Senhor, how much is beauty worth? Can you live without it? If you destroy the beauty of the rain forest, on what would you feast your eyes?"

A child from the Yanomamo tribe who lived in the rain forest knelt over the sleeping man. He murmured in his ear: "Senhor, when you awake, please look upon us all with new eyes."

The man awoke with a start. Before him stood the rain forest child, and all around him, staring, were the creatures who depended upon the great Kapok tree. What wondrous and rare animals they were!

The man looked about and saw the sun streaming through the canopy. Spots of bright light glowed like jewels amidst the dark green forest. Strange and beautiful plants seemed to dangle in the air, suspended from the great Kapok tree.

The man smelled the fragrant perfume of their flowers. He felt the steamy mist rising from the forest floor. But he heard no sound, for the creatures were strangely silent.

The man stood and picked up his ax. He swung back his arm as though to strike the tree. Suddenly he stopped. He turned and looked at the animals and the child.

He hesitated. Then he dropped the ax and walked out of the rain forest.

THINK IT OVER

1. What do you think the author's purpose was in writing this story?

2. What are some of the things that people and animals lose when trees in a rain forest are chopped down?

3. At the end of the story, why does the man drop his ax and walk out of the rain forest?

4. A bee in the story says that all living things depend on one another. Do you agree? Explain why you think as you do.

WRITE

Write a descriptive paragraph that tells what you think your world would be like if there were no trees.

Words from the Author and Illustrator:
Lynne Cherry

There has been an incredible response to *The Great Kapok Tree.* I must get 100 letters a week about it. Children tell me they've been recycling at their schools and using the money to buy land in a rain forest in order to protect it. There's a group called the Children's Rainforest, and at last count they've purchased 17,000 acres in the Costa Rican rain forest to help save it.

Questioning when my interest in nature began would be like asking when did I start eating or breathing. As long as I can remember, I have had an interest in the world around me. Many of my books are about environmental issues and helping other living creatures. A recent book, *Archie Follow Me,* which I originally wrote when I was 10 years old, is about going into the woods and seeing through my cat's eyes and listening through his ears. When I was growing up, I used to go into the woods behind my house and stand very still, like a statue. The animals would hop around me, as if I wasn't there. That land behind my house was my playground. Going out by the stream, looking under rocks, waiting for animals to come to me— those things always made me feel a part of nature.

COME ON INTO MY TROPICAL GARDEN

from *Come on
into My Tropical
Garden*

by
Grace Nichols

Come on into my tropical garden
Come on in and have a laugh in
Taste my sugar cake and my pine drink
Come on in please come on in

And yes you can stand up in my hammock
and breeze out in my trees
you can pick my hibiscus
and kiss my chimpanzees

O you can roll up in the grass
and if you pick up a flea
I'll take you down for a quick dip-wash
in the sea
believe me there's nothing better
for getting rid of a flea
than having a quick dip-wash in the sea

Come on into my tropical garden
Come on in please come on in

above:
*Flower Garden and Bungalow,
Bermuda. 1899.*
Winslow Homer
The Metropolitan Museum of
Art, Amelia B. Lazarus Fund,
1910

facing page:
*Still Life with Apples on a Pink
Tablecloth. 1924.*
Henri Matisse
National Gallery of Art,
Washington, D.C.
Chester Dale Collection

WILDFLOWER

from *Flower Moon Snow*

by Kazue Mizumura

ALA Notable Book

Is it waiting just for me,
This one wildflower
In the empty lot?

APPLE TREE

from *Remembering and Other Poems*

by Myra Cohn Livingston

Award-Winning Author

One branch is low enough to hold,
to bend,
to swing into the gold
of apples hanging on our tree.
Climbing higher,
I can see
across the empty lilacs
where
the poplars,
like green soldiers,
bare
of round fruit,
wish that they could be
wearing apples—
like our tree.

All spring and summer, strange "animals" abound in the woods, fields, swamps and gardens.

Some are enormous; some are tiny. Some look wild and fierce; some look gentle and sweet. Some smell wonderful; some have a terrible smell.

When you're out for a walk, keep an eye peeled. You'll meet "tigers" and "snakes," little white "mice," and a host of other "beastly" creatures.

They are all plants. They have leaves or stalks or flowers that remind you, somehow, of animals—or parts of animals: noses, tails, paws, wings. It may be something in their shapes or their colors. Or it might be the way they "behave."

There's a real "menagerie" out there—growing out of the ground, not waiting to pounce but to be found.

TIGER LILIES

Wild "tigers" are galloping through the field. They are down by the stream, too, and along the road. Their shiny orange heads lift in the summer breeze.

These tigers are different from the orange tiger at the zoo. It has black stripes and it growls. These tigers are orange too but they have colored spots instead of stripes and they never make a sound. They are tiger lilies—so called for their tiger-like colors.

Tiger lilies were once kept in gardens, just as the tiger is kept in the zoo. But the tiger lilies escaped. They spread fast—in wet and dry ground, in sun and shade. (They grow *best* in light, rich soil that isn't too wet.)

You can't miss them. Their bright, shiny flowers stand high in a field.

Up close, you can see the six spotted petals turn back from the flower's deep center. The whole flower looks like a Turkish hat. *Stamens* poke out from the flower's center. They look like little pickaxes on long, bending handles. The long, seed-bearing part in the middle is the *pistil*.

It's no wonder tiger lilies spread fast. New plants can start in so many ways. Lilies may grow from seeds. They also grow from white bulbs. The bulbs stay in the ground all winter and send up stems in the spring. New plants also come from "bulbils" (little black bulbs that grow at the base of the leaves). The bulbils drop from the stems and root themselves.

ELEPHANT'S EARS

The "elephants" are all ears. They have no long, swaying trunks or log-shaped legs. Only ears. The ears turn slowly as the air whispers by. They look as if they're listening, but, of course, they can't hear a thing. They are the leaves of the elephant's-ear plants.

The leaves grow two and even three feet long, often touching the ground. Each leaf is as wide as a knight's shield. You can easily hide behind a big, thick, green "ear."

The tiny flowers of an elephant's-ear plant hide, too. They're almost lost among the huge leaves.

Elephant's ears grow from starchy *tubers*. In the South Pacific Islands and in some southern states, the tubers of certain elephant's-ear plants are grown as food. These *edible* (eatable) plants are called "taro" or "eddo" or "dasheen," depending on where they grow.

In Hawaii, taro roots are steamed, peeled, mashed, mixed with water and strained to make "poi," a famous and deliciously sticky Hawaiian dish.

The elephant's-ear tubers are *never* eaten raw. The raw tubers contain sharp crystals—like slivers of glass. The slivers would cut your mouth. Cooking, however, destroys the dangerous glassy bits.

If you'd like to grow big, beautiful elephant's ears—to enjoy, not to eat—just plant some tubers in good, rich soil. Beside a pool is a good place. In about seven months you'll have something to whisper to or hide behind—or just to look at as the giant ears turn slowly this way and that.

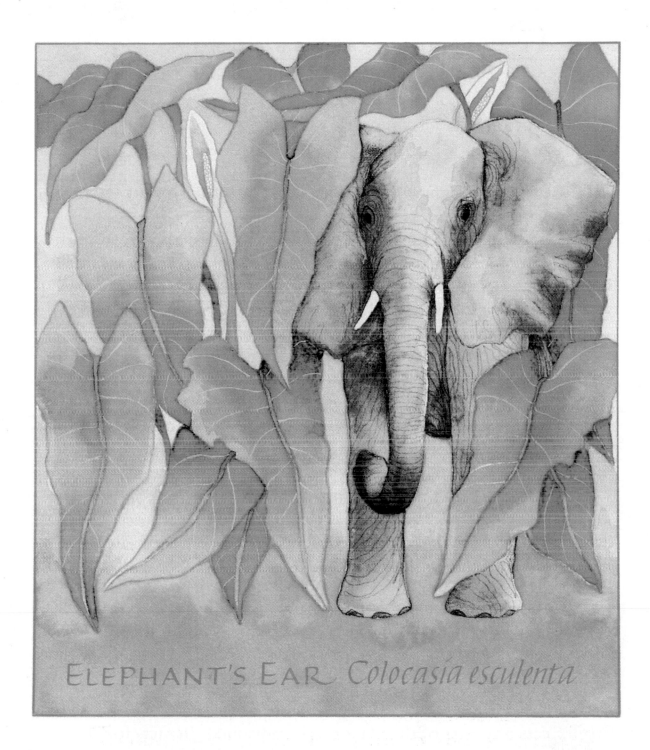

ELEPHANT'S EAR *Colocasia esculenta*

FOXGLOVES

Can you imagine a fox wearing gloves? Not easily.

Yet, look! Foxgloves are out there in the back yard. They are strewn all over the fields and in clearings in the woods too. They are foxglove flowers.

Watch for them in May. They'll be around through September. Most often you see purple blossoms, but some flowers are rose, or pink, or white, or yellow or blue. They grow in *racemes,* bunched along a long stem. Some plants have as many as eighty flowers on one stalk.

Pick five foxglove flowers. Slip the little tubes on the ends of your fingers. It's something like wearing the fingertips snipped from a velvet-soft glove.

Look inside a bell-shaped blossom. See the spots on the lower lip? Now stand aside for a while. Most likely you'll see a bumblebee alight—right on the spots. The bee will probably follow the spotted trail into the flower. The spots are sometimes called the "honey line," because they lead to the sweet *nectar* deep inside the open flower.

When the bee leaves, you can bet it'll carry pollen away. When the pollen reaches another foxglove flower, seeds will be able to grow. Then, when the seeds are ripe, they'll be scattered by the wind. Some seeds are planted in gardens.

Foxgloves help people. A special chemical called *digitalis* is in the plant's long, hairy leaves. The chemical is used to make a medicine that is good for certain kinds of heart disease.

Unfortunately, foxgloves can hurt people too. Whoever eats any part of the plant can be poisoned. In fact, foxgloves are sometimes called "dead men's bells."

FOXGLOVE
Digitalis purpurea

If you find it hard to imagine a fox wearing gloves, try thinking of the flowers as "folks' gloves." The plant goes by that name, too. But mostly you hear "foxgloves," so stretch your imagination enough to picture a fox with gloves on its paws!

Watch where you step as you cross the lawn. There's a "mouse!" There's another. And another. Tiny ears twitch as you go by. The mice won't run away. They are mouse-ear plants.

You'll find wild "mouse-ears" in fields, woods, and along roadsides. They like to live in wet places, but they settle in dry places too. When they scatter themselves in lawns and gardens mouse-ears bother people. That's because their tough roots are very hard to dig up. Some people *like* some kinds of mouse-ears because they look pretty in gardens.

Pick a mouse-ear plant. Feel the furry leaves and stem? Now, close your eyes and imagine you are holding a small mouse!

Each flower has five notched petals. (You might find a blossom with only four petals, but hardly ever; they are as scarce as four-leaf clovers.)

Mouse-ears grow from seeds. Small *capsules* hold the seeds until they are ripe, in September or October. Then the capsules open, and the seeds scatter—all over the place. Mouse-ear plants multiply in a big way.

Mouse-ears have many cousins. They all belong to one family called "chickweed." Chickens love to eat chickweed, and that's how the family name came about. This is probably the first time you've heard of a chicken eating a mouse's ear!

MOUSE·EAR
Cerastium vulgatum

TIGER LILY
Lilium tigrinum

THINK IT OVER

1. *In what ways are the plants in this article alike?*

2. *Where can tiger lilies be found?*

3. *For what reasons are two of the plants in this article dangerous to eat?*

4. *Which beastly plant would you like to have? Explain why.*

WRITE

Think of a plant that you are familiar with that is not featured in this article. On a poster, draw the plant and list its beastly characteristics.

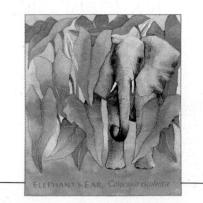

ELEPHANT'S EAR *Colocasia esculenta*

FOXGLOVE
Digitalis purpurea

MOUSE-EAR
Cerastium vulgatum

GARDEN VARIETY

The selections and poems you read describe many different kinds of plants and where they grow. Which of the plants that you read about would you most like to find in your own yard or neighborhood? Tell why.

· ·

How are our lives richer because of plants? Use examples from the selections and poems to support your ideas.

· ·

WRITER'S WORKSHOP Look through a book on plants to find others with unusual names or interesting characteristics. Choose one and gather information about it. Then write a how-to paragraph telling how to care for the plant you chose.

263

THEME

HARVEST HUMOR

Have you ever heard an amazing story about a plant? Did you believe the story? The following riddles, selection, and words from the author will test your knowledge about the plant world in ways that will make you smile.

CONTENTS

265

FRUIT AND VEGETABLE STEW

from Alexander
the Grape
compiled by
Charles Keller

illustrated by Tuko Fujisaki

AWARD-WINNING
AUTHOR

266

Why aren't bananas ever lonely?
Because they come in bunches.

What vegetable do you get when you drop a tomato?
Squash.

Why do watermelons contain so much water?
They are planted in the spring.

How do you make gold stew?
Add fourteen carrots.

What's the most dangerous vegetable to have on a boat?
A leek.

Why did the cornstalk get mad at the farmer?
He kept pulling its ears.

When are vegetables like music?
When there are two beets to the measure.

What do you call a twisted path through an Indian cornfield?
A maize.

Why did the tomato go out with the prune?
Because he couldn't find a date.

McBroom
Tells The
Truth

BY SID FLEISCHMAN

ILLUSTRATIONS
DOUG PANTON

THERE HAS BEEN so much tomfool nonsense told about McBroom's wonderful one-acre farm that I had better set matters straight. I'm McBroom. Josh McBroom. I'll explain about the watermelons in a minute.

I aim to put down the facts, one after the other, the way things happened—exactly.

It began, you might say, the day we left the farm in Connecticut. We piled our youngsters and everything we owned in our old air-cooled Franklin automobile. We headed West.

To count noses, in addition to my own, there was my dear wife Melissa and our eleven red-headed, freckle-faced youngsters. Their names were Will*jill*hester-*chester*peter*polly*tim*tom*mary-*larry*andlittle*clarinda*.

It was summer, and the trees along the way were full of bird-song. We had got as far as Iowa when my dear wife Melissa made a startling discovery. We had *twelve* children along—one too many! She had just counted them again.

I slammed on the brakes and raised a cloud of dust.

"Will*jill*hester*chester*peter*polly* tim*tom*mary*larry*and-little*clarinda*!" I shouted. "Line up!"

The youngsters tumbled out of the car. I counted noses and there were twelve. I counted again. Twelve. It was a baffler as all the faces were familiar. Once more I made the count—but this time I caught Larry slipping around behind. He was having his nose counted twice, and the mystery was solved. The scamp! Didn't we laugh, though, and stretch our legs in the bargain.

Just then a thin, long-legged man came ambling down the road. He was so scrawny I do believe he could have hidden behind a flagpole, ears and all. He wore a tall stiff collar, a diamond stickpin in his tie, and a black hat.

"Lost, neighbor?" he asked, spitting out the pips of a green apple he was eating.

"Not a bit," said I. "We're heading West, sir. We gave up our farm—it was half rocks and the other half tree stumps. Folks tell us there's land out West and the sun shines in the winter."

The stranger pursed his lips. "You can't beat Iowa for farmland," he said.

"Maybe so," I nodded. "But I'm short of funds. Unless they're giving farms away in Iowa we'll keep a-going."

The man scratched his chin. "See here, I've got more land than I can plow. You look like nice folks. I'd like to have you for neighbors. I'll let you have eighty acres cheap. Not a stone or a tree stump anywhere on the place. Make me an offer."

"Thank you kindly, sir," I smiled. "But I'm afraid you would laugh at me if I offered you everything in my leather purse."

"How much is that?"

"Ten dollars exactly."

"Sold!" he said.

Well, I almost choked with surprise. I thought he must be joking, but quick as a flea he was scratching out a deed on the back of an old envelope.

"Hector Jones is my name, neighbor," he said. "You can call me Heck—everyone does."

Was there ever a more kindly and generous man? He signed the deed with a flourish, and I gladly opened the clasp of my purse.

Three milky white moths flew out. They had been gnawing on the ten dollar bill all the way from Connecticut, but enough remained to buy the farm. And not a stone or tree stump on it!

Mr. Heck Jones jumped on the running board and guided us a mile up the road. My youngsters tried to amuse him along the way. Will wiggled his ears, and Jill crossed her eyes, and Chester twitched his nose like a rabbit, but I reckoned Mr. Jones wasn't used to youngsters. Hester flapped her arms like a bird, Peter whistled through his front teeth, which were missing, and Tom tried to stand on his head in the back of the car. Mr. Heck Jones ignored them all.

Finally he raised his long arm and pointed.

"There's your property, neighbor," he said.

Didn't we tumble out of the car in a hurry? We gazed with delight at our new farm. It was broad and sunny, with an oak tree on a gentle hill. There was one defect, to be sure. A boggy looking pond spread across an acre beside the road. You could lose a cow in a place like that, but we had got a bargain—no doubt about it.

"Mama," I said to my dear Melissa. "See that fine old oak on the hill? That's where we'll build our farmhouse."

"No you won't," said Mr. Heck Jones. "That oak ain't on your property."

"But, sir—"

"All that's yours is what you see under water. Not a rock or a tree stump in it, like I said."

I thought he must be having his little joke, except that there wasn't a smile to be found on his face. "But *sir*!" I said. "You clearly stated that the farm was eighty acres."

"That's right."

"That marshy pond hardly covers an acre."

"That's wrong," he said. "There are a full eighty acres—one piled on the other, like griddle cakes. I didn't say your farm was all on the surface. It's eighty acres deep, McBroom. Read the deed."

I read the deed. It was true.

"*Hee-haw! Hee-haw!*" he snorted. "I got the best of you, McBroom! Good day, neighbor."

He scurried away, laughing up his sleeve all the way home. I soon learned that Mr. Heck was always laughing up his sleeve. Folks told me that when he'd hang up his coat and go to bed, all that stored-up laughter would pour out his sleeve and keep him awake nights. But there's no truth to that.

I'll tell you about the watermelons in a minute.

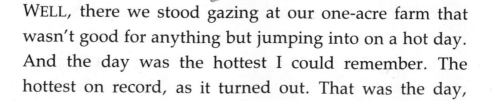

WELL, there we stood gazing at our one-acre farm that wasn't good for anything but jumping into on a hot day. And the day was the hottest I could remember. The hottest on record, as it turned out. That was the day, three minutes before noon, when the cornfields all over Iowa exploded into popcorn. That's history. You must have read about that. There are pictures to prove it.

I turned to my children. "Will*jill*hester*chester*-peter*polly*tim*tom*mary*larry*andlittle*clarinda*," I said. "There's always a bright side to things. That pond we bought is a mite muddy, but it's wet. Let's jump in and cool off."

That idea met with favor and we were soon in our swimming togs. I gave the signal, and we took a running jump. At that moment such a dry spell struck that we landed in an acre of dry earth. The pond had evaporated. It was very surprising.

My boys had jumped in head first and there was nothing to be seen of them but their legs kicking in the air. I had to pluck them out of the earth like carrots. Some of my girls were still holding their noses. Of course, they were sorely disappointed to have that swimming hole pulled out from under them.

But the moment I ran the topsoil through my fingers, my farmer's heart skipped a beat. That pond bottom felt as soft and rich as black silk. "My dear Melissa!" I called. "Come look! This topsoil is so rich it ought to be kept in a bank."

I was in a sudden fever of excitement. That glorious topsoil seemed to cry out for seed. My dear Melissa had a sack of dried beans along, and I sent Will and Chester to fetch it. I saw no need to bother plowing the field. I directed Polly to draw a straight furrow with a stick and Tim to follow her, poking holes in the ground. Then I came along. I dropped a bean in each hole and stamped on it with my heel.

Well, I had hardly gone a couple of yards when something green and leafy tangled my foot. I looked behind me. There was a beanstalk traveling along in a hurry and looking for a pole to climb on.

"Glory be!" I exclaimed. That soil was *rich!* The stalks were spreading out all over. I had to rush along to keep ahead of them.

By the time I got to the end of the furrow the first stalks had blossomed, and the pods had formed, and they were ready for picking.

You can imagine our excitement. Will's ears wiggled. Jill's eyes crossed. Chester's nose twitched. Hester's arms flapped. Peter's missing front teeth whistled. And Tom stood on his head.

"Will*jill*hester*chester*peter*polly*tim*tom*mary*larry*and-little*clarinda*," I shouted. "Harvest them beans!"

Within an hour we had planted and harvested that entire crop of beans. But was it hot working in the sun! I sent Larry to find a good acorn along the road. We planted it, but it didn't grow near as fast as I had expected. We had to wait an entire three hours for a shade tree.

WE MADE CAMP under our oak tree, and the next day we drove to Barnsville with our crop of beans. I traded it for various seeds—carrot and beet and cabbage and other items. The storekeeper found a few kernels of corn that hadn't popped, at the very bottom of the bin.

But we found out that corn was positively dangerous to plant. The stalk shot up so fast it would skin your nose.

Of course, there was a secret to that topsoil. A government man came out and made a study of the matter. He said there had once been a huge lake in that part of Iowa. It had taken thousands of years to shrink up to our pond, as you can imagine. The lake fish must have got packed in worse than sardines. There's nothing like fish to put nitrogen in the soil. That's a scientific fact. Nitrogen makes things grow to beat all. And we did occasionally turn up a fish bone.

It wasn't long before Mr. Heck Jones came around to pay us a neighborly call. He was eating a raw turnip. When he saw the way we were planting and harvesting cabbage his eyes popped out of his head. It almost cost him his eyesight.

He scurried away, muttering to himself.

"My dear Melissa," I said. "That man is up to mischief."

Folks in town had told me that Mr. Heck Jones had the worst farmland in Iowa. He couldn't give it away. Tornado winds had carried off his topsoil and left the hardpan right on top. He had to plow it with wedges and a sledge hammer. One day we heard a lot of booming on the other side of the hill, and my youngsters went up to see what was happening. It turned out he was planting seeds with a shotgun.

Meanwhile, we went about our business on the farm. I don't mind saying that before long we were showing a handsome profit. Back in Connecticut we had been lucky to harvest one crop a year. Now we were planting and harvesting three, four crops a *day*.

But there were things we had to be careful about. Weeds, for one thing. My youngsters took turns standing weed guard. The instant a weed popped out of the ground, they'd race to it and hoe it to death. You can imagine what would happen if weeds ever got going in rich soil like ours.

We also had to be careful about planting time. Once we planted lettuce just before my dear Melissa rang the noon bell for dinner. While we ate, the lettuce headed up and went to seed. We lost the whole crop.

One day back came Mr. Heck Jones with a grin on his face. He had figured out a loophole in the deed that made the farm ours.

"*Hee-haw!*" he laughed. He was munching a radish. "I got the best of you now, Neighbor McBroom. The deed says you were to pay me *everything* in your purse, and you *didn't*."

"On the contrary, sir," I answered. "Ten dollars. There wasn't another cent in my purse."

"There were *moths* in the purse. I seen 'em flutter out. Three milky white moths, McBroom. I want three moths by three o'clock this afternoon, or I aim to take back the farm. *Hee-haw!*"

And off he went, laughing up his sleeve.

Mama was just ringing the noon bell so we didn't have much time. Confound that man! But he did have his legal point.

"Willjillhesterchesterpeterpollytimtommarylarryand-littleclarinda," I said. "We've got to catch three milky white moths! Hurry!"

We hurried in all directions. But moths are next to impossible to locate in the daytime. Try it yourself. Each of us came back empty-handed.

My dear Melissa began to cry, for we were sure to lose our farm. I don't mind telling you that things looked dark. Dark! That was it! I sent the youngsters running down the road to a lonely old pine tree and told them to rush back with a bushel of pine cones.

Didn't we get busy though! We planted a pine cone every three feet. They began to grow. We stood around anxiously, and I kept looking at my pocket watch. I'll tell you about the watermelons in a moment.

Sure enough, by ten minutes to three, those cones had grown into a thick pine forest.

It was dark inside, too! Not a ray of sunlight slipped through the green pine boughs. Deep in the forest I lit a lantern. Hardly a minute passed before I was surrounded by milky white moths—they thought it was night. I caught three on the wing and rushed out of the forest.

There stood Mr. Heck Jones waiting with the sheriff to foreclose.

"*Hee-haw! Hee-haw!*" old Heck laughed. He was eating a quince apple. "It's nigh onto three o'clock, and you can't catch moths in the day-time. The farm is mine!"

"Not so fast, Neighbor Jones," said I, with my hands cupped together. "Here are the three moths. Now, skedaddle, sir, before your feet take root and poison ivy grows out of your ears!"

He scurried away, muttering to himself.

"My dear Melissa," I said. "That man is up to mischief. He'll be back."

IT TOOK A GOOD BIT of work to clear the timber, I'll tell you. We had some of the pine milled and built ourselves a house on the corner of the farm. What was left we gave away to our neighbors. We were weeks blasting the roots out of the ground.

But I don't want you to think there was nothing but work on our farm. Some crops we grew just for the fun of it. Take pumpkins. The vines grew so fast we could hardly catch the pumpkins. It was something to see. The youngsters used to wear themselves out running after those pumpkins. Sometimes they'd have pumpkin races.

Sunday afternoons, just for the sport of it, the older boys would plant a pumpkin seed and try to catch a ride. It wasn't easy. You had to grab hold the instant the blossom dropped off and the pumpkin began to swell. Whoosh! It would yank you off your feet and take you whizzing over the farm until it wore itself out. Sometimes they'd use banana squash, which was faster.

And the girls learned to ride cornstalks like pogo sticks. It was just a matter of standing over the kernel as the stalk came busting up through the ground. It was good for quite a bounce.

We'd see Mr. Heck Jones standing on the hill in the distance, watching. He wasn't going to rest until he had pried us off our land.

Then, late one night, I was awakened by a hee-hawing outside the house. I went to the window and saw old Heck in the moonlight. He was cackling and chuckling and heeing and hawing and sprinkling seed every which way.

I pulled off my sleeping cap and rushed outside.

"What mischief are you up to, Neighbor Jones!" I shouted.

"Hee-haw!" he answered, and scurried away, laughing up his sleeve.

I had a sleepless night, as you can imagine. The next morning, as soon as the sun came up, that farm of ours broke out in weeds. You never saw such weeds! They heaved out of the ground and tumbled madly over each other—chickweed and milkweed, thistles and wild morning glory. In no time at all the weeds were in a tangle several feet thick and still rising.

We had a fight on our hands, I tell you! "Willjill-hesterchesterpeterpollytimtommarylarryandlittleclarinda!" I shouted. "There's work to do!"

We started hoeing and hacking away. For every weed we uprooted, another reseeded itself. We were a solid month battling those weeds. If our neighbors hadn't pitched in to help, we'd still be there burning weeds.

HARVEST HUMOR

The writers of the riddles and selection asked silly questions and stretched the truth about plants. How were the plants that you read about different from real plants?

Choose from the riddles a fruit or vegetable that McBroom did not grow on his land. Describe how that crop might have grown in McBroom's rich soil.

WRITER'S WORKSHOP Suppose that McBroom had not been able to find three moths. What do you think would have happened to the family and to the land? Would they have left and traveled west? Do you think McBroom would have thought of another way to save his land? Brainstorm ideas and write another ending to the silly story.

CONNECTIONS

IROQUOIS HARVEST CELEBRATIONS

Native Americans have made huge contributions to the world food supply by being the first to cultivate many important crops, including corn. Newcomers to America were saved from starving by corn provided by Native Americans.

As they did long ago, people of the Iroquois nations still hold ceremonies to give thanks for nature's gifts. The Green Corn Festival is held at harvesttime. In midwinter, a great thanksgiving feast begins the new year.

■ *Look in copies of* National Geographic World *magazine and other sources to find out what other ethnic groups or countries celebrate harvest festivals. Make a poster report about a group or country, illustrating the foods, costumes, dances, and other activities of its festival.*

Iroquois men, dressed in bear skins and dried cornhusks, go from house to house announcing the New Year's festival.

288

PLEASE DON'T PICK THE FLOWERS

Every plant deserves its own celebration. Choose a national park, and make a map of it. In the border of the map, draw some wild plants that are protected there. Give facts that tell why each plant is valuable and why it needs protection. Display your map on a class bulletin board.

A SEASON FOR EVERYTHING

Why didn't the Iroquois plant corn year-round? They knew that plants grow well only if certain needs are met. Research four plants known to early American settlers. Find out how much heat or cold, water, and time each requires to grow. Report your findings to your classmates.

You might record what you learn on charts like the one shown.

Name of plant	
Regions it grows in	
Temperature needs	
Water needs	
Planting season	
Length of growing season	

DISCOVERIES

People in all cultures make discoveries. In this unit, you will read about a young boy from Ethiopia who discovers a secret about a game board. You'll follow a hometown detective as he sets out to solve a mystery. You'll share in the discovery of ancient treasures in Mexico. As you journey through this unit, try to feel the thrill of discovery shared by people all over the world.

FUN AND GAMES

SOLVE IT!

HIDDEN RICHES

BOOKSHELF

JACE THE ACE
BY JOANNE ROCKLIN

Ten-year-old Jason Caputo, who prefers to be called "Jace the Ace, junior photo-journalist," learns some valuable lessons as he solves the case of a "spy" named Sky.

HBJ LIBRARY BOOK

THE DISCOVERY OF THE AMERICAS
BY BETSY AND GIULIO MAESTRO

This nonfiction book tells how our part of the world was discovered and rediscovered by early explorers. AWARD-WINNING AUTHOR AND ILLUSTRATOR

WINDCATCHER
BY AVI

Tony does not look forward to spending the summer with his grandmother on the coast of Connecticut. But when he buys a small sailboat and learns about a sunken treasure, Tony's summer turns into an adventure. AWARD-WINNING AUTHOR

KNEE•KNOCK RISE
BY NATALIE BABBITT

Egan visits his relatives in the town of Instep and makes a discovery that the townspeople do not want to accept. NEWBERY HONOR, ALA NOTABLE BOOK

GRANDFATHER TANG'S STORY
BY ANN TOMPERT

Little Soo listens and watches as Grandfather Tang uses puzzles called tangrams to tell a story. She learns about a pair of foxes that make an important discovery. NOTABLE CHILDREN'S TRADE BOOK IN THE FIELD OF SOCIAL STUDIES

FUN AND GAMES

Do you remember a time when you were bored and you couldn't find anything to do? The characters in the next three selections experience that same boredom. Then suddenly their ordinary days overflow with unexpected adventures.

C O N T E N T S

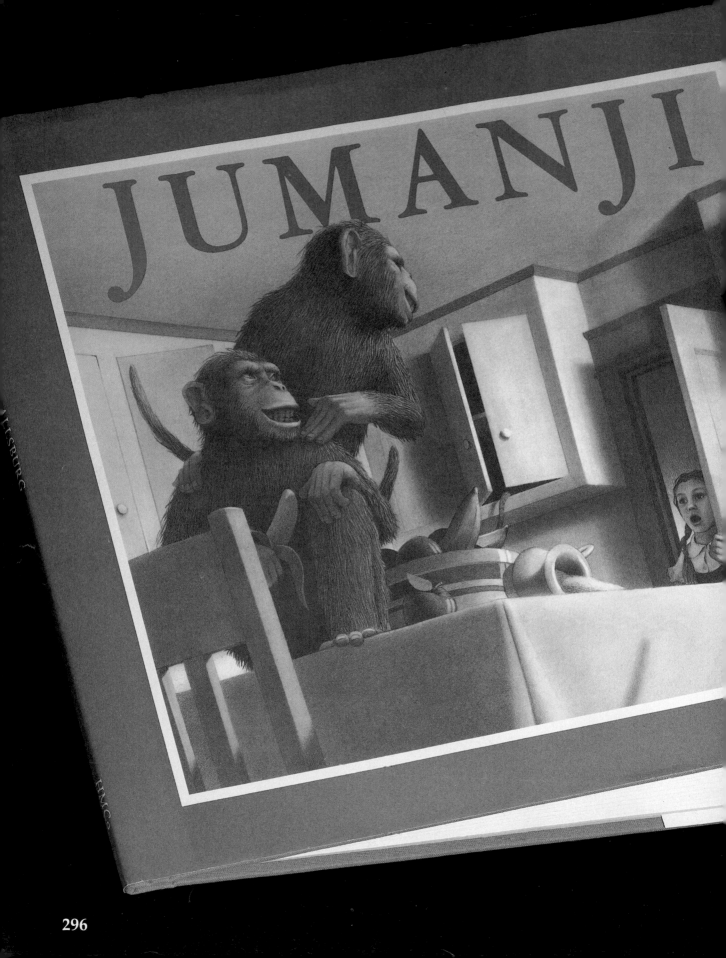

"Now remember," Mother said, "your father and I are bringing some guests by after the opera, so please keep the house neat."

"Quite so," added Father, tucking his scarf inside his coat.

Mother peered into the hall mirror and carefully pinned her hat in place, then knelt and kissed both children good-bye.

When the front door closed, Judy and Peter giggled with delight. They took all the toys out of their toy chest and made a terrible mess. But their laughter slowly turned to silence till finally Peter slouched into a chair.

"You know what?" he said. "I'm really bored."

Written and Illustrated by

CHRIS VAN ALLSBURG

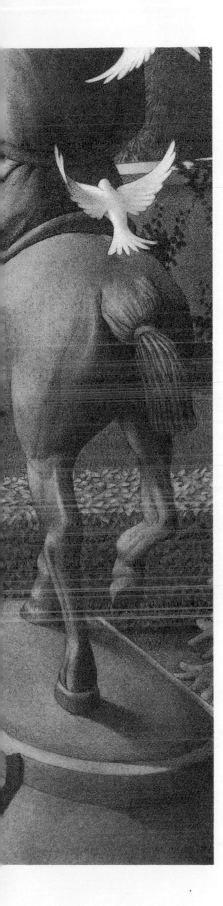

"Me too," sighed Judy. "Why don't we go outside and play?"

Peter agreed, so they set off across the street to the park. It was cold for November. The children could see their breath like steam. They rolled in the leaves and when Judy tried to stuff some leaves down Peter's sweater he jumped up and ran behind a tree. When his sister caught up with him, he was kneeling at the foot of the tree, looking at a long thin box.

"What's that?" Judy asked.

"It's a game," said Peter, handing her the box.

"'JUMANJI,'" Judy read from the box, 'A JUNGLE ADVENTURE GAME.'"

"Look," said Peter, pointing to a note taped to the bottom of the box. In a childlike handwriting were the words "Free game, fun for some but not for all. P.S. Read instructions carefully."

"Want to take it home?" Judy asked.

"Not really," said Peter. "I'm sure somebody left it here because it's so boring."

"Oh, come on," protested Judy. "Let's give it a try. Race you home!" And off she ran with Peter at her heels.

At home, the children spread the game out on a card table. It looked very much like the games they already had. There was a board that unfolded, revealing a path of colored squares. The squares had messages written on them. The path started in the deepest jungle and ended up in Jumanji, a city of golden buildings and towers. Peter began to shake the dice and play with the other pieces that were in the box.

"Put those down and listen," said Judy. "I'm going to read the instructions: 'Jumanji, a young people's jungle adventure especially designed for the bored and restless.

"'A. Player selects piece and places it in deepest jungle. B. Player rolls dice and moves piece along path through the dangers of the jungle. C. First player to reach Jumanji and yell the city's name aloud is the winner.'"

"Is that all?" asked Peter, sounding disappointed.

"No," said Judy, "there's one more thing, and this is in capital letters: 'D. VERY IMPORTANT: ONCE A GAME OF JUMANJI IS STARTED IT WILL NOT BE OVER UNTIL ONE PLAYER REACHES THE GOLDEN CITY.'"

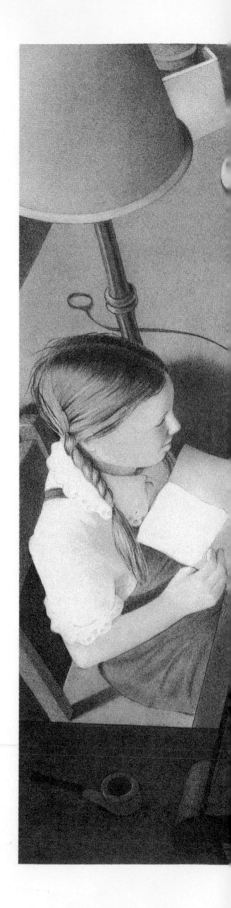

BALDW

"Oh, big deal," said Peter, who gave a bored yawn.

"Here," said Judy, handing her brother the dice, "you go first."

Peter casually dropped the dice from his hand.

"Seven," said Judy.

Peter moved his piece to the seventh square.

"'Lion attacks, move back two spaces,'" read Judy.

"Gosh, how exciting," said Peter, in a very unexcited voice. As he reached for his piece he looked up at his sister. She had a look of absolute horror on her face.

"Peter," she whispered, "turn around very, very slowly."

The boy turned in his chair. He couldn't believe his eyes. Lying on the piano was a lion, staring at Peter and licking his lips.

The lion roared so loud it knocked Peter right off his chair. The big cat jumped to the floor. Peter was up on his feet, running through the house with the lion a whisker's length behind. He ran upstairs and dove under a bed. The lion tried to squeeze under, but got his head stuck. Peter scrambled out, ran from the bedroom, and slammed the door behind him. He stood in the hall with Judy, gasping for breath.

"I don't think," said Peter in between gasps of air, "that I want . . . to play . . . this game . . . anymore."

"But we have to," said Judy as she helped Peter back downstairs. "I'm sure that's what the instructions mean. That lion won't go away until one of us wins the game."

Peter stood next to the card table. "Can't we just call the zoo and have him taken away?" From upstairs came the sounds of growling and clawing at the bedroom door. "Or maybe we could wait till Father comes home."

"No one would come from the zoo because they wouldn't believe us," said Judy. "And you know how upset Mother would be if there was a lion in the bedroom. We started this game, and now we have to finish it."

Peter looked down at the game board. What if Judy rolled a seven? Then there'd be two lions. For an instant Peter thought he was going to cry. Then he sat firmly in his chair and said, "Let's play."

Judy picked up the dice, rolled an eight, and moved her piece. "'Monkeys steal food, miss one turn,'" she read. From the kitchen came the sounds of banging pots and falling jars. The children ran in to see a dozen monkeys tearing the room apart.

"Oh boy," said Peter, "this would upset Mother even more than the lion."

"Quick," said Judy, "back to the game."

Peter took his turn. Thank heavens, he landed on a blank space. He rolled again. "'Monsoon season begins, lose one turn.'" Little raindrops began to fall in the living room. Then a roll of thunder shook the walls and scared the monkeys out of the kitchen. The rain began to fall in buckets as Judy took the dice.

"'Guide gets lost, lose one turn.'" The rain suddenly stopped. The children turned to see a man hunched over a map.

"Oh dear, I say, spot of bad luck now," he mumbled. "Perhaps a left turn here then . . . No, no . . . a right turn here . . . Yes, absolutely, I think, a right turn . . . or maybe . . ."

"Excuse me," said Judy, but the guide just ignored her.

". . . around here, then over . . . No, no . . . over here and around this . . . Yes, good . . . but then . . . Hm . . ."

Judy shrugged her shoulders and handed the dice to Peter.

". . . four, five, six," he counted. "'Bitten by tsetse fly, contract sleeping sickness, lose one turn.'"

Judy heard a faint buzzing noise and watched a small insect land on Peter's nose. Peter lifted his hand to brush the bug away, but then stopped, gave a tremendous yawn, and fell sound asleep, his head on the table.

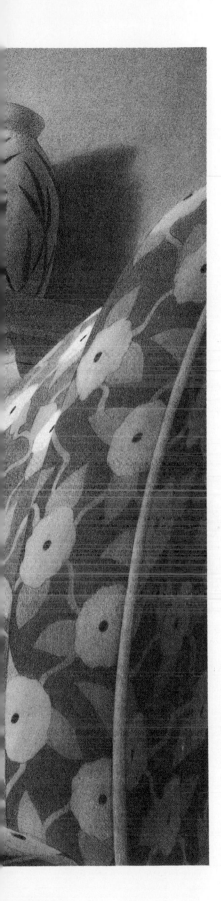

"Peter, Peter, wake up!" cried Judy. But it was no use. She grabbed the dice and moved to a blank. She rolled again and waited in amazement. "'Rhinoceros stampede, go back two spaces.'"

As fast as he had fallen asleep, Peter awoke. Together they listened to a rumble in the hallway. It grew louder and louder. Suddenly a herd of rhinos charged through the living room and into the dining room, crushing all the furniture in their path. Peter and Judy covered their ears as sounds of splintering wood and breaking china filled the house.

Peter gave the dice a quick tumble. "'Python sneaks into camp, go back one space.'"

Judy shrieked and jumped up on her chair.

"Over the fireplace," said Peter. Judy sat down again, nervously eyeing the eight-foot snake that was wrapping itself around the mantel clock. The guide looked up from his map, took one look at the snake, and moved to the far corner of the room, joining the monkeys on the couch.

Judy took her turn and landed on a blank space. Her brother took the dice and rolled a three.

"Oh, no," he moaned. "'Volcano erupts, go back three spaces.'" The room became warm and started to shake a little. Molten lava poured from the fireplace opening. It hit the water on the floor and the room filled with steam. Judy rolled the dice and moved ahead.

"'Discover shortcut, roll again.' Oh dear!" she cried. Judy saw the snake unwrapping itself from the clock.

"If you roll a twelve you can get out of the jungle," said Peter.

"Please, please," Judy begged as she shook the dice. The snake was wriggling its way to the floor. She dropped the dice from her hand. One six, then another. Judy grabbed her piece and slammed it to the board. "JUMANJI," she yelled, as loud as she could.

The steam in the room became thicker and thicker. Judy could not even see Peter across the table. Then, as if all the doors and windows had been opened, a cool breeze cleared the steam from the room. Everything was just as it had been before the game. No monkeys, no guide, no water, no broken furniture, no snake, no lion roaring upstairs, no rhinos. Without saying a word to each other, Peter and Judy threw the game into its box. They bolted out the door, ran across the street to the park, and dropped the game under a tree. Back home, they quickly put all their toys away. But both children were too excited to sit quietly, so Peter took out a picture puzzle. As they fit the pieces together, their excitement slowly turned to relief, and then exhaustion. With the puzzle half done Peter and Judy fell sound asleep on the sofa.

"Wake up, dears," Mother's voice called.

Judy opened her eyes. Mother and Father had returned and their guests were arriving. Judy gave Peter a nudge to wake him. Yawning and stretching, they got to their feet.

Mother introduced them to some of the guests, then asked, "Did you have an exciting afternoon?"

"Oh yes," said Peter. "We had a flood, a stampede, a volcano, I got sleeping sickness, and—" Peter was interrupted by the adults' laughter.

"Well," said Mother, "I think you both got sleeping sickness. Why don't you go upstairs and put your pajamas on? Then you can finish your puzzle and have some dinner."

When Peter and Judy came back downstairs they found that Father had moved the puzzle into the den. While the children were working on it, one of the guests, Mrs. Budwing, brought them a tray of food.

"Such a hard puzzle," she said to the children. "Daniel and Walter are always starting puzzles and never finishing them." Daniel and Walter were Mrs. Budwing's sons. "They never read instructions either. Oh well," said Mrs. Budwing, turning to rejoin the guests, "I guess they'll learn."

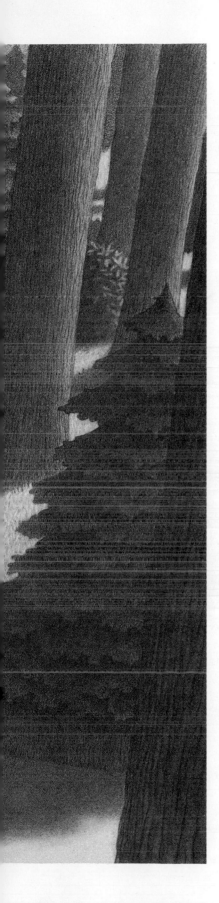

Both children answered, "I hope so," but they weren't looking at Mrs. Budwing. They were looking out the window. Two boys were running through the park. It was Danny and Walter Budwing, and Danny had a long thin box under his arm.

THINK IT OVER

1. *Why was winning Jumanji so important?*

2. *Why didn't Peter want to take the Jumanji game home from the park?*

3. *Peter and Judy had different feelings at different points in the story. What were some of the different feelings they had?*

4. *What does it take to win a game of Jumanji?*

WRITE

The message on the Jumanji game box read, "fun for some but not for all." Write a message telling what you think about the game for the next person who finds it.

AN
INTERVIEW
WITH THE
AUTHOR
AND
ILLUSTRATOR:

Chris Van Allsburg

Chris Van Allsburg is both an author and an illustrator. He has written and illustrated many books about strange happenings. Read what he told writer Ilene Cooper about how his mind works when he writes and draws.

MS. COOPER: Where did you get the idea for *Jumanji*?

MR. VAN ALLSBURG: I see images in my mind's eye. Usually they're images of things that are unexplainable. With *Jumanji*, it wasn't a jungle scene, but more the idea of something not being where it's supposed to be.

MS. COOPER: Like a lion on top of the piano?

MR. VAN ALLSBURG: Yes, but first I saw the idea of a house, which we like to think of as a safe place, being overrun by beasts of some sort.

MS. COOPER: What about the board game?

316

MR. VAN ALLSBURG: One thing about board games is that they require your imagination to make them fun. When you play some board games, even when you win, you're not rich, so the excitement of the game really comes from inside your head. So with *Jumanji*, I thought of this game that wouldn't require an imagination. Those animals really are there. In the game, the object is to get to the Golden City, but what the kids understand at the end is that the real payoff is to get your world back to where it was.

MS. COOPER: Did you think about being a writer when you were young?

MR. VAN ALLSBURG: No, I never thought about writing for anyone, adults or children. Even now, when I know the challenges and the opportunities of being a writer, I still am a writer who is motivated by the images that I see in my mind.

THE GAME BOARD

AWARD-WINNING AUTHOR

from *The Fire on the Mountain and Other Ethiopian Stories*
by Harold Courlander and Wolf Leslau
illustrated by Jaimie Bennett

Once a man in the town of Nebri carved a beautiful gebeta[1] board for his son. He made it from the wood of an olive tree. When he was finished he showed his son how to play games upon it. The boy was very glad to have such a beautiful thing, and in the morning when he went out with the cattle to the valley where they grazed he took his gebeta board along. Everywhere he went he carried his board under his arm.

While he followed the cattle, he came upon a group of wandering Somalis with their camels, gathered around a small fire in a dry riverbed.

"Where in this country of yours can a man get wood?" the Somalis asked.

"Why, here is wood," the boy said. And he gave them the fine gebeta board, which they put into the fire.

As it went up in flames, the boy began to cry:

"Oh, now where is my fine gebeta board that my father has carved for me?"

"Do not make such turmoil," the Somalis said, and they gave him a fine new knife in place of the game board.

The boy took the knife and went away with his cattle. As he wandered he came to a place where a man was digging a well in the sand of the riverbed, so that his goats could drink.

"The ground is hard," the man said. "Lend me your knife to dig with."

The boy gave the man the knife, but the man dug so vigorously with it that it broke.

"Ah, what has become of my knife?" the boy wailed.

---

[1]gebeta [geh' beh · tah]: an Ethiopian version of a counting game played throughout Africa with beans or seeds on a carved board (actually two boards that fit together) having nine carved playing positions and a pocket at each end for winnings

"Quiet yourself," the man said. "Take this spear in its place." And he gave the boy a beautiful spear trimmed with silver and copper.

The boy went away with his cattle and his spear. He met a party of hunters. When they saw him one of them said:

"Lend me your spear, so that we may kill the lion we are trailing."

The boy gave him the spear, and the hunters went out and killed the lion. But in the hunt the shaft of the spear was splintered.

"See what you've done with my spear!" the boy cried.

"Don't carry on so," the hunter said. "Here is a horse for you in place of your spear."

The hunter gave him a horse with fine leather trappings, and he started back toward the village. On the way he came to where a group of workmen were repairing the highway. As they worked they caused a landslide, and the earth and rocks came down the mountain with a great roar. The horse became frightened and ran away.

"Where is my horse?" the boy cried. "You have made him run away!"

"Don't grieve," the workman said. "Here is an ax." And he gave the boy a common iron ax.

The boy took the ax and continued toward the village. He came to a woodcutter who said:

"Lend me your large ax for this tree. My ax is too small."

He loaned the woodcutter the ax, and the woodcutter chopped with it and broke it.

The boy cried, and the woodcutter said: "Never mind, here is a limb of a tree."

The boy took the limb upon his back and when he came near the village a woman said:

"Where did you find the wood? I need it for my fire."

The boy gave it to her, and she put it in the fire. As it went up in flames he said:

"Now where is my wood?"

"Here," the woman said, "here is a fine gebeta board."

He took the gebeta board under his arm and went home with the cattle. As he entered his house his father smiled and said:

"What is better than a gebeta game board to keep a small boy out of trouble?"

THINK IT OVER

1. *How did the boy end up with the same kind of object that he had when he left home?*

2. *Do you think that the gebeta board kept the young boy out of trouble? Explain your answer.*

WRITE

Think about something special that you own. Write sentences that tell what you would trade your possession for and why you would trade it.

CLOSE ENCOUNTER OF A WEIRD KIND

by A. F. Bauman • illustrated by Jeffrey Mangiat
from *Space and Science Fiction Plays for Young People*

Characters

MR. WILSON
MRS. WILSON
THERESA WILSON ⎰ *twins, 12*
TOM WILSON ⎱
JIM WILSON, *9*
THREE LETONIANS, *creatures from the planet Leto*

TIME: *Evening, the present.*

SETTING: *Living room of the Wilson home. Exit to bedrooms is left; door to outside is center back, with windows on either side; exit to kitchen is right. A coffee table is in middle of room, with couch and chairs arranged around it. A board game is set up on coffee table. Magazines and an evening bag are on couch.*

AT RISE: TOM, THERESA, *and* JIM *are sitting around coffee table, playing the board game.*

JIM (*Moving his piece on the board game*):   One, two, three! Hooray! I landed on Boardwalk. I'll buy it.

TOM: Sorry, Jim, you can't. You spent most of your money the last time around buying your third railroad.

THERESA: Yes, Jim. You've got to be careful how you use your money in this game.

JIM: Stop telling me how to spend my money, Theresa! (MR. *and* MRS. WILSON *enter right.*)

MRS. WILSON (*To* JIM *and* THERESA):   Did I hear you two fighting again? I thought you all said you'd be good tonight.

TOM: We will, Mom. Don't worry.

MRS. WILSON: All right. I guess I'm a little uneasy about leaving you children here alone.

TOM (*Reassuringly*):   Sure, Mom. We understand. But we really are old enough to take care of ourselves.

MR. WILSON (*To* MRS. WILSON):   Yes, dear. Tom and Theresa can handle things much better than that last babysitter we had.

JIM: All she did was yell at me. She wouldn't let me play games or watch TV or anything. We just had to be quiet all evening while she talked to her boyfriend on the phone.

MR. WILSON (*Sternly, to* JIM):   That's enough, Jim.

THERESA: We'll keep all the lights on, Mom, and all the doors and windows locked. Don't worry.

TOM: And we've got the fire department and police phone numbers right here. (TOM *holds up a small piece of paper.*) And the number of the place where you'll be.

THERESA: Besides, you'll only be gone two or three hours.

MRS. WILSON (*To* THERESA):   All right. But, Theresa, just one more thing—don't you tell Jim any ghost stories. You know what an imagination he has. Those stories of yours give him bad dreams for a week.

THERESA: O.K., Mom, I promise. Go ahead and have a good time.

TOM: Everything's cool. Enjoy yourselves.

MR. WILSON (*To* MRS. WILSON):   Come on, dear, we'll be late. (*He picks up evening bag from couch and hands it to her.*)

MRS. WILSON (*To* MR. WILSON):   I wouldn't be so worried if we lived in town. Out here the nearest house is two miles away.

MR. WILSON: Everything will be fine, honey. Come on, it's late. Let's go. (*They exit center.* TOM, THERESA, *and* JIM *go to window left, wave, then return to the game.*)

TOM: I think it was my turn. (*They ad lib playing game.*)

THERESA: Jim, isn't it about time you put your cat outside?

JIM: I almost forgot. Reginald's in the kitchen. I'll go let him out the back door. (JIM *exits.*)

TOM: Whose turn is it now?

THERESA: Jim's. We'll have to wait for him. (JIM *returns and sits.*)

TOM: It's your turn, Jim. Throw the dice. (*Suddenly, sound of a loud "boom" is heard, followed by a bright flash of light, seen through windows. Then a blinking light is seen through right window.* TOM, JIM, *and* THERESA *jump up, startled.*) What could that be?

JIM: Maybe it's a thunderstorm!

THERESA: No, Jim, the moon is bright, and the stars are out.

TOM: It's not a fire. That light keeps going on and off.

JIM (*Excitedly*): I don't smell any smoke.

TOM (*Trying to be calm*): It can't be burglars. They would sneak in quietly.

THERESA: It's O.K. We're safe. All the doors are locked.

JIM (*Sheepishly*): They *were'* locked. But remember when I put out the cat?

THERESA: You left the back door unlocked! Oh, no!

TOM: But nobody is coming in, yet. (*Bravely*) I'm going over to the window to see what's making that light. (TOM *walks to window right and peers out.*) Look at that! A huge round thing as big as a fifty-foot-wide saucer.

THERESA: What? Let me see. (*She walks to window.* JIM *follows close behind.*) It does look like a saucer. And it's got a big flashing light on top!

JIM (*Looking out window*): Look—something's opening up on the bottom—it's a set of stairs unfolding down to the ground!

THERESA (*Watching*): And three weird creatures are climbing down!

TOM (*Trying to remain calm*): Well, gang, I guess we've got a UFO right in our own back yard.

THERESA: Those creatures are walking over to our back door! (TOM, JIM, *and* THERESA *run left, huddling close to one another. Sound of footsteps is heard from offstage.*)

JIM: They must be inside the house! What are we going to do?

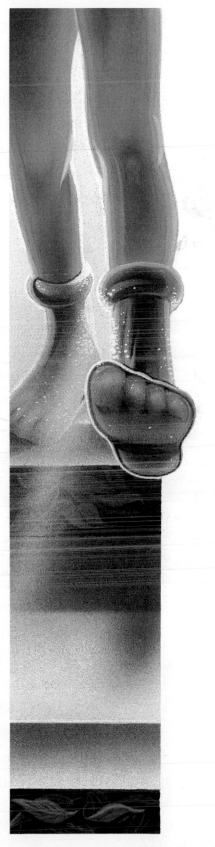

TOM: There's nothing we can do. Just try to stop shaking and be cool. (THREE LETONIANS *enter right, walking stiffly, wearing silvery costumes and green leotards. They lift their visors, revealing green faces.* TOM, JIM, *and* THERESA *jump back, frightened.* LETONIANS *speak in robot-like monotones.*)

1ST LETONIAN: Do not be afraid.

2ND LETONIAN: We will not harm you.

TOM (*Trying to be calm*): Who are you?

3RD LETONIAN: We are from the planet Leto.

THERESA (*Scared*): What do you want?

1ST LETONIAN: We are on a special mission. We have been sent to bring something back from the earth to our planet.

2ND LETONIAN: You earthlings have what we need.

1ST LETONIAN: On earth, you have something that will keep cold things cold for a long time. The same device will keep hot things hot for a long time.

2ND LETONIAN: This is a strange but useful item. We do not know how it can tell whether to keep things cold or hot.

3RD LETONIAN: This is our assignment: To bring this invention back to Leto.

1ST LETONIAN: Can you help us?

JIM (*Helpfully*): I know what you need! I'll go get it! (JIM *runs, exits right.*)

THERESA: I wonder what he's going after?

TOM: I sure don't know. With his imagination, he can think up just about anything. (JIM *returns, carrying a bowl of ice. He hands it to* 2ND LETONIAN.)

JIM: Here's what you need!

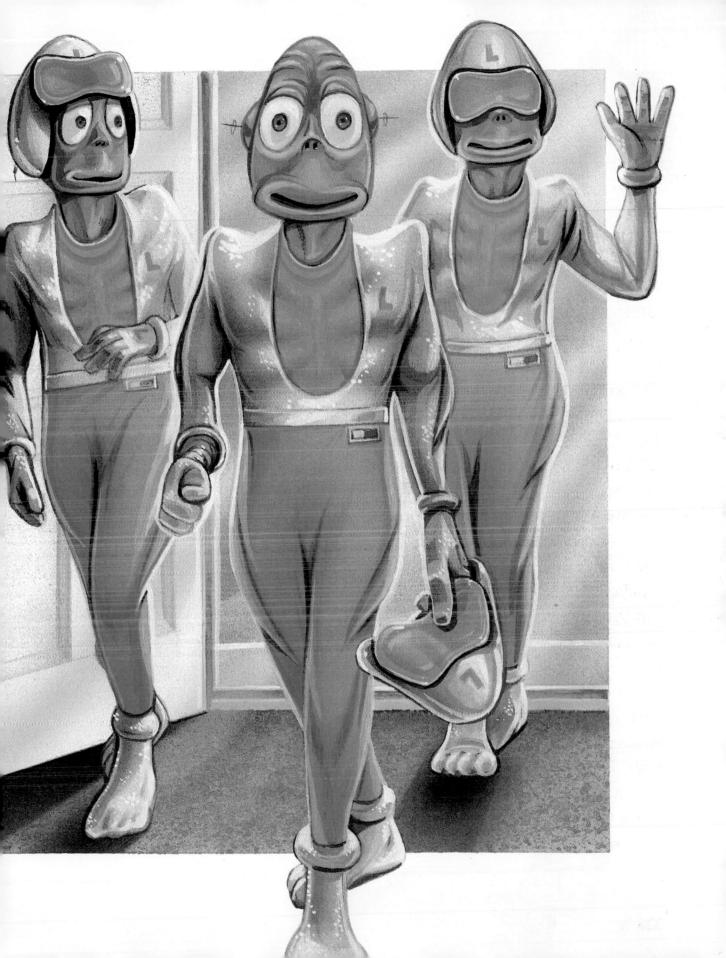

2ND LETONIAN (*Looking in bowl*): We have ice on Leto. Thank you, but this is not what we need.

THERESA: Besides, Jim, ice certainly won't keep hot things hot.

JIM: Oh, now I know! Wait a second; I know just where it is! (JIM *exits right and quickly returns with an immersion heater.*) Mom uses this to heat up her coffee. (*Excited,* 1ST LETONIAN *takes off gloves, revealing green hands. He tries to stuff gloves into pocket, but one falls to floor and remains there, unnoticed.* 1ST LETONIAN *takes immersion heater from* JIM *and examines it.*)

2ND LETONIAN (*To* JIM): Will it keep hot things hot?

JIM: Sure. Mom can keep the coffee in her mug hot all day with that thing.

3RD LETONIAN (*To* JIM): And will it keep things cold?

JIM: No, it won't.

1ST LETONIAN: This is not what we want.

2ND LETONIAN: Our commander will be disappointed if we return from our trip without this invention.

3RD LETONIAN: We are told that it does not cost a lot of—of—of—what is it called?

THERESA: Money?

3RD LETONIAN: Yes, it does not cost a lot of money.

2ND LETONIAN: Our commander told us that almost every household in America has one.

TOM (*Wondering*): What could it be?

THERESA (*Thinking*): Beats me. Let's see—it keeps cold things cold for a long time.

1ST LETONIAN: And hot things hot for a long time.

TOM: And it doesn't cost a lot and most Americans have it in their homes.

JIM: At lunchtime, I always have a cold drink.

THERESA: And I always have a hot drink with my lunch.

TOM (*Triumphantly*):   Hey, we've got what you need, Letonians! Wait right here. (TOM *runs off stage to kitchen carrying immersion heater, and comes back quickly with a thermos bottle.*) Here it is!

THERESA (*Excited*):   Of course! A thermos! Nice going, Tom! Why didn't we think of that before?

JIM (*Also excited*):   Yes, the same thing keeps hot things hot and cold things cold!

1ST LETONIAN (*Puzzled*):   What is this great invention?

TOM: We call it a thermos bottle. (*Shows thermos to* THREE LETONIANS.) Here, let me show you how it works. You take the lid off, like this, see? Then you put in whatever you want to stay hot or cold.

THERESA: Then you make sure the lid is on tight. (*She takes thermos and lid from* TOM *and screws lid on thermos.*)

1ST LETONIAN: Will it keep cold things cold for a long time?

JIM (*Proudly*):   Sure it will! My mom puts ice cubes in it in the morning when she fixes my cold drink. By lunchtime at school, the ice isn't even melted and my drink is icy cold.

2ND LETONIAN: Does this same invention keep hot things hot for a long time?

THERESA: Easily! Every morning Mom makes hot chocolate and puts it in my thermos. When I open it hours later for lunch, the hot chocolate is steaming.

3RD LETONIAN: How does it know which is which, to keep hot or cold?

TOM: Gosh, I sure don't know. But it works.

THERESA: And it's really easy to use!

JIM (*Proudly*): That thermos bottle is the one from *my* lunchbox. You can have it if you like. (THERESA *gives thermos to* 1ST LETONIAN.)

1ST LETONIAN (*Taking thermos carefully*): Thank you. Our special mission is completed. Now we can return to Leto.

2ND LETONIAN (*Slowly*): A thermos bottle. A thermos bottle. A thermos bottle. (3RD LETONIAN *hits him gently on the back.*)

3RD LETONIAN: Thank you, earthlings, for sharing this great invention with us.

2ND LETONIAN: Our commander will be satisfied with this thermos bottle, thermos bottle, thermos bottle. (1ST LETONIAN *hits* 2ND LETONIAN *on the back.*)

1ST LETONIAN: We do not need to write down the name of this invention. My co-captain (*Pointing to* 2ND LETONIAN) knows the name well.

3RD LETONIAN: We are very grateful for your help.

1ST LETONIAN: We must return to our planet now. Let us get back to our space vehicle.

JIM: O.K. I'll lock the door after you. (LETONIANS *and* JIM *walk off stage right.* THERESA *and* TOM *walk to window right, look out.*)

TOM: Look, Theresa. They're walking over to their spacecraft.

THERESA: And there they go up the steps. I can't see them any more.

TOM: The steps are folding back up into the spacecraft. (*There is another loud boom and flash of bright light. Flicker of light is seen, then fades and goes off.*)

JIM (*Walking quickly onstage from right*): Wow! What weird visitors!

THERESA: Boy, was I ever scared when they walked into the house.

TOM: Me, too. Maybe they were just as scared of us. But you could never tell by the way they talked.

JIM (*Imitating* LETONIANS): Yes, we are scared of you, too, but we have a special mission.

THERESA: Wasn't that something? All they wanted was a thermos bottle.

JIM: Some special mission! I really liked the way they looked.

TOM: Just like space creatures in the movies. (MR. *and* MRS. WILSON *open center door and enter.*)

MR. WILSON (*Taking* MRS. WILSON's *coat*): How did it go, kids? Everything O.K.?

JIM (*Running up to* MR. *and* MRS. WILSON): Mom! Dad! A flying saucer landed in our back yard!

MRS. WILSON (*Humoring* JIM): Really, Jim?

JIM: Yes, Mom. Three space people from the planet Leto came inside our house!

MRS. WILSON (*Still humoring* JIM): My, what an adventure! Jimmy, you've got a big imagination. (TOM *sits and shakes his head.*)

THERESA: But he's right, Mother. They're called Letonians and they came here on a special mission. They talked funny and had green skin and silver suits and gloves and helmets!

MRS. WILSON: Now, Theresa, were you telling Jimmy scary stories again?

THERESA (*Exasperated*): No, Mother. It really happened.

MRS. WILSON: Theresa, you should write books. You're so good at thinking up stories that now even you are beginning to believe them. Anyway, I'm glad you had a nice evening.

MR. WILSON (*Looking around room*): It looks as if playing that game is about all you did while we

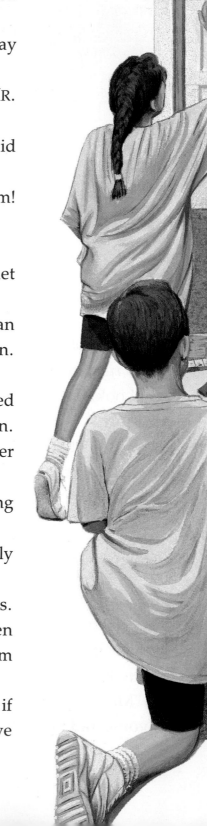

were gone. Everything's all right. The doors and windows are still locked. (*To* MRS. WILSON) See, honey, I told you nothing would happen.

JIM (*Exasperated*): But it did! It really happened! Honest! The Letonians were here, right in our own living room.

MRS. WILSON: Yes, dear. Now you three put away your game and get ready for bed. (*To* MR. WILSON) Let's go and get some coffee, dear. (MR. *and* MRS. WILSON *exit.*)

JIM (*Exasperated*): But, Theresa, why won't they believe us? (TOM *and* THERESA *start putting the game away.*)

THERESA: It's hard to convince them it really happened. The whole thing sounds so unbelievable I almost think I imagined it myself.

TOM: Mom and Dad would never in a million years believe our story about those Letonians. Let's just keep it a secret for ourselves.

JIM: Just wait till Mom tries to find my thermos!

THERESA: Come on, let's go to bed. (*They exit left.* MR. *and* MRS. WILSON *enter right, holding coffee mugs.*)

MR. WILSON: That story about the spaceship is ridiculous!

MRS. WILSON: Flying saucer, indeed! Theresa always did have a vivid imagination. (*Pause*) I wonder what my immersion heater was doing out on the counter? (MRS. WILSON *sets down her mug and begins straightening pillows on the couch.*)

MR. WILSON (*Sitting left*): You probably forgot to put it away in your rush getting ready to go out.

MRS. WILSON (*Straightening magazines on coffee table*):   But I wasn't in any rush. I had everything put away when we left.

MR. WILSON: O.K., dear, O.K. (*He drinks coffee.* MRS. WILSON *walks toward the chair on right where* 1ST LETONIAN *dropped his glove. With a quizzical look, she goes over and picks it up, holding it up for* MR. WILSON *to see.*)

MRS. WILSON: But where did this silver glove come from? I've never seen anything like it before! (*Musing*) I wonder if the children were telling the truth, after all? (*Quick curtain*)

THE END

THINK IT OVER

1. *What does the title of this play mean?*

2. *What landed in the Wilsons' back yard?*

3. *Why did the Letonians visit Earth?*

4. *Do you think Mr. and Mrs. Wilson believed that the Letonians really visited their home? Why do you think as you do?*

WRITE

Suppose you were traveling to another planet. Write a list of useful items you would take along. Include the reason you would take each thing.

FUN AND GAMES

The characters in the selections you read had interesting days. Do you think Judy and Peter would have reacted differently from the way the Wilson children did if they had been visited by the Letonians? Tell why you think as you do.

. . . .

Which adventure would you most like to have shared in? Support your choice with reasons.

. . . .

WRITER'S WORKSHOP Suppose the Letonians brought a weird game with them to exchange for the thermos. Make up a name, an object, and rules for the game. Then write a paragraph of information about the game. Include the steps of how to play. Share your paragraph with a group of classmates. You may wish to design a game board and play the game with your classmates.

SOLVE IT!

Donald J. Sobol writes about brilliant detectives who are challenged by mysterious crimes. Read the following cases and author interview to see how the characters solve the puzzling crimes that Mr. Sobol creates.

C O N T E N T S

"I didn't become a serious reader until I went to college and decided I wanted to be a writer and I had better develop a pleasure in reading all kinds, not just for information, which is the kind of reading I'd mainly been doing."

Donald J. Sobol

Since he began writing, Donald Sobol has won many awards for his mysteries. He began by writing a newspaper column called "Two-Minute Mysteries." But Mr. Sobol is perhaps best known for his Encyclopedia Brown detective stories. It has been thirty years since the first story about the crime-solving boy detective was published. The next two selections were written by Donald Sobol. See if you can match wits with Dr. Haledjian and Encyclopedia Brown to solve the cases.

THE CASE OF THE LOCKED ROOM

from *Two-Minute Mysteries*

by Donald J. Sobol

"I think I've been taken for ten thousand dollars, but I can't figure out how it was done," said Archer Skeat, the blind violinist, to Dr. Haledjian, as the two friends sat in the musician's library.

"Last night Marty Scopes dropped by," continued Skeat. "Marty had a ginger ale—and we got to chatting about the locked room mysteries till I made this crazy ten-thousand-dollar bet.

"Marty then went to the bar over there, filled a glass with six cubes of ice and gave it to me. He took a bottle of ginger ale and left the room.

"I locked the door and the windows from the inside, felt to make sure that Marty's glass held only ice, and put it into the wall safe behind you. Then I turned off the lights and sat down to wait.

"The bet was that within an hour Marty could enter the dark, locked room, open the locked safe, take out the glass, remove the ice, pour in half a glass of ginger ale, lock the safe, and leave the room, locking it behind him—all without my hearing him!

illustrated by Steven Meyers

"When the alarm rang after an hour, I had heard nothing. Confidently, I unlocked the door. I kept Marty whistling in the hall when I crossed the room to the opposite wall and opened the safe. The glass was inside. By heavens, it was half filled with ginger ale and only ginger ale. I tasted it! How did he do it?"

"Undoubtedly by means of an insulated bag," replied Haledjian after a moment's thought. "There is nothing wrong with your hearing. But no man could have heard—"

Heard what?

Solution

Ice melting. Marty had brought with him frozen cubes of ginger ale. After setting up the bet, he had slipped the ginger ale cubes into the glass. While they melted in the glass inside the safe, Marty waited in the hall!

THINK IT OVER

1. Describe the mystery that Archer Skeat was trying to solve.

2. Why was it important that Marty keep whistling while Archer Skeat crossed the room to open the safe?

WRITE

Write a clue that would have helped Archer Skeat solve the mystery.

An Interview with the Author:

DONALD J. SOBOL

Donald J. Sobol works hard to write the mysteries that never seem to stump the amazing Encyclopedia Brown. In this interview, Mr. Sobol shares with writer Ilene Cooper some of the tricks of his trade and some good tips for future writers.

MS. COOPER: How do you write the Encyclopedia Brown books? I've read that you keep files where you store all kinds of interesting facts you might use in stories.

MR. SOBOL: That's correct, Ms. Cooper, I keep files. And what goes into my files are simply what I call gimmicks. I think I have forty categories in all. What happens in the construction of the mystery story for me is that I pull out a file and the heading is, let's say, "food," and I rifle through whatever notes I have in that file under "food" until something ignites, or sparks me. I use that as the solution. I do not start to write the mystery until I already know how the story's going to end, who did it, how it was done, and so forth. The solution takes about two weeks. The rest of the writing takes about two days.

MS. COOPER: Where do you get these gimmicks, these kernels of ideas that you use?

MR. SOBOL: Everywhere. They come from my five senses, but mainly from what I see and what I read. We all know that reading is the other side of writing and if you don't read, you probably won't enjoy writing. For those who want to write, it's especially important, but even for those who don't want to pursue writing as a career, you're going to deprive yourself of an awful lot of pleasure down through the years if you don't read.

MS. COOPER: What advice do you have for young writers?

MR. SOBOL: I tell them to keep at it, keep reading, keep writing, and keep trying to find out what makes people and everything around you tick.

THE CASE OF THE MILLION PESOS

from *Encyclopedia Brown Gets His Man*

by Donald J. Sobol

Encyclopedia solved mysteries at the dinner table. He solved mysteries in the garage. He solved mysteries at the scene of the crime.

There were no other places in Idaville, he thought, to solve mysteries.

He was wrong.

There was second base.

While sitting on second base, he solved a robbery that had taken place in a country a thousand miles away.

Duffy Gomez

illustrated by Steven Meyers

Encyclopedia got his start as an international detective during an evening baseball game. His grounder slipped through Benny Breslin at short-stop. Encyclopedia wound up with a double.

Tim Gomez, the next batter, ended the inning by striking out. The game was immediately called on account of darkness. The score was 12 to 3.

Encyclopedia sat down on second base, discouraged. Benny Breslin flopped upon the grass beside him.

"We were going good," said Encyclopedia. "All we needed were nine runs to tie."

"I'm glad they stopped it," said Benny, a home-run hitter. "I've raced around the bases five times. My legs are falling off."

Sally walked over from first base. She looked troubled.

"What's bothering Tim Gomez?" she asked Encyclopedia. "He struck out six times in a row. Something is on his mind."

"Baseballs," said Benny. "He fielded every fly with the top of his head. He didn't catch one all game."

"Be quiet," whispered Encyclopedia, for Tim was passing near them.

"Sorry," Tim apologized. "I played like a cow on crutches."

"Forget it," said Encyclopedia.

"Aren't you feeling well?" asked Sally.

"I'm worried about my uncle, Duffy Gomez," said Tim. "He's in jail in Mexico City."

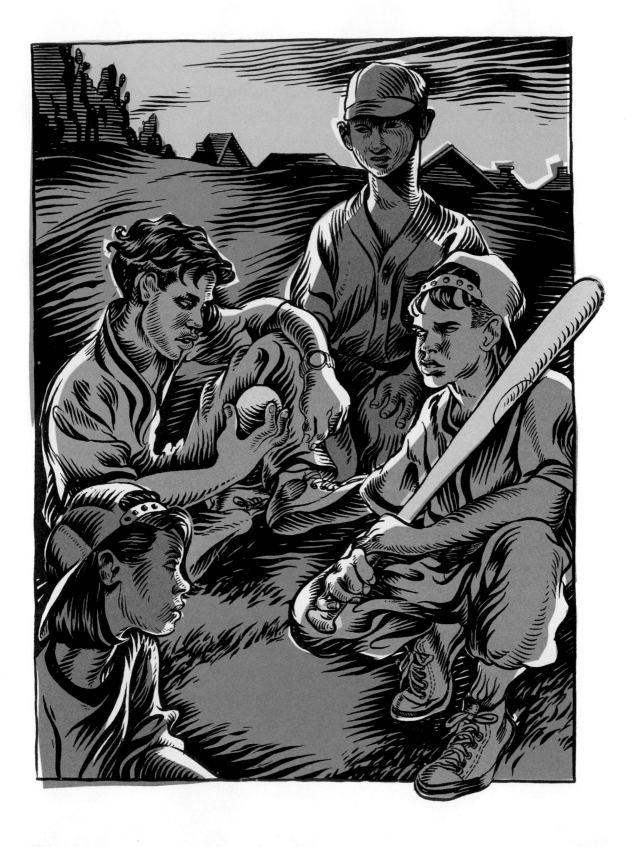

Duffy Gomez, Mexico's greatest baseball player, in jail! Encyclopedia, Sally, and Benny were stunned by the news.

"What did he do?" asked Benny.

"The police say he robbed a bank," answered Tim. "But I don't believe it!"

"What does your uncle say?" asked Encyclopedia.

"He says he's innocent," replied Tim. "The police threw him in jail just the same. He's being framed!"

"By whom?" asked Sally.

"By a man named Pedro Morales. He's hated my uncle for years," said Tim. "Pedro was in love with my Aunt Molly. She turned him down to marry Uncle Duffy."

"So Pedro accused your uncle of robbing a bank," said Sally. "What a low way to get back!"

"Doesn't your uncle have an alibi?" asked Encyclopedia. "Can't he prove he was somewhere else when the bank was robbed?"

"He was at a movie. Nobody saw him, though," said Tim. "Uncle Duffy wears a fake beard when he goes out in public. If he didn't disguise himself, baseball fans would mob him."

"Being at a movie is a pretty weak alibi," said Encyclopedia regretfully. "Your uncle will have a hard time making a judge and jury believe him."

"The real robber is bound to be caught," said Sally. "Don't you worry, Tim."

"There isn't much time left," said Tim. "Uncle Duffy goes on trial next week. Pedro will testify against him."

Sally glanced at Encyclopedia for help.

"Don't ask me," mumbled Encyclopedia.

"You *can't* say no," urged Sally. "Give it a try, Encyclopedia!"

"I can tell you everything about the case," said Tim eagerly. "I've read the newspaper stories my uncle sent from Mexico."

Encyclopedia considered the problem; namely, trying to solve a bank robbery in Mexico while sitting on second base in Idaville.

"You can't do Tim's uncle any harm," said Sally.

Encyclopedia couldn't argue with that. "You win," he said. "Tell me what you know, Tim."

"The National Bank of Mexico City was robbed last month by two masked men. They got away with a million pesos in one-peso bills," said Tim.

"That's about eighty thousand dollars," exclaimed Encyclopedia.

"Two weeks later," continued Tim, "Pedro Morales says he passed my uncle's house. It was late at night. There was a light in the living room. Pedro says he saw my uncle arguing with another man."

"Did Pedro overhear what was said?" asked Encyclopedia.

"Yes, the window was open," replied Tim. "Pedro claims my uncle said that he had counted the money again that afternoon. His share wasn't half the million pesos—it was a thousand pesos short."

"What happened next?" said Sally.

"According to Pedro," said Tim, "the other man got excited. He threw some money into my uncle's face and shouted, 'There's a thousand pesos. I never want to see your ugly face again!'"

"How did Pedro know they were talking about the stolen money?" asked Encyclopedia.

"Pedro says he didn't know—then," replied Tim. "Some of the one-peso bills the man threw at my uncle flew out the open window. Pedro picked them up. On a hunch, he brought them to the police. The numbers on the bills proved they were stolen from the bank."

"If Pedro had some of the stolen money," said Sally, "he must have had something to do with the robbery himself!"

"I agree," said Encyclopedia. "Pedro lied. His story just doesn't add up!"

WHAT WAS PEDRO'S LIE?

Solution

Pedro's mistake was in claiming that Tim's uncle said that he had "counted the money again that afternoon," and that "his share wasn't half the million pesos."

Remember, the stolen money was in the form of one million one-peso bills.

Tim's uncle could not have counted half a million bills, his share, in one afternoon.

It would have taken him five days—counting day and night!

THINK IT OVER

1. *How did Encyclopedia Brown help Tim Gomez?*

2. *Why was Uncle Duffy's alibi weak?*

3. *How did Encyclopedia know that Duffy Gomez was innocent?*

4. *Would you go to Encyclopedia Brown if you had a mystery to solve? Explain your answer.*

WRITE

Write a letter to Encyclopedia Brown telling him why you think he is or is not a good detective.

SOLVE IT!

Think about the mysteries and detectives that Donald Sobol created. Do you think that solving mysteries is a tough job? Explain why you think as you do.

· ·

How are Dr. Haledjian and Encyclopedia Brown alike and how are they different? What characteristics that they share make them good detectives?

· ·

WRITER'S WORKSHOP Pretend that you are a mystery writer like Donald Sobol. Write a letter to Mr. Sobol, explaining an idea for another two-minute mystery that he might like to write about in one of his books. Remember to include a possible solution in the body of your letter.

HIDDEN RICHES

Sometimes when you are searching for something, you find a more valuable treasure along the way. The following selection and poem tell about some hidden riches that change the people who discover them.

CONTENTS

THE GOLD COIN

by Alma Flor Ada

illustrated by Neil Waldman

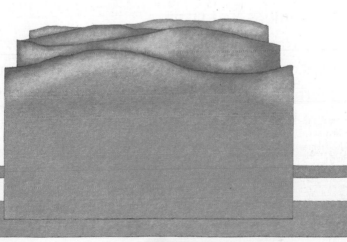

Juan had been a thief for many years. Because he did his stealing by night, his skin had become pale and sickly. Because he spent his time either hiding or sneaking about, his body had become shriveled and bent. And because he had neither friend nor relative to make him smile, his face was always twisted into an angry frown.

One night, drawn by a light shining through the trees, Juan came upon a hut. He crept up to the door and through a crack saw an old woman sitting at a plain, wooden table.

What was that shining in her hand? Juan wondered. He could not believe his eyes: It was a gold coin. Then he heard the woman say to herself, "I must be the richest person in the world."

Juan decided instantly that all the woman's gold must be his. He thought that the easiest thing to do was to watch until the woman left. Juan hid in the bushes and huddled under his poncho, waiting for the right moment to enter the hut.

Juan was half asleep when he heard knocking at the door and the sound of insistent voices. A few minutes later, he saw the woman, wrapped in a black cloak, leave the hut with two men at her side.

Here's my chance! Juan thought. And, forcing open a window, he climbed into the empty hut.

He looked about eagerly for the gold. He looked under the bed. It wasn't there. He looked in the cupboard. It wasn't there, either. Where could it be? Close to despair, Juan tore away some beams supporting the thatch roof.

Finally, he gave up. There was simply no gold in the hut.

All I can do, he thought, is to find the old woman and make her tell me where she's hidden it.

So he set out along the path that she and her two companions had taken.

It was daylight by the time Juan reached the river. The countryside had been deserted, but here, along the riverbank, were two huts. Nearby, a man and his son were hard at work, hoeing potatoes.

It had been a long, long time since Juan had spoken to another human being. Yet his desire to find the woman was so strong that he went up to the farmers and asked, in a hoarse, raspy voice, "Have you seen a short, gray-haired woman, wearing a black cloak?"

"Oh, you must be looking for Doña Josefa," the young boy said. "Yes, we've seen her. We went to fetch her this morning, because my grandfather had another attack of—"

"Where is she now?" Juan broke in.

"She is long gone," said the father with a smile. "Some people from across the river came looking for her, because someone in their family is sick."

"How can I get across the river?" Juan asked anxiously.

"Only by boat," the boy answered. "We'll row you across later, if you'd like." Then turning back to his work, he added, "But first we must finish digging up the potatoes."

The thief muttered, "Thanks." But he quickly grew impatient. He grabbed a hoe and began to help the pair of farmers. The sooner we finish, the sooner we'll get across the river, he thought. And the sooner I'll get to my gold!

It was dusk when they finally laid down their hoes. The soil had been turned, and the wicker baskets were brimming with potatoes.

"Now can you row me across?" Juan asked the father anxiously.

"Certainly," the man said. "But let's eat supper first."

Juan had forgotten the taste of a home-cooked meal and the pleasure that comes from sharing it with others. As he sopped up the last of the stew with a chunk of dark bread, memories of other meals came back to him from far away and long ago.

By the light of the moon, father and son guided their boat across the river.

"What a wonderful healer Doña Josefa is!" the boy told Juan. "All she had to do to make Abuelo better was give him a cup of her special tea."

"Yes, and not only that," his father added, "she brought him a gold coin."

Juan was stunned. It was one thing for Doña Josefa to go around helping people. But how could she go around handing out gold coins—*his gold coins*?

When the threesome finally reached the other side of the river, they saw a young man sitting outside his hut.

"This fellow is looking for Doña Josefa," the father said, pointing to Juan.

"Oh, she left some time ago," the young man said.

"Where to?" Juan asked tensely.

"Over to the other side of the mountain," the young man replied, pointing to the vague outline of mountains in the night sky.

"How did she get there?" Juan asked, trying to hide his impatience.

"By horse," the young man answered. "They came on horseback to get her because someone had broken his leg."

"Well, then, I need a horse, too," Juan said urgently.

"Tomorrow," the young man replied softly. "Perhaps I can take you tomorrow, maybe the next day. First I must finish harvesting the corn."

So Juan spent the next day in the fields, bathed in sweat from sunup to sundown.

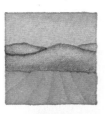

Yet each ear of corn that he picked seemed to bring him closer to his treasure. And later that evening, when he helped the young man husk several ears so they could boil them for supper, the yellow kernels glittered like gold coins.

While they were eating, Juan thought about Doña Josefa. Why, he wondered, would someone who said she was the world's richest woman spend her time taking care of every sick person for miles around?

The following day, the two set off at dawn. Juan could not recall when he last had noticed the beauty of the sunrise. He felt strangely moved by the sight of the mountains, barely lit by the faint rays of the morning sun.

As they neared the foothills, the young man said, "I'm not surprised you're looking for Doña Josefa. The whole countryside needs her. I went for her because my wife had been running a high fever. In no time at all, Doña Josefa had her on the road to recovery. And what's more, my friend, she brought her a gold coin!"

Juan groaned inwardly. To think that someone could hand out gold so freely! What a strange woman Doña Josefa is, Juan thought. Not only is she willing to help one person after another, but she doesn't mind traveling all over the countryside to do it!

"Well, my friend," said the young man finally, "this is where I must leave you. But you don't have far to walk. See that house over there? It belongs to the man who broke his leg."

The young man stretched out his hand to say good-bye. Juan stared at it for a moment. It had been a long, long time since the thief had shaken hands with anyone. Slowly, he pulled out a hand from under his poncho. When his companion grasped it firmly in his own, Juan felt suddenly warmed, as if by the rays of the sun.

But after he thanked the young man, Juan ran down the road. He was still eager to catch up with Doña Josefa. When he reached the house, a woman and a child were stepping down from a wagon.

"Have you seen Doña Josefa?" Juan asked.

"We've just taken her to Don Teodosio's," the woman said. "His wife is sick, you know—"

"How do I get there?" Juan broke in. "I've got to see her."

"It's too far to walk," the woman said amiably. "If you'd like, I'll take you there tomorrow. But first I must gather my squash and beans."

So Juan spent yet another long day in the fields. Working beneath the summer sun, Juan noticed that his skin had begun to tan. And although he had to stoop down to pick the squash, he found that he could now stretch his body. His back had begun to straighten, too.

Later, when the little girl took him by the hand to show him a family of rabbits burrowed under a fallen tree, Juan's face broke into a smile. It had been a long, long time since Juan had smiled.

Yet his thoughts kept coming back to the gold.

The following day, the wagon carrying Juan and the woman lumbered along a road lined with coffee fields.

The woman said, "I don't know what we would have done without Doña Josefa. I sent my daughter to our neighbor's house, who then brought Doña Josefa on horseback. She set my husband's leg and then showed me how to brew a special tea to lessen the pain."

Getting no reply, she went on. "And, as if that weren't enough, she brought him a gold coin. Can you imagine such a thing?"

Juan could only sigh. No doubt about it, he thought, Doña Josefa is someone special. But Juan didn't know whether to be happy that Doña Josefa had so much gold she could freely hand it out, or angry for her having already given so much of it away.

When they finally reached Don Teodosio's house, Doña Josefa was already gone. But here, too, there was work that needed to be done. . . .

Juan stayed to help with the coffee harvest. As he picked the red berries, he gazed up from time to time at the trees that grew, row upon row, along the hillsides. What a calm, peaceful place this is! he thought.

The next morning, Juan was up at daybreak. Bathed in the soft, dawn light, the mountains seemed to smile at him. When Don Teodosio offered him a lift on horseback, Juan found it difficult to have to say good-bye.

"What a good woman Doña Josefa is!" Don Teodosio said, as they rode down the hill toward the sugarcane fields. "The minute she heard about my wife being sick, she came with her special herbs. And as if that weren't enough, she brought my wife a gold coin!"

In the stifling heat, the kind that often signals the approach of a storm, Juan simply sighed and mopped his brow. The pair continued riding for several hours in silence.

Juan then realized he was back in familiar territory, for they were now on the stretch of road he had traveled only a week ago—though how much longer it now seemed to him. He jumped off Don Teodosio's horse and broke into a run.

This time the gold would not escape him! But he had to move quickly, so he could find shelter before the storm broke.

Out of breath, Juan finally reached Doña Josefa's

hut. She was standing by the door, shaking her head slowly as she surveyed the ransacked house.

"So I've caught up with you at last!" Juan shouted, startling the old woman. "Where's the gold?"

"The gold coin?" Doña Josefa said, surprised and looking at Juan intently. "Have you come for the gold coin? I've been trying hard to give it to someone who might need it," Doña Josefa said. "First to an old man who had just gotten over a bad attack. Then to a young woman who had been running a fever. Then to a man with a broken leg. And finally to Don Teodosio's wife. But none of them would take it. They all said, 'Keep it. There must be someone who needs it more.'"

Juan did not say a word.

"You must be the one who needs it," Doña Josefa said.

She took the coin out of her pocket and handed it to him. Juan stared at the coin, speechless.

At that moment a young girl appeared, her long braid bouncing as she ran. "Hurry, Doña Josefa, please!" she said breathlessly. "My mother is all alone, and the baby is due any minute."

"Of course, dear," Doña Josefa replied. But as she glanced up at the sky, she saw nothing but black clouds. The storm was nearly upon them. Doña Josefa sighed deeply.

"But how can I leave now? Look at my house! I don't know what has happened to the roof. The storm will wash the whole place away!"

And there was a deep sadness in her voice.

Juan took in the child's frightened eyes, Doña Josefa's sad, distressed face, and the ransacked hut.

"Go ahead, Doña Josefa," he said. "Don't worry about your house. I'll see that the roof is back in shape, good as new."

The woman nodded gratefully, drew her cloak about her shoulders, and took the child by the hand. As she turned to leave, Juan held out his hand.

"Here, take this," he said, giving her the gold coin. "I'm sure the newborn will need it more than I."

THINK IT OVER

1. *In what way was Doña Josefa rich? Explain your answer.*
2. *How many gold coins did Doña Josefa have?*
3. *Describe the trouble Juan had in getting the gold coin.*
4. *What made Juan give back the gold coin?*

WRITE

Do you know someone who is like Doña Josefa? Write a poem telling how that person is special and how you feel about him or her.

Pearls

from *Hey World, Here I Am!*
by Jean Little
illustrated by Denise Hilton Putnam

Dad gave me a string of pearls for my birthday.
They aren't real pearls but they look real.
They came nested in deep, deep blue velvet
    in a hinged box with a silvery lid.
His sister had some like them when she was my age.
She was thrilled.
He thought I'd really like them.
I said I did.

I love the box.

HIDDEN RICHES

Many people think that having money or jewels makes them rich. In what ways did the main characters in "The Gold Coin" feel rich?

. . . .

Think about the treasures that Juan and the girl in the poem discovered. Would you rather have a friend like Doña Josefa or a priceless box?

. . . .

WRITER'S WORKSHOP Think about a treasure that you own. Is it something you had to look for or was it given to you? Write a personal narrative telling about how you first found it or when you first received your treasure. Tell why it is valuable to you.

CONNECTIONS

Mexican girl with festive mask

MEXICAN MASKS

Dr. Eduardo Matos Moctezuma of Mexico has directed many archaeological projects in order to learn more about the ancient people of his country. Dr. Moctezuma and other archaeologists around the world often are puzzled by what they find.

Many ancient Mexican masks have been discovered, but we can't be sure why these masks were made and worn. We know more about the Mexican masks of recent centuries. Generations of carvers handed down the art of maskmaking. Their striking masks were worn by dancers acting out folktales.

Mexican masks have made their way north. Today you might see the masks on the actors of a Mexican American theater group. Or you might see them displayed in a museum as the work of modern artists.

■ *With your classmates, choose a Mexican folktale or one from another culture. Then create masks for all the characters.*

MYSTERIES OF THE MAYA

Who were the mysterious people who created the early masks of Mexico? Read about one of the Mexican native groups, such as the Maya, the Aztecs, or the Toltecs. Use what you learn to create a bulletin board display. List some questions that archaeologists have answered and some they have not answered.

Mexican Indian cat mask

This chart might help you organize information.

Name of group	
A question	
Why this is a question	
What the answer is OR Why there is no answer	

WHAT IS IT?

Archaeologists are often puzzled by the things they find. Puzzle your classmates in the same way by drawing a useful object that doesn't exist. Design the object so that its use makes sense once someone knows what it is. Challenge your classmates to tell what the object is for and to name it.

People from many different places traveled to America looking for a new way of life. Often they did not know where their road would take them. You'll learn about traditions and ideas that some European and Asian travelers brought with them to their new homes. You'll also learn about traditions of Native Americans who were already here. As you read the selections, think about how exciting it is to live in a country settled by people from so many cultures.

BOOKSHELF

PUEBLO STORYTELLER
BY DIANE HOYT-GOLDSMITH

April, a ten-year-old Native American girl, learns many crafts and pueblo traditions from her storyteller grandparents. AWARD-WINNING AUTHOR

HBJ LIBRARY BOOK

MAKING A NEW HOME IN AMERICA
BY MAXINE B. ROSENBERG

This nonfiction book tells of five young people who have come to America from different countries. Their stories describe their feelings about America and about their homelands. AWARD-WINNING AUTHOR

ON THE BANKS OF PLUM CREEK

BY LAURA INGALLS WILDER

In the fourth book of Ms. Wilder's *Little House* series, Laura and her family move to Walnut Grove, Minnesota, and settle on the banks of Plum Creek. NEWBERY HONOR

THE CHICKENHOUSE HOUSE

BY ELLEN HOWARD

Until their new home is built, Alena's family must live in a chickenhouse. Alena finds that although the chickenhouse is cramped, it has its comforts.
AWARD-WINNING AUTHOR

MEET KIRSTEN, AN AMERICAN GIRL

BY JANET SHAW

In 1854, Kirsten and her family leave their home in Sweden to come to America. This story tells of the hardships they face during their journeys to and across America.

PIONEERS

Imagine what it would have been like to live long ago in the wide, open spaces of the West. The characters in the following selections face challenges every day while settling the western frontier.

C O N T E N T S

379

Runaway

from *On the Banks of Plum Creek*

by Laura Ingalls Wilder
illustrated by Garth Williams

When Pa, Ma, and little Carrie went into town for the day, Laura and Mary were left alone with Jack, their dog, to take care of everything. After lunch, the three were faced with a big problem. The cattle were tearing into the hay-stacks and eating all the hay. Jack and Laura and Mary finally were able to chase the cattle into the high prairie grasses away from the banks of Plum Creek.

ALL that long, quiet afternoon they stayed in the dugout. The cattle did not come back to the hay-stacks. Slowly the sun went down the western sky. Soon it would be time to meet the cattle at the big grey rock, and Laura and Mary wished that Pa and Ma would come home.

Again and again they went up the path to look for the wagon. At last they sat waiting with Jack on the grassy top of their house. The lower the sun went, the more attentive Jack's ears were. Often he and Laura stood up to look at the edge of the sky where the wagon had gone, though they could see it just as well when they were sitting down.

Finally Jack turned one ear that way, then the other. Then he looked up at Laura and a waggle went from his neck to his stubby tail. The wagon was coming!

They all stood and watched till it came out of the prairie. When Laura saw the oxen, and Ma and Carrie on the wagon seat, she jumped up and down, swinging her sunbonnet and shouting, "They're coming! They're coming!"

"They're coming awful fast," Mary said.

Laura was still. She heard the wagon rattling loudly. Pete and Bright were coming very fast. They were running. They were running away.

The wagon came bumpity-banging and bouncing. Laura saw Ma down in a corner of the wagon box, hanging onto it and hugging Carrie. Pa came bounding in long jumps beside Bright, shouting and hitting at Bright with the goad.

He was trying to turn Bright back from the creek bank.

He could not do it. The big oxen galloped nearer and nearer the steep edge. Bright was pushing Pa off it. They were all going over. The wagon, Ma and Carrie, were going to fall down the bank, all the way down to the creek.

Pa shouted a terrible shout. He struck Bright's head with all his might, and Bright swerved. Laura ran screaming. Jack jumped at Bright's nose. Then the wagon, Ma, and Carrie flashed by. Bright crashed against the stable and suddenly everything was still.

Pa ran after the wagon and Laura ran behind him.

"Whoa, Bright! Whoa, Pete," Pa said. He held onto the wagon box and looked at Ma.

"We're all right, Charles," Ma said. Her face was grey and she was shaking all over.

Pete was trying to go on through the doorway into the stable, but he was yoked to Bright and Bright was headed against the stable wall. Pa lifted Ma and Carrie out of the wagon, and Ma said, "Don't cry, Carrie. See, we're all right."

Carrie's pink dress was torn down the front. She snuffled against Ma's neck and tried to stop crying as Ma told her.

"Oh, Caroline! I thought you were going over the bank," Pa said.

"I thought so, too, for a minute," Ma answered. "But I might have known you wouldn't let that happen."

"Pshaw!" said Pa. "It was good old Pete. He wasn't running away. Bright was, but Pete was only going along. He saw the stable and wanted his supper."

But Laura knew that Ma and Carrie would have fallen down into the creek with the wagon and oxen, if Pa had not run so fast and hit Bright so hard. She crowded against Ma's hoopskirt and hugged her tight and said, "Oh, Ma! Oh, Ma!" So did Mary.

"There, there," said Ma. "All's well that ends well. Now, girls, help bring in the packages while Pa puts up the oxen."

They carried all the little packages into the dugout. They met the cattle at the grey rock and put Spot into the stable, and Laura helped milk her while Mary helped Ma get supper.

At supper, they told how the cattle had got into the hay-stacks and how they had driven them away. Pa said they had done exactly the right thing. He said, "We knew we could depend on you to take care of everything. Didn't we, Caroline?"

They had completely forgotten that Pa always brought them presents from town, until after supper he pushed back his bench and looked as if he expected something. Then Laura jumped on his knee, and Mary sat on the other, and Laura bounced and asked, "What did you bring us, Pa? What? What?"

"Guess," Pa said.

They could not guess. But Laura felt something crackle in his jumper pocket and she pounced on it. She pulled out a paper bag, beautifully striped with tiny red and green stripes. And in the bag were two sticks of candy, one for Mary and one for Laura!

They were maple-sugar-coloured, and they were flat on one side.

Mary licked hers. But Laura bit her stick, and the outside of it came off, crumbly. The inside was hard and clear and dark brown. And it had a rich, brown, tangy taste. Pa said it was hoarhound candy.

After the dishes were done, Laura and Mary each took her stick of candy and they sat on Pa's knees, outside the door in the cool dusk. Ma sat just inside the dugout, humming to Carrie in her arms.

The creek was talking to itself under the yellow willows. One by one the great stars swung low and seemed to quiver and flicker in the little wind.

Laura was snug in Pa's arm. His beard softly tickled her cheek and the delicious candy-taste melted on her tongue.

After a while she said, "Pa."

"What, little half-pint?" Pa's voice asked against her hair.

"I think I like wolves better than cattle," she said.

"Cattle are more useful, Laura," Pa said.

She thought about that a while. Then she said, "Anyway, I like wolves better."

She was not contradicting; she was only saying what she thought.

"Well, Laura, we're going to have a good team of horses before long," Pa said. She knew when that would be. It would be when they had a wheat crop.

THINK IT OVER

1. *What exciting event happened in this story?*

2. *Why do you think the oxen started running away?*

3. *What did Pa bring Laura and Mary from town?*

WRITE

Write a paragraph comparing and contrasting your life today with Laura's life more than 100 years ago. Tell how your lives are different and how they are the same.

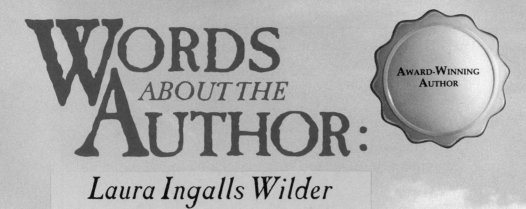

WORDS ABOUT THE AUTHOR:

Laura Ingalls Wilder

AWARD-WINNING AUTHOR

If the characters in "Runaway" seem real, it's because Laura Ingalls Wilder was writing about her own family. She wanted to write down her memories of growing up as a pioneer girl because she felt "they were stories that needed to be told." Even though Ms. Wilder's stories are set long ago, they appeal to young readers today.

Laura was born in a little log cabin in the big woods of Wisconsin in 1867. In *Little House in the Big Woods*, her first book, she wrote about her experiences growing up.

In her next book, *Little House on the Prairie*, which is also the title of a television series based on the family's experiences, Laura described the wagon-train trip that took the Ingalls family from Wisconsin to the Kansas prairie. The landscape of the prairie was very different from that of the Wisconsin woods. On the prairie, the sky seemed to go on forever. There weren't many other settlers, but there were Indians living on the land, which had once been their hunting ground.

When it appeared that the government was going to return the land to the Indians, the Ingalls family went back to Wisconsin, but Pa soon had an "itchy foot" and wanted to try the West again. This time, the family settled in Walnut Grove, Minnesota, which is the setting for "Runaway."

Hard times eventually forced the Ingalls family to move west again, to the Dakota Territory. By that time, Laura's older sister, Mary, had become blind from a fever, and there were still more troubles ahead. The frigid winter of 1880–1881 was so cold that people could barely stay warm and find enough food. The story of how the Ingallses managed to survive is told in Laura's book *The Long Winter*.

When she was 17, Laura was courted by a local farmer, Almanzo Wilder. They married in 1885. Laura described her early years of marriage in *The First Four Years*. She also wrote about Almanzo's childhood in *Farmer Boy*.

Laura didn't start writing until she was 65 years old. She wanted children to understand "more about the beginnings of things—what it is that made America." As you read Laura Ingalls Wilder's books, you feel like a pioneer child too because she wrote so vividly about an exciting period in history.

SAILING

from *Grasshopper Summer*

by Ann Turner

illustrated by Joel Spector

Sam White did not want to leave Kentucky, but his father was ready to look for their future in Dakota Territory. So, Ma, Pa, brother Billy, and Sam set out in a covered wagon, with their dog, Jake, on their journey to a new home.

THE LAND WAS CHANGING. The smaller hills and red rocks of the South were gone, and day by day, the land got more and more like a blanket—a brown-green, rumpled one. Grandma'd want to pull it neat and flat, but I liked it. Like the sea was supposed to be, and sometimes I felt we were on a boat sailing over an ocean.

We went over so many miles of grass, it all began to look the same. We got quieter the farther north we traveled. Sometimes the only sound I heard was the wind flapping our canvas top. Something about that wide blue sky, that endless grass, made us quiet. Like our voices were a fire we had to save.

389

After a few weeks of rolling over the new grass, Pa turned to us. "We're in Dakota Territory now. We got here!"

Billy said, "Looks just the same to me, Pa. Grass and grass and sky and wind."

Pa frowned.

"I like it, Pa," Billy hurried to say. "It's just it doesn't look any different."

Ma patted his arm and I silently agreed. I wondered if she was thinking about living in the ground, the way Pa said we would. Dig into a hill with the wind at our backs, he said. I wondered if it would feel like a grave instead of a house, but I didn't tell Billy that.

After another week, we came to the first town we'd seen in some time.

"What's that?" Billy asked.

You could hardly tell it was a town at first. There were just some bumpy bits on the horizon. Then, as the wagon rolled on, they became house roofs, then walls, and a dusty street snaked between them.

Pa stopped Ham and Duke outside the town, and Ma fidgeted with her handkerchief. She dabbed at her cheeks and hands, and pushed her straggly hair under the dusty bonnet.

"Walter, do I look all right?"

"You always look lovely, Ellen," Pa said.

She shook her head. "Bonnets are no use in this country—all that wind and sun." She "tcched." "You boys smooth down your hair and neaten up."

Billy stared at me and I stared at him. I straightened his dusty jacket and he brushed off my shoulders and we laughed. Used to be that I'd fuss at him and he'd fuss back. But ever since that time weeks ago when he was almost lost, I'd stopped picking at him quite so much.

Pa chirruped to the horses, and we went into town. There were five or six houses on either side, cows in back, and horses tied in front of the "Comfort Hotel." It was a skinny, gray building like an old lady trying to pretty herself up. Faded pink curtains hung inside the windows, and the glass was smeary.

There were people all over the street, calling and talking to each other. "Harry!" someone shouted, and my ears hurt. "How's your boy? Alice doing well?" "Sure!" the other shouted back. Didn't they know you didn't need to shout on the prairie? That it was so quiet a whisper would do?

The only ones who were quiet were Indians. We'd seen a few on horseback when we traveled, but not many. Here an older man stood straight as a gun by the Comfort Hotel, and a younger one stood beside him. In the shadows crouched a woman. They didn't talk to each other, but the quiet around them seemed to join them up somehow, and we just looked noisy and silly compared to them.

Ma said, "Indians!"

"Hush," Pa said. "They have a right to be here, too. Just go about your business and don't fuss."

"What's that, Pa?" Billy pointed to a long line of men outside a shabby building.

"That's probably the land claim office, Billy, and those men are waiting to file on their claims."

Pa stopped the horses by the general store and said, "You boys can come with us or stay here."

Billy jumped down and went in with Ma and Pa, but I stayed in the wagon. "Come on, Sam." He waved to me.

I shook my head, and couldn't explain to him that there were too many people and too many voices, and I just wasn't used to it. Made my neck itch, and I scrunched down to watch people while Ma and Pa bought supplies. Most folks looked like us, kind of tattered. Nobody was too neat—men had scrungy beards and blue denim overalls. Women were in calico with kids tugging at their hands. One yellow mutt with a sad tail lay in the street.

After a long, noisy time they came back, and Pa heaved a sack of flour into the wagon while Ma tucked a bag beside it.

"Glad I got that map, Ellen," Pa said. Even his voice sounded loud to me.

"Yes, Walter—I was glad to have a little conversation with the storekeeper. News!" Ma said.

"What news?" I asked. "I bet it's still the same. Storms. Woman has five babies. Horses run amok and little boy squashed. Tornadoes in the South and—"

"Railroads, Sam!" Billy broke in. "You forgot the railroads."

"Coming this way," Pa said. "It makes me think. . . ."

"Think what, Walter?" Ma hopped up onto the seat.

"Think that we may be getting near to stopping."

"It would be so wonderful to stop, just to sit for a while. Not to move," Ma sighed.

"The storekeeper drew me a rough map, Ellie, of the territory still open around here. Just in case."

Pa smiled at her, flicked the reins, and we set off down the street. I was so glad to be going again, to get out of that town and beyond all those voices and legs and arms. I didn't know if I wanted to stop moving or not.

"Sam, you should have seen the candy! And guns and knives and fishing poles!"

"Mmmph," was all I said to Billy.

I watched the prairie roll by, and it swept my mind clean—the cool wind and the sky so wide and high. Who wanted to look at candy?

Suddenly, Billy nudged me and pointed out the back. Two hawks dove after a pigeon. They screamed at that bird as it zigzagged and flew low.

"Come on, pigeon!" Billy called. "Fly faster!"

It whizzed to one side, raced to the other, gained height, dove, but the hawks stayed close behind. One of the hawks rose higher and higher, then screamed again. It sped down the sky and hit the pigeon so hard its feathers exploded into the air.

"Whooh! Hate to be that pigeon!" Billy sucked in a breath.

"Me, too." I looked through the back. There was no one out here on the prairie except us—us and those screaming hawks and the pigeon exploded into nothing. The wind blew the feathers away, it blew away the hawks' calls. I shivered and couldn't stop.

A NIGHT AND A DAY AFTER WE LEFT THAT DRAB town, Pa turned to Ma on the wagon seat.

"Ellie, it's about time we thought of making a claim."

"How are we going to choose, Walter?"

Pa stopped and unfolded the map he'd got in town. He ran his finger down the paper. "It's divided into sections, Ellen, and each section is one hundred sixty acres."

Ma studied the map. Pa said, "These are the sections that are still unclaimed. The ones closer to town are already gone. But we could try to find something near the next town—about forty miles away."

"Forty miles!" Ma jumped down from the wagon and dusted off her dress. She looked around and breathed in. To the left, the plain ran up to a little hump, flattened, and stretched out to some hills far away. They were purple and brown, with cloud shadows racing over them. To the right, the grass was brown and green. Birds popped up from it and swung on the stems. Ham and Duke lowered their heads to graze. Jake rolled on his back in the grass.

"What's wrong with this?" Ma said.

"Here? But I thought you wanted neighbors, to be closer to town. The last one's more than a day away."

"I know. I know it's contrary of me, but . . ." She walked back and forth, taking deep breaths. Billy and I jumped down beside her. The ground was springy and soft, and I threw myself on it, rolling and kicking my feet. Earth. Land that didn't move under the wagon wheels.

Billy rolled beside me, and we rooted and snorted like two spring pigs. Jake bounced from my head to Billy's, pretending to snap at us.

"Boys!" Ma reproved. But her mouth twitched.

Pa laughed and jumped down beside us. "If this doesn't beat all." He swung Ma around until her bonnet fell off and her hair streamed out behind.

"Walt! Put me down." He did, and she looked like an Indian woman then, with her brown face and hands and dark hair. Grandma'd hate it. She'd want to stuff Ma's hair under the bonnet and dab cornstarch on her skin.

"Well, boys"—Pa kept his hand on Ma's waist—"what do you think?"

We scrambled to our feet and Billy said, "If there's water nearby, this looks fine to me."

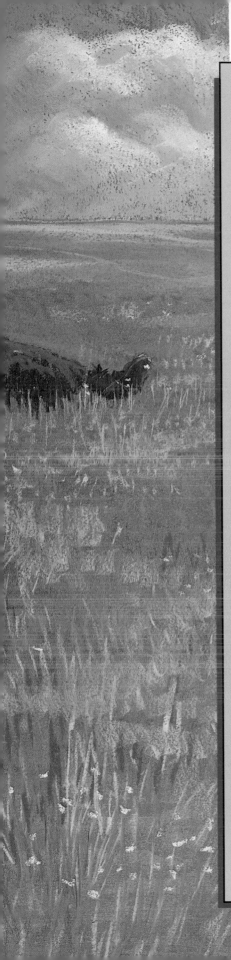

He sure was getting practical all of a sudden. I hadn't even thought of water.

Pa pointed to some trees in the distance. "Those are willows. Should mean a creek over there."

"If this section's free," Ma said, pinning up her hair. "*And* if no one else wants it." She got the map from the wagon, and she and Pa pored over it, murmuring—"That track there—meant to be a road—goes through the middle of these four sections—that pine there. . . ." I guess they were figuring out landmarks. Billy and I lay down in the grass and looked up at the sky while they talked.

"You could fall into it," Billy said.

"Or swim around in it, like a blue sea."

"The air smells good!" He chewed on some grass. "Clean, like laundry."

"Or potatoes baking."

"Mmm, I like it here." Billy rolled onto his side. Pa yelled to us. "We're clear, boys!" He ran over and pretended to put his foot on each of our chests. "We declare this to be Walter T. White's—"

"And Ellen A. White's—" Ma put in.

"And Billy and Sam White's land," we all finished together.

Pa rubbed his chin. "Who'll come with me to look for water?"

Billy jumped up and they set off together, singing, while Ma pulled grass out of a circle to make a fire. "Sam, help me get dinner started." Of course Billy *would* get to go exploring while I had to help with supper.

"In a minute, Ma." I did something strange, then, something I never told anyone about, not even Billy. I went off behind the wagon, where no one could see me, and dug a tiny hole with my knife. The grass roots tangled up the dirt and it took a while. I sniffed the wet earth smell. Then I spat into the hole three times and mixed it in, tamping the grass hard on top.

"Samuel, you come here!" Ma's voice rose.

"Coming." I felt strange doing such a thing. But when I saw Pa and Billy running back toward the wagon, waving their hats and shouting, "We found water!" I knew why. I'd put a piece of myself into the earth. Samuel Theodore White, a Kentucky boy, had made his mark on Dakota Territory.

THINK IT OVER

1. *What was life like in 1874 for a family who traveled West?*

2. *What did the land look like in Dakota Territory?*

3. *Why didn't Sam want to go into the general store?*

4. *How did Sam feel about Dakota Territory? Tell how you know.*

WRITE

Would you like to have traveled to Dakota Territory with Sam and his family? Write a list of reasons that support your decision.

PIONEERS

Life was difficult for pioneer families. Which of the hardships challenging the families you read about do you think was the most difficult to face? Tell why you think as you do.

. . . .

In what ways was life on the Minnesota prairie like life in the Dakota territory?

. . . .

WRITER'S WORKSHOP Choose another pioneer that you have heard about or read about. Remember that a pioneer is a person who settles in a new country or region. Read about and take notes on how that person lived and what he or she contributed to the settling of the frontier. Organize your notes into an outline. Then write a research report about the pioneer you chose and share your report with your classmates.

IMMIGRANTS

Did you ever wonder what it would be like to move to a new country or travel far, far away? The following poem and selection tell about the many problems some people face when they travel to faraway places.

CONTENTS

FAR, FAR WILL I GO

from *Beyond the High Hills* • by Knud Rasmussen
illustrated by Bryan Haynes

Far, far will I go,
Far away beyond the high hills,
Where the birds live,
Far away over yonder, far away over yonder.

Two pieces of rock barred the way,
Two mighty rocks,
That opened and closed
Like a pair of jaws.
There was no way past,
One must go in between them
To reach the land beyond and away,
Beyond the high hills,
The birds' land.

Two land bears barred the way,
Two land bears fighting
And barring the way.
There was no road,
And yet I would gladly pass on and away
To the farther side of the high hills,
To the birds' land.

CHANAH'S

from *The Cat Who Escaped from Steerage*

Chanah and her family are crossing the Atlantic Ocean to begin a new life in America. Her parents, Rifke and Yonkel, and her brother, Benjamin, are traveling with cousins Raizel, Yaacov, and Schmuel, and Grandmother Tante Mima.

Chanah is sad because Pitsel, the cat she found before they boarded, has escaped from her basket. Chanah and Yaacov last saw Pitsel on the third-class deck, where they made friends with a woman with a feather in her hat. If Chanah leaves the ship without Pitsel, she will never see her again.

As the ship nears land, the family wonders if they will pass inspection because Yaacov is deaf. A ship's officer who knows the secret has written a note for the inspectors at Ellis Island.

AWARD-WINNING BOOK

JOURNEY

by Evelyn Wilde Mayerson   illustrated by Mike Dooling

THE NEXT MORNING they awoke to an awful din. Eager to find out what all the commotion was about, Chanah's family ran out on deck in an awkward cluster, banging into other people, even knocking over a cooking pot and a checkerboard. Each one holding the hand of another, they quickly saw that everything was veiled in an early-morning mist as dense as steam from a kettle.

Then something wondrous appeared. To their left, rising before them, stood a giant statue of a woman holding aloft a torch in one hand and clutching a book in the other. Rays like the spokes on a wheel poked from her head.

Tante Mima tried to cover Chanah's eyes. "Don't look," she said. "She's in her nightgown."

405

"If the Americans want to put the Statue of Liberty in a nightdress," said Yonkel, "it's their business."

Everyone in steerage began to shout at the same moment. Some began to cry. Parents picked up babies and small children and held them up to see the lady with the torch. Chanah felt as if the lady were looking right at her. She did not really believe it, but it was nice to pretend until Benjamin spoiled it by saying that she was only made of copper.

Things happened quickly after that. A booming gun salute was fired from an island to their right. Crewmen ran shouting among the passengers in the steerage hold with orders for all people to wear their tickets in plain sight, the men to fasten them to their caps, the women to their dresses. Then, carrying bills of lading in their trembling hands, the steerage passengers gathered on deck with their bundles, trunks, boxes, baskets, while the passengers on the upper decks threw down coins or waved to people waiting on the wharf.

"Don't pick up their pennies," warned Yonkel. "Soon we will be richer than rich."

"I," said Rifke, "will settle for a roof over my head and a floor that doesn't rock."

They were poked and shoved into a long line that led down the gangplank, where they were herded into waiting ferries. At this moment, Yaacov's mother thought she saw her husband, Shimson, waiting on the wharf. She began to wave to a man who waved back, but before she could be certain, she was rudely shoved along with everyone else into a ferry.

"Wave to your father, Schmuel," she shouted.

"Where?" asked Schmuel. "I don't see him."

"Why do you tell them that that man is Shimson," asked Rifke, "when you are not sure? When you cannot even see his face?"

"It will help to have something good to think about," replied Yaacov's mother, "while we wait in that place." She pointed in the direction of Ellis Island, to which they were headed.

Chanah paid attention to none of this. She was taking one last look at the ship that had been her home for the last two weeks. If there was any hope of ever seeing Pitsel again, it would be gone the minute she stepped foot on the ferry. Her deep sigh went unheard when passengers suddenly began to tug and shout as their baggage was torn from them and thrown into the ferry's lower deck. Most had not been separated from their possessions since they had left their homes, and having their personal belongings yanked from their hands was an unsettling experience.

For Chanah's family it was less so, mainly because they had so little of value. Whatever was important, like the silver cups, the brass candlesticks, and the gold coins, was carried on their persons.

Chanah wondered about the woman from third class. Did she have to go to Ellis Island? Did they tug the luggage from her hands, too?

"Where are we going now?" asked Tante Mima. "Are they sending us back already?"

"Not back, Mama," replied Yonkel. "Just to Ellis Island."

"What for?" asked Tante Mima.

"To look us over. To make sure that we're fit to enter." He said this softly, so that Yaacov's mother wouldn't have more to worry about than she already had.

THE FERRY RIDE to Ellis Island was brief, only fifteen minutes by Yonkel's pocket watch, the time it takes to pluck a chicken, pinfeathers and all. As Chanah and her family stepped on the dock, they were surrounded by guards who looked as if they did not know how to smile, all scowling and gesturing, shouting commands, pulling the immigrants into separate groups, then counting them and shoving them into line when they did not move quickly enough.

Chanah and her family were pushed into a red-brick building, where they climbed a staircase, lugging their bundles and their baskets one step at a time. At the top of the staircase they were stopped by a team of doctors in long gray coats who inspected their faces, hair, necks, and hands, with careful attention to their eyes, then listened to their hearts. Others did not pass inspection and were taken out of line, including the Russian family, who were all being detained to determine if they were carrying disease.

When the doctors finally waved them through, Chanah and her family stepped down another flight of stairs into a great hall. Yaacov, Schmuel, and Raizel were right behind them. The conclusion that none of them dared make was that the note from the ship's officer had somehow been lost.

The great hall below was divided into a maze of passageways for the immigrants to pass through, clearance lines bound by iron pipe railings with benches to sit on. There they waited to be called before an inspector who would ask them twenty-nine questions. Everything depended on the answers they gave. Even though they might be prepared, there was always the fear that the all-powerful officials would find cause to send one back. Parents could be separated from children, husbands from wives. Everyone had heard of someone who had had that experience.

Chanah's family moved along a few feet of bench space at a time in a string of human beads jerking forward one by one. After what seemed like forever, they were next.

The first question was directed to Yonkel. "Who paid for your fare?" the inspector asked through an interpreter.

Yonkel straightened his collarless jacket. "I did," he replied proudly.

"Do you have a job waiting for you?"

"Yes. In Woodbine, New Jersey. I go to work on a farm."

"Is anyone meeting you?"

"No."

This answer seemed to bother the inspector, who made a note on a piece of paper.

Yonkel was next asked if he and Rifke were married. Rifke, offended, jumped up. "Of course we are married," she shouted. "What do you think we are?"

"When and where?" demanded the inspector. Rifke gave him the date and the name of the village. She would have told him more, but Yonkel gave her a warning look and she sat down, her arms angrily crossed.

"How much money do you have?"

Yonkel wanted no unexpected whacks on the head from thieves in the night. "Five dollars in gold," he whispered.

"Show it to me," demanded the inspector.

This presented a problem. Should Yonkel show his coins, which he had kept so

carefully hidden, and risk losing them? Yet, without money, they were considered public charges. If the authorities decided that this was so, they would all have to wait in detention rooms from which hardly anyone was released except to be sent back to where they came from.

Yonkel reluctantly took off his shoes while the inspector and the interpreter laughed. Then each family member was asked his or her name, after which a miracle occurred. The inspector issued landing cards for all of them, including Tante Mima, whose answers were not always on the mark, especially when they asked if she knew where she was and she replied that she wasn't sure, but it was definitely not the Taj Mahal.

"Thank you," said Yonkel, using up two of his eleven English words.

Dragging their belongings, they passed through the maze of iron railings. Then they waited on the other side behind a mesh fence for Yaacov, Schmuel, and Raizel, close enough to hear what the inspector was saying to them.

Yaacov stood before the high bench in his knickers and visored hat. When the inspector asked him his name, his mother stepped forward. "He has a sore throat," she explained. "Not a sickness. Just hoarse. From calling geese. See, I have wrapped his neck in flannel."

"You've been on the ship for two weeks," said the inspector when the interpreter had relayed Raizel's answer. "As far as I know, there was not a goose among you." He laughed at his own joke.

Then things took a serious turn. The officials conferred. One stepped behind Yaacov and clapped his hands behind Yaacov's head. Chanah, who saw this coming, pointed from the fence and Yaacov turned.

"He seems to hear all right," said the interpreter.

"I'm not so sure," said the inspector. "He was slow in turning. Whisper your name, boy. Even with a sore throat, you can whisper."

"He wants your name," said the interpreter.

Yaacov drew an imaginary line down the center of his body, turned in one direction, then the other.

"What is he doing?" asked the inspector. "Is he having some kind of fit? If that's what he's doing, the interview is over."

Chanah broke from her family, ducked beneath the iron pipe, and ran to the high bench. "I know what he's doing."

The inspector leaned over his desk to peer at Chanah. "Who are you to him?" he asked.

"He's my cousin. He can talk," insisted Chanah. "He just talks with his hands. Tell him something else," she said to Yaacov.

Yaacov pointed to the inspector's pocket watch, made rippling hand motions, then a pinch of his thumb and forefinger.

"He's saying you have a drop of water inside your watchcase."

The inspector looked. Sure enough, there was a tiny drop of water under the case.

"At least we know his eyesight is good," he said.

Yonkel decided it was time to join the protest. "A different language," he shouted through the mesh. "Like all the different languages here. You need an interpreter, that's all."

Then the inspector lost his temper. "Get that little girl out of here!" he shouted. "Things are getting out of hand. Tell them to be quiet or we'll send them all back."

The inspector appeared to be troubled. He seemed to be thinking, You let in someone who's deaf, then you let in someone else who's blind. Where's it all going to end?

When the inspector shook his head, no one needed an interpreter to figure out that Yaacov would not be permitted to enter.

A great scream went up from Raizel, the kind that rattles from the throat and makes all within hearing feel their scalps crawl. Rifke began to wail, Yonkel to shout.

The interpreter, used to such scenes, explained, "The boy has to return. The mother and the other boy can stay, but this one has to go back to Poland."

Raizel began to shriek and tear at her dress, while every other mother and father in the waiting room pressed forward with their hands at their hearts, their throats, knowing that at any time, this could happen to them.

Yaacov's mother was in a painful dilemma. What to do? Her choice was simple, yet terrible: to return with Yaacov, and perhaps never see her husband, Shimson, again; worse, to let Yaacov return alone to live with distant relatives, perhaps never to see him again.

413

Chanah broke free from Benjamin's clutch, ducked beneath the railing, and again approached the inspector's bench. This time one of her black stockings had fallen to her high-topped shoes, but she made no move to pick it up. "He knows everything," she said. "He can tell you what you had for breakfast this morning and what you had for lunch. Ask him."

"The boy is entitled to an appeal," said the interpreter to the inspector. "You and I both know that can include the testimony of either relatives or lawyers."

"We can't afford a lawyer," shouted Yonkel.

Suddenly weary, the inspector's shoulders sagged. "All right," he said. "Tell him to tell me what I had to eat today."

Chanah asked Yaacov. Yaacov in turn made hand motions that Chanah interpreted.

"He said you had sausage and bread for lunch with coffee to drink, and eggs for breakfast."

"I'll be," said the inspector. "How did he do that?"

Chanah conferred with Yaacov. "He smells the sausage on your breath, and he sees the coffee on your teeth, the bread crumbs on your beard, and the eggs on your mustache."

The inspector cocked an eye. He reminded Chanah of a rooster that used to strut in a neighbor's yard. "How does he know that I didn't have the eggs for lunch?"

"Because the egg on your mustache is dry. If you had had it for lunch, the pieces would still be damp."

The two men looked at each other while the others held their breath. Then the inspector winked at the interpreter. "I say we let in a kid with a sore throat." No translation was needed. The smiles told it all.

When the inspector stamped a landing permit for Yaacov, Yaacov's mother grabbed his hand and kissed it.

"Oh, now," said the inspector, "don't be making me out to be some saint." Then he became all business. "Next," he shouted, "we haven't got all day," as another family with patient, hopeful eyes came forward, bringing their belongings on their backs and their children in their arms.

--*•◆•*--

Chanah's family's last stop before they took the return ferry was the money exchange booth. Yonkel decided to cash only one gold coin and save the other for emergencies, which, in a family, come along at a fearsome rate. Besides, he reasoned, paper money can tear, paper money can burn, paper money can go out of fashion if one's country loses a war. But a gold coin . . . you cannot even bite into a gold coin.

Yonkel made another choice, one that cost him some of his money. A boat was available to take them directly to New Jersey, but Yonkel wanted to be sure that his cousin Shimson's family were safely met. He would take the ferry with them to New York City. It would cost him extra. A few pennies, he thought. What did it matter? If he and his entire family, including Yaacov, could make it safely through the inspection at Ellis Island, earning money would be easier than slapping a potato pancake on a griddle.

THE FAMILY RAN from the shelter of the pier to the streets and back again, looking for Shimson. If the docks of New York City were a confusion, the streets beyond were more so, with horse-drawn carriages, cable cars whirring from overhead tracks, and once in a while, when one could take one's eyes from the tops of the tall buildings, a true wonder, a horseless carriage.

Yonkel decided that they were better off waiting under the shelter of the pier. Sooner or later, Shimson would find them. Yonkel led them to the exit ramp of the ferries, where they stood rooted like trees among a horde of immigrants heading for the crowded streets.

Some were vaguely familiar. Some they knew, like the German couple who stopped to say good-bye, the father carrying the chair carved with lions, the mother proudly holding their new baby with the red ribbon pinned to her swaddling shawl.

As the waiting grew tiresome, Chanah and her family sat on their bundles until Yaacov suddenly began flicking each side of his waist and pointing excitedly to someone in the crowd.

"Look," shouted Chanah. "Yaacov is making the fringe on his father's prayer shawl!" Then Shimson appeared, excusing himself as he pushed through the crowd, looking exactly like an American. Yonkel said it was his beard, which had been shaved off. Rifke said it was more likely his suit of clothes, made of first-class American material.

"Shimson!" shouted Raizel, who had not seen her husband in two years. "Papa," shouted Schmuel, who bolted clumsily on his fat, stubby legs. Yaacov ran smiling and silent, flicking his hands at his waist.

417

Shimson was all good news. He had a job in the garment industry, an excellent one. He was a pants presser. In fact, he had jobs lined up for every member of his family. Raizel would sew at home while he would take the boys, both of them, to the shop, where Schmuel would sweep and Yaacov would pull threads.

"Why can't I pull threads?" complained Schmuel. "Why isn't he the one to sweep?"

Shimson paid no attention to his older son and turned to Yonkel. "Stay in New York," he advised. "With all the family working, you will be able to put aside some money."

"I don't think so," replied Yonkel. "I have made up my mind to go to New Jersey."

Rifke whispered in his ear.

"Besides," added Yonkel, "my children will go to school."

"The girl, too?" asked Shimson, with some surprise.

Yonkel wanted to say, *Especially* the girl, especially after what she did this day for your son, but such comments would make Benjamin feel unworthy. Instead he said, "Why not the girl?"

While Shimson gathered his family's belongings, assigning to each a parcel to carry, Yaacov pulled his hat over one eye and looked over his shoulder.

Chanah turned and recognized the woman from third class standing alone in the throng, like a pebble in a stream only feet from where they stood. Chanah approached the woman timidly.

"There you are," said the woman with a great sigh. "I was getting ready to let it go."

"Let what go?" asked Chanah, wondering if she meant the feather.

"See for yourself." The woman handed Chanah her blue flower-printed hatbox. Scratching sounds could be heard coming from inside.

"Go on," said the woman. "Open it."

Chanah carefully lifted the lid of the hatbox. Inside was a scrawny, tired-looking, unhappy cat. Chanah bent down, tears shining in her eyes, picked up the creature, and held her to her chest. "Pitsel. I thought I would never, never see you again," she crooned.

"And a fine mess it made of my hatbox," said the woman. "I can never use it again, I can tell you that."

Then Yonkel came shouting through the crowd. "There you are! Didn't I tell you never to leave our side? Never! Your mother is beside herself. Why would you give us such a fright?"

Chanah wiped the tears that streamed down her face. "Look, Papa," she said. "The lady kept her for me."

"What was I to do?" said the woman. "The creature followed me to my cabin. It must have been the smoked fish I had wrapped inside a napkin. Once it was inside, there was the problem of getting rid of it. I didn't want anyone to think it belonged to me. So I hid it in my hatbox, which, I might add, will never be the same."

"Thank you," said Chanah in English.

"What did she say?" asked the woman.

"She spoke English," replied Yonkel. "And she thanked you, as I do. Is anyone meeting you?" he asked.

"My sister and her husband. They were supposed to be here two hours ago. I decided that as long as I was waiting for them, I would watch to see if you came out."

"If they don't show up," he said, "you are welcome to come with us to New Jersey. We are going to a farm community where there is work for all who want it and plenty of room."

"Heaven forbid," she said. "I grew up on a farm. I have no intention of going back to one, especially in a place I never heard of. Besides, I will soon have my own apartment."

Just then a woman yelled, "There she is! Looking like a greenhorn!" and a couple broke from the crowd to wrap the woman from third class in a warm embrace. The man picked up her baggage and they led her away while the woman said, "You can't sleep on the couch. Stan's cousin is sleeping there. But we made a bed for you in the kitchen."

Rifke had been standing behind Yonkel's shoulder. "No one wants to go with us to New Jersey," she said. "Maybe they know something we don't." She forgot about New Jersey when she saw the cat. Cats carried typhus, ringworm, and heaven knows what else. They were even known to suck the breath from a sleeping baby. Rifke put her hands on her hips. "No cat," she said.

Then Benjamin did something he seldom did. He put in a good word. "Cats also kill mice, Mama," he said. "And there are a lot of mice in the country."

Raizel also intervened. "Rifke, if it wasn't for Chanah, I hate to think what would have happened today."

Tante Mima had the last word. "Let the child have her cat," she said, "so we can go and I can get off my feet."

Rifke, outnumbered, gave in. "All right," she said. "But not in the house." She turned to Yonkel. "We are going to have a house, aren't we?"

"There will be a house," replied Yonkel. He did not add, Maybe not today. Neither did he say, Maybe not tomorrow. All he said was, "In this country, everything is possible."

With tears and promises to write and visit, Chanah and her family said good-bye to Shimson, Raizel, Schmuel, and Yaacov and boarded the ship for New Jersey.

Chanah stood at the railing, with the basket partially opened so Pitsel could feel the sea breeze on her face. The cat, who seemed to know that all was going reasonably well, poked her head out of the basket and sniffed the salt air.

"That's some terrible-looking animal," said Rifke to Yonkel.

"I wouldn't worry," said Yonkel. "In New Jersey, you will not be able to tell her from an American cat. Mark my words."

Then Tante Mima, too weary to stand, sat on her baggage. "This is positively the last boat they'll ever get me on again. I may be an old lady, but I can still put my foot down."

"What does it mean, Bubbi," asked Chanah, "to put your foot down?"

"It means to be stubborn. It means to say yes or no and mean it. Like what you did today for your cousin. You put your foot down. And they listened." Tante Mima bent over to pull up Chanah's stocking. "Chanah, Chanah," she said, "what a little woman you are going to be."

THINK IT OVER

1. *Describe Chanah's adventures as an immigrant arriving in a new country.*

2. *How did Yaacov communicate?*

3. *What did Chanah do to help Yaacov enter the United States?*

4. *Do you think it was difficult to travel to an unfamiliar country as an immigrant? Explain why you think as you do.*

WRITE

Imagine that you have a friend who is immigrating to the United States. Write a letter to this friend that tells why his or her trip will be worth the effort.

IMMIGRANTS

Throughout history, people have traveled great distances for many reasons. What does America have to offer immigrants? Support your ideas with examples from the poem and selection you read.

. . . .

Look back at the poem and the selection. How was the Eskimo's journey like the trip that Chanah and her family made to America?

. . . .

WRITER'S WORKSHOP   Imagine that Chanah, Benjamin, Yaacov, and Schmuel are new students in your school and that they are nervous about being in a new school and in a new land. What could you say to convince them that they will grow to like America? Write one or more persuasive paragraphs telling them what a great land America is. Share your writing with your classmates.

425

TRADITIONS

Traditions are important to many people. They are usually customs that began many years ago and have been passed down from one generation to another. The characters in the following selections find personal honor in their cultural traditions.

C O N T E N T S

427

CHIN CHIANG
AND THE DRAGON'S DANCE

WRITTEN AND ILLUSTRATED BY
IAN WALLACE

AWARD-WINNING
ILLUSTRATOR

**F**rom the time Chin Chiang stood
only as high as his grandfather's knees, he had dreamed of
dancing the dragon's dance. Now the first day of the Year
of the Dragon had arrived and his dream was to come true.
Tonight he would dance with his grandfather. But instead
of being excited, Chin Chiang was so scared he wanted to
melt into his shoes. He knew he could never dance well
enough to make Grandfather proud of him.

He stopped sweeping the floor of his family's shop and looked into the street where his mother and father were busy with other shopkeepers, hanging up paper lanterns shaped like animals, fish and birds.

"It's time to practice our parts in the dragon's dance for the last time before the other dancers arrive, Chin Chiang. The afternoon is almost over," called Grandfather Wu from the bakeroom behind the shop.

"If I were a rabbit, I could run far away from here," Chin Chiang said to himself, "but then Mama, Papa and Grandfather really would be ashamed of me." So very slowly he walked into the bakeroom where Grandfather Wu stood waiting. He was wearing the splendid fierce dragon's head that he would put on again that night for the parade.

"Pick up the silk tail on the floor behind me," said his grandfather from inside the dragon's head, "and together we will be the most magnificent dragon that anyone has ever seen."

Chin Chiang did as he was asked, but as his grandfather started to dance, Chin Chiang did not move. "Grandfather can hide under the dragon's head," he whispered, "but if I trip or fall, I have nowhere to hide. Everyone will say, 'There goes clumsy Chin Chiang.'"

Grandfather Wu stopped dancing. "A dragon must have a tail as well as a head," he said gently.

Chin Chiang looked down at his shoes. "I can't dance the dragon's dance," he said.

"You have trained for a long time, Chin Chiang. Tonight, when you dance, you will bring tears of pride to your parents' eyes. Now come, join me and practice just as we have practiced before."

But when Chin Chiang tried to leap he tripped,
stumbled and fell. Why had he ever thought he could
dance the dragon's dance? Why had he ever wanted to?
He was much too clumsy.

431

He jumped up and ran—away from his grandfather, out of the shop, into the market street. He stopped long enough to pick up a rabbit lantern, poke two holes for eyes and shove it over his head.

"Look, look. It's the dragon's tail!" called Mrs. Lau, dangling a speckled salmon for Chin Chiang to see. "Tonight, when you dance, the Great Dragon who lives in the clouds above the mountains will be honored, and next year he will fill our nets with beautiful fish like this."

Chin Chiang turned away.

"And he will grow oranges of a size and color never seen before," called Mr. Koo.

"What they say is true," added Mr. Sing. "The Great Dragon will bring prosperity and good fortune, if your dance pleases him."

But Chin Chiang remembered what one of the other dancers had once told him. If the dance was clumsy, the Great Dragon would be angry. Then he might toss the fruit from the trees and flood the valley. *It will all be my fault*, thought Chin Chiang. *Grandfather Wu will have to choose someone else to dance with him.* He waited to hear no more and raced across the market street.

"Our fish!" called Mrs. Lau.

"Our oranges!" called Mr. Koo.

Chin Chiang turned the corner.

"Our dance," called Grandfather Wu, from the doorway.

Looking out through the lantern, Chin Chiang hurried along the road by the sea to the public library, which he

had visited many times when he wanted to be alone. He opened the door and ran up the stairs, round and round, higher and higher, up, up, up, to the door at the top that led out to the roof.

433

From his perch in the sky he could see the mountains rising above the sea and below him the animal lanterns, which would glow like tiny stars tonight. Chin Chiang felt happier than he had for many days.

"I never expected to meet a rabbit on top of this roof," called a strange voice.

Chin Chiang turned around quickly. A woman carrying a mop and pail was coming toward him.

"I'm not a rabbit," he said shyly. "I am Chin Chiang," and he pulled off the lantern.

"Oh, that is much better," she said. "Greetings, Chin Chiang. My name is Pu Yee. May I enjoy the view with you?" She didn't wait for a reply. "In a little while I'll be watching the New Year's parade from here. I used to dance the dragon's dance when I was young, but not any more. My feet are too old, and they are covered with corns."

"My grandfather dances the dragon's dance," said Chin Chiang, "and his corns are as old as yours."

Pu Yee laughed. "His old shoes may move his old bones, but my feet will never dance again."

A wonderful idea suddenly came to Chin Chiang. What if he had found someone to dance in his place? He would show Pu Yee his part in the dance right now. No one would see them if they tripped or fell. "You can help me practice what my grandfather taught me," he said.

"Oh, my creaky bones, what a funny sight that will be," said Pu Yee.

"You can dance," he told her. Cautiously Chin Chiang gave a little jump. Pu Yee jumped too. He shook slowly at first and she shook too. Next they leaped into the air, landed together and spun on their heels. Before long Pu Yee had forgotten her creaky bones. Then Chin Chiang stumbled and fell.

"Let's try again," said Pu Yee, picking him up.

While they danced, darkness had crept down slowly from the mountains to the city below. Then, from far off, Chin Chiang heard the lilting tune of pigeons with whistles tied to their tail feathers. They had been set free from their cages in the marketplace and were flying high above the buildings. Chin Chiang knew this meant that the New Year Festival had begun.

"We must go, Pu Yee. We're late," said Chin Chiang. "The pigeons are flying free."

"I'm not late," she replied. "I'm staying here."

But Chin Chiang pulled her by the hand, and they hurried down the stairs together —round and round, down, down, down, to the market street. The sound of firecrackers exploded in their ears while the eager crowd buzzed and hummed. Chin Chiang pushed his way forward, but Pu Yee pulled back. In the noise and confusion Chin Chiang let go of her hand, and suddenly he came face to face with the dragon whose head was wreathed in smoke.

"Where have you been, Chin Chiang? I have been sick with worry," called Grandfather Wu in a muffled voice. Chin Chiang did not reply. "Come now, take up the tail before the smoke disappears and everyone can see us."

Chin Chiang stood still, his feet frozen to the ground. The clamor of the street grew louder, stinging his ears. "I can't dance, Grandfather," he said.

Grandfather Wu turned away. "You can dance, Chin Chiang. Follow me."

"Look, look. Here comes the dragon!" called Mr. Sing. The crowd sent up a cheer that bounced off windows and doors and jumped into the sky.

Chin Chiang was trapped. Slowly he stooped and picked up the tail. Grandfather Wu shook the dragon's head fiercely until Chin Chiang started to kick up his heels to the beat of the thundering drum.

Then, suddenly, Chin Chiang stumbled, but instead of falling he did a quick step and recovered his balance. Excitedly, he leaped into the air, and again, and higher again. And as the dance went on, Chin Chiang's feet moved more surely, his steps grew firmer and his leaps more daring. Mrs. Lau and Mr. Koo cheered from their market shops while people poured out of their houses onto balconies and sidewalks, filling the streets. High in the sky flags of fire and falling moons burst into light. They sizzled and sparkled, rocketed straight up and whistled to the ground.

Just then Chin Chiang caught sight of a familiar face in the crowd. It was Pu Yee. Chin Chiang leaped to the sidewalk and pulled her into the street.

"I can't, Chin Chiang," she said, pulling away. "My
bones. My corns. My knees."

"Pu Yee, yes, you can," Chin Chiang assured her.
"Look at me!" Hesitantly she took hold of the tail and
together they kicked up their heels just as they had on the
rooftop, while the throngs of people cheered them on. Up
one street and down another they danced, to the beat of
the thundering drum.

All too soon the dragon lifted its head and shook its
tail for the last time. The dance was over. Pu Yee hugged
Chin Chiang close.

Grandfather Wu smiled inside the dragon's head. "Bring your new friend to our home for dinner, Chin Chiang," he said. Pu Yee and Chin Chiang hopped quickly over the doorstep and into the bakeshop.

The family exchanged gifts of fine teas in wooden boxes, new clothes and small red envelopes of Lucky Money. Then they sat together to share plates of meat dumplings and carp, bowls of steaming soup and trays of delicious pastries and cakes and fresh fruit.

"To Chin Chiang, the very best dragon's tail I have ever seen," said Grandfather Wu, raising his glass in a toast.

Chin Chiang's face glowed with pride. "To a prosperous Year of the Dragon," he said, raising his glass to his mama, papa, grandfather and his new friend Pu Yee.

THINK IT OVER

1. *How did Pu Yee and Chin Chiang help each other?*

2. *Why didn't Chin Chiang want to dance the dragon's dance?*

3. *When Chin Chiang ran away from the bakeshop, where did he go?*

4. *Do you think Chin Chiang should have run away from what he feared? Explain why you think as you do.*

WRITE

Write a news story that tells about Chin Chiang's dance.

440

TOTEM POLE

BY DIANE HOYT-GOLDSMITH • PHOTOGRAPHS BY LAWRENCE MIGDALE

My name is David. I live in a small town called Kingston in Washington State. In the summer, I like to hunt for salmonberries and blackberries in the fields near our house.

My brother and I like to look out over Puget Sound, watching for the ferry from Seattle. Sometimes, we spot a pair of eagles flying high overhead. This makes us feel lucky because our family belongs to the Eagle Clan, which is our family group within the Tsimshian *(TSIM-shee-an)* tribe.

Our father is an Indian. He was brought up by his grandparents in Metlakatla *(MET-lah-CAT-lah),* on Annette Island in Alaska. He was raised in the old ways and traditions. He learned how to hunt, to fish, and to carve.

In our tribe, a person belongs to the same clan as his mother does. Our mother is not Indian. Her ancestors emigrated to the United States from Europe many generations ago. When I was two years old, she was adopted in a special ceremony by two members of the Eagle Clan in Metlakatla. This makes my brother and me members of the Eagle Clan too.

My father is an artist, a wood-carver. Ever since I was little, I have watched him take a piece of wood and carve a creature from it. Sometimes it is a wolf, sometimes a bear, and sometimes an eagle, the symbol and totem of our clan.

441

My father has a special cedar box. It is very important to him because it was made by my great-great-grandfather five generations ago. My father painted an eagle on the lid, and now he keeps his carving tools inside.

The box was first used to store food. When my father was a young boy, he was in charge of keeping the food box safe. When his family went out to hunt or fish, he carried the box from the boat up to the camp and stored it in a safe place. The foods his family had prepared for the journey were kept inside the box—the dried meat and fish, and the hardtack. These were the only foods the family would have to eat while they were camping.

My father says that even now, when he opens the box to take out a tool, he can smell the foods that were once stored inside. The faint scent brings him strong memories of the salt air, the hardtack, the fresh salmon, and even the smoke of the cooking fire where his family gathered. These memories are precious to him. The smells make the past come alive, he says.

When I open the box, all I can smell are the steel and leather tools inside. But the past comes alive for me when I hear the strike of the adze and hear my father tell his stories. He likes to tell me what it was like to grow up in Alaska.

One of my favorite stories is a Tsimshian tale called "The Legend of the Eagle and the Young Chief." Maybe I like it best because I belong to the Eagle Clan.

When my father first began to teach me about the Tsimshian songs, dances, and legends, he made some special clothes for me to wear. These clothes are called "regalia." They are worn for certain ceremonies, dances, and celebrations.

Sometimes in the afternoons, I go to my father's workshop. I look inside the trunk that holds all the regalia he has made. I dress in my special clothes to practice the dances my father taught me.

The first thing my father made for me is a headdress out of leather and decorated with ermine skins. On the front, there is a small eagle's face carved from a piece of cedar wood and painted blue and brown. This is called a frontlet. The eagle is shown on all our regalia because the eagle is our family crest. My Indian name is Lap'aigh laskeeg (lah-pah-AG-a-lah-SKEEK). It means "He Who Flies Like the Eagle" in the Tsimshian language.

My father made me an apron out of deerskin which is painted with an eagle design. I have leggings made of soft leather. They have a fringe with deer hooves hanging down. The hooves knock together as I dance and make a rattling sound as I move.

I also have a button blanket that I wear. On the back there is another large eagle design. It is outlined in hundreds of tiny white buttons. In the old days, the Tsimshian blankets were first woven from cedar bark and then decorated with rows of tiny white shells. But in the 1800s, when Europeans began to trade with the tribes along the coast, the Indians began to use bright red "trade cloth" for the blankets and machine-made buttons of mother-of-pearl for decoration.

The first step in making a totem pole is to find a straight tree. It must be wide enough to make a strong pole. The best trees for a totem pole have few branches. Where a branch joins the trunk a knot forms, making the carving very difficult.

Nearly all totem poles are carved from cedar logs. Cedar trees grow very straight and are common in the evergreen forests along the coastline near our home. The wood of the cedar is soft and easy to carve. It does not rot and insects will not destroy it. A totem pole carved from a cedar log can last a hundred years or more.

After the right tree is found and cut down, all the branches are removed with an axe and the bark is stripped from the outside of the log. In the old days, the Indians had no saws or axes, so even cutting the tree down was a harder job than it is today. Back then, the carvers used a hammer and chisel to cut a wedge at the base of the tree. This weakened the tree, and in a strong wind storm, the tree would fall.

When the log is ready to be carved, my father makes a drawing of how the pole will look when it is finished. He draws the animals for the totem pole on a sheet of paper. He might begin by drawing each animal separately, but before he starts to carve he will draw a picture of how the completed pole will look.

Next he uses a stick of charcoal to make a drawing on the log itself. Then he stands up on the log to see how the figures and animals look. When he is satisfied with the drawing, he takes up his tools and begins to carve.

The totem pole for the Klallam tribe has six figures, one on top of the other. At the very top of the pole is the Thunderbird. He brings good luck to the Klallam village. The Klallam people believe the Thunderbird lives on the Olympic mountain range, across the water from their reservation, in the place where the mountains touch the sky. They say that when Thunderbird catches the great Killer Whale, you can hear thunder and see lightning in the sky.

Thunderbird

Klallam Figure

Below Thunderbird is the figure who represents the Klallam people. The figure holds Killer Whale by the tail. Together, they tell the legend of a tribal member named Charlie who rode out to sea on the back of a Killer Whale.

Killer Whale

The fourth animal on the pole is Bear, who provided the Indian people with many important things. His fur gave warmth and clothing. His meat gave food. His claws and teeth were used for trinkets and charms and to decorate clothing.

Bear

The next figure is Raven, who brought light to the Indian people by stealing the Sun from Darkness. Raven is the great trickster. Sometimes he does things that are good, but sometimes he does things that are bad.

Raven

The last figure on the pole is a Klallam Chief. The chief on the pole holds a "speaker stick," a symbol of his leadership and his important position in the tribe. In the Klallam culture, when a chief holds the speaker stick, all the people pay attention and listen to what he says.

Klallam Chief

As my father carves the pole, he brings all of these characters to life. He works on the pole every day. He uses many tools: the adze, chisels, and handmade knives. He even uses a chain saw for the largest cuts!

This totem pole is special to me. I am finally old enough to help my father with the work. He lets me sweep away the wood shavings as he carves. I can also take care of the tools he uses—the adze, the saws, the handmade knives, and the chisels.

As I get older, I'll learn how to use my father's carving tools safely and to help him really carve a pole. But for now, I just practice on some bits of wood I find lying around. Like my father, I look for the animal shapes hidden inside the wood.

In the old days, it used to take a year to carve a totem pole. In those days, the blade of the adze was made of stone and was nearly as sharp as the steel blades my father uses today. Knives, for the carving of fine details, were made from beaver teeth or from large shells.

My father says that it is the artist's skill with the adze that makes a totem pole great. Each artist has his own way of carving. The strokes of the adze create a pattern in the wood, like small ripples across the wide water.

My father makes the work look easy. He cuts into the wood quickly, as if it were as soft as soap. I know carving is much harder than he makes it look. I know because I've tried it.

After all the figures and animals are carved into the log, I help my father paint the pole. We make the eyes dark. We paint the mouths red. Whale's back and dorsal fins are black. Raven and Thunderbird have wings with patterns of red and black. The colors my father shows me are taken from the old traditions of the Tsimshian people. From a distance, the pole will look powerful and strong.

Finally, after two months of hard work, my father puts away his tools and packs up his paintbrushes. The totem pole is finished.

RAISING THE POLE

The Klallam tribe decides to hold a special ceremony to raise the totem pole. It will follow the ancient traditions of the Northwest Coast Indian people. After the ceremony, there will be a feast like the potlatch of the old days. There will be many guests. There will be traditional songs and dances, and food prepared by the villagers. If this were a traditional potlatch, the Klallam would give money or gifts to every guest.

On the day of the ceremony, we arrive on the Klallam Reservation early. I look at the pole, lying on its back in the early morning light. Each figure on the pole is strong. Looking at the totem pole, I can hardly believe my father made it.

Soon the guests begin to arrive. Many are from the Klallam village. Others are from Seattle and the surrounding towns. Some people have even come from other states.

My father and I dress in our regalia. Although my little brother is too young to dance, he wears his button blanket and headdress for the occasion. Most of my family have come to celebrate the raising of the pole. My mother is here with my grandmother and grandfather. I know my father wishes that *his* grandfather could be here too. Although my great-grandfather is in Alaska, we know he is thinking about us today.

When all the guests have arrived, my father invites everyone to help carry the pole to the place where it will be raised. It weighs over three thousand pounds and it takes fifty strong men and women to carry it. Long pieces of wood are placed underneath the back of the pole. Standing two by two, the people lift the pole when my father gives the command. They carry it slowly down the road to the place where it will stand.

In the old days, every totem pole stood so it faced the water. This was because the visitors to a village would always arrive by canoe. But today, things are different. Since people come to the reservation by car, the pole is placed to face the road.

It used to be that a totem pole was raised in position by hand, with many people pulling it up with ropes. The modern way is to use a powerful truck with a crane attached. The crane slowly lifts the pole while a group of singers chant and dance.

As the pole is raised higher and higher, their voices grow louder and louder. It takes a number of tries to get the pole in the right position, but finally it is done. The pole stands straight, facing south toward the road that leads into the Klallam Reservation.

Now it is time for my father and me to dance. Holding ceremonial wooden adzes, we begin to perform the Carver's Dance at the base of the totem pole. This dance was created by my father to show that the work on the pole is finished. We dance to show how proud we are.

THINK IT OVER

1. *What things has David learned from his father or his Indian tribe?*

2. *Why is the cedar box important to David's father?*

3. *Why is the totem pole important to the Northwest Coast Indians?*

WRITE

Write a journal entry telling about a tradition that your family practices. Explain why you would want to share this tradition with others.

TRADITIONS

Cultural traditions are important to many people. In what ways does learning traditions enrich the lives of Chin Chiang and David?

How are the traditions of Chin Chiang's and David's families similar? In what ways are the traditions different?

WRITER'S WORKSHOP Choose a tradition that you and your family share. How is the celebration of this tradition similar to and different from the celebration that Chin Chiang or David took part in? Write one or more paragraphs that compare and contrast your family tradition with one of the traditions in the selections.

Bullet trains side by side

RIDING JAPAN'S RAILS

In Japan, many travelers are whisked over the land so quickly that they seem to fly. They are riding in a "bullet train," which reaches speeds up to 135 miles (217 km) per hour.

The Japanese became worried about overcrowded roads, wasted fuel resources, and air pollution, so they made great improvements to their high-speed train system. In 1964, new rails were opened in Japan, and today more than a half million people use the trains each day.

■ *Find out how other countries, including the United States, are solving their transportation problems. Post pictures and facts on a bulletin board in a display titled "The Road to Tomorrow."*

ON THE MOVE

Find out more about how transportation methods have changed in the United States since 1750. Set up a classroom museum by displaying models and pictures.

You might use a chart like the one below to help you organize information.

Type of transportation		
Time period when used		
Rate of travel		
Advantages		
Disadvantages		

COMIN' ROUND THE MOUNTAIN

Travelers often sing traveling songs to make the time pass more quickly. You probably know many songs about sailing on the sea, riding on the road, and flying in the sky. Collect some traveling songs and sing them as a group. Talk about when and where the songs were first sung.

DREAMERS

. . . i'm gonna beat
out my own rhythm
                    Nikki Giovanni

Everyone has a dream and a rhythm, a way of making that dream come true. Dr. Martin Luther King, Jr., had one of the most important dreams of our times. Do you dream of growing up to be like him or like another adult whom you admire? Or do you dream of winning a prize or leading a team to victory? As you read the selections in this unit, think about your own dream. You may find someone who shares it.

ACHIEVERS

YOUNG AT HEART

STARGAZERS

BOOKSHELF

CARVER
BY RUTH YAFFE RADIN

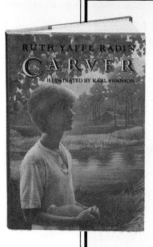

Jon, blind since he was two years old, wants to carve wood just as his father used to. With the help of an old sculptor, Jon sees that it is possible to achieve his dreams in spite of his handicap. AWARD-WINNING AUTHOR

HBJ LIBRARY BOOK

GO FISH
BY MARY STOLZ

Thomas is tired of resting his broken ankle. Then Grandfather suggests that the two of them go fishing. During their time together, Thomas learns to appreciate Grandfather's wisdom. AWARD-WINNING AUTHOR

WHAT ARE YOU FIGURING NOW? A STORY ABOUT BENJAMIN BANNEKER

BY JERI FERRIS

Benjamin Banneker had many talents and was always eager to try new things. His biography tells of his wonderful accomplishments.

THE RING AND THE WINDOW SEAT

BY AMY HEST

When she was a little girl, Great-Aunt Stella learned a valuable lesson. She tells Annie the story of how she discovered what is important in life. AWARD-WINNING AUTHOR

YEH-SHEN: A CINDERELLA STORY FROM CHINA

BY AI-LING LOUIE

With the help of her fish friend, Yeh-Shen becomes a queen. This Asian tale is a retelling of the familiar Cinderella story. ALA NOTABLE BOOK, CHILDREN'S CHOICE, SLJ BEST BOOKS OF THE YEAR

ACHIEVERS

Do you remember a time when you did not live up to the expectations of others? How did you feel about what you had not done? Some characters in the following folktales are told what to do to help themselves or others, but the directions are not easy to follow.

C O N T E N T S

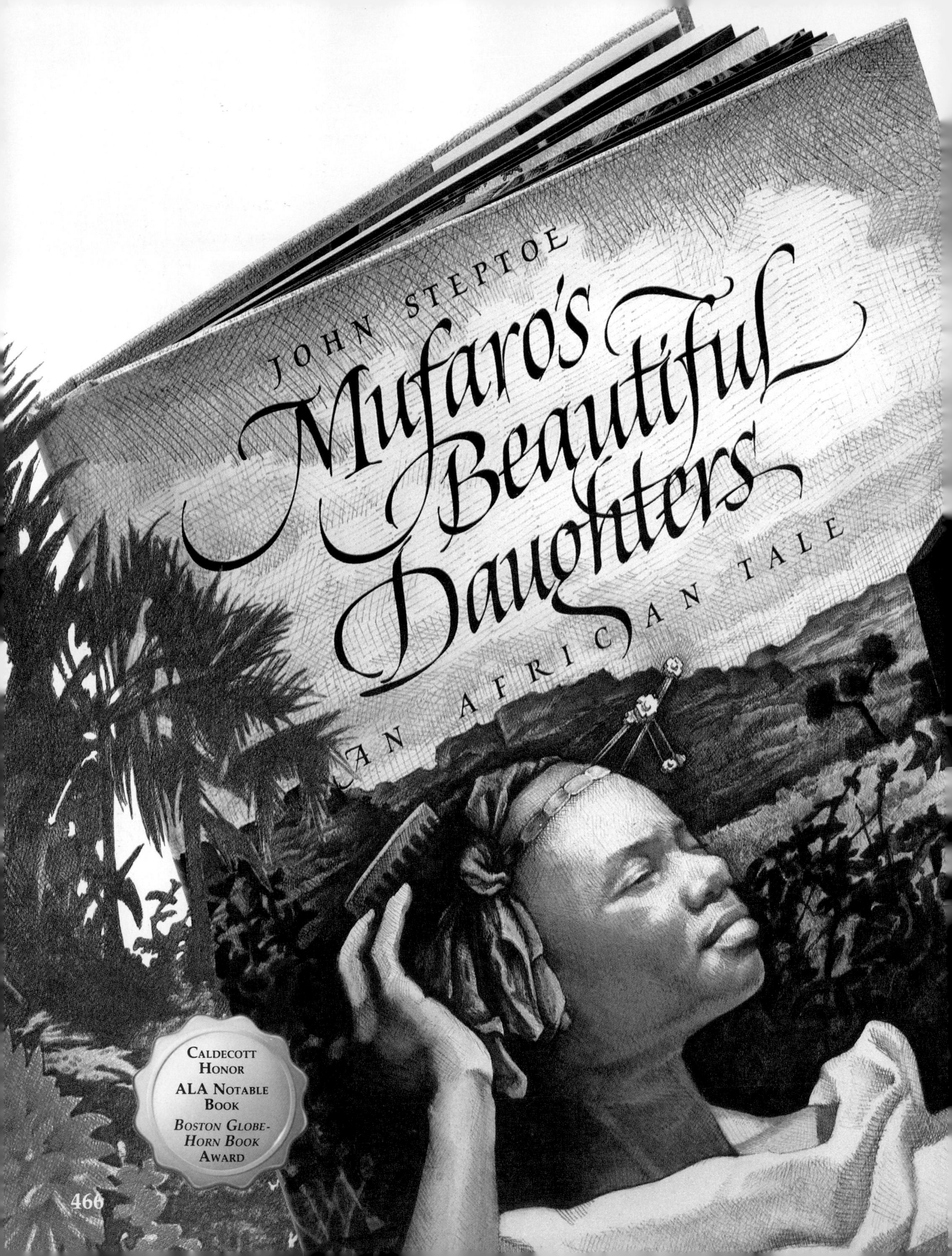

JOHN STEPTOE

Mufaro's Beautiful Daughters

AN AFRICAN TALE

CALDECOTT
HONOR

**ALA Notable
Book**

*Boston Globe-
Horn Book
Award*

A LONG TIME AGO, in a certain place in Africa, a small village lay across a river and half a day's journey from a city where a great king lived. A man named Mufaro lived in this village with his two daughters, who were called Manyara and Nyasha. Everyone agreed that Manyara and Nyasha were very beautiful.

Manyara was almost always in a bad temper. She teased her sister whenever their father's back was turned, and she had been heard to say, "Someday, Nyasha, I will be a queen, and you will be a servant in my household."

"If that should come to pass," Nyasha responded, "I will be pleased to serve you. But why do you say such things? You are clever and strong and beautiful. Why are you so unhappy?"

"Because everyone talks about how kind *you* are, and they praise everything you do," Manyara replied. "I'm certain that Father loves you best. But when I am a queen, everyone will know that your silly kindness is only weakness."

Nyasha was sad that Manyara felt this way, but she ignored her sister's words and went about her chores. Nyasha kept a small plot of land, on which she grew millet, sunflowers, yams, and vegetables. She always sang as she worked, and some said it was her singing that made her crops more bountiful than anyone else's.

One day, Nyasha noticed a small garden snake resting beneath a yam vine. "Good day, little Nyoka," she called to him. "You are welcome here. You will keep away any creatures who might spoil my vegetables." She bent forward, gave the little snake a loving pat on the head, and then returned to her work.

From that day on, Nyoka was always at Nyasha's side when she tended her garden. It was said that she sang all the more sweetly when he was there.

Mufaro knew nothing of how Manyara treated Nyasha. Nyasha was too considerate of her father's feelings to complain, and Manyara was always careful to behave herself when Mufaro was around.

Early one morning, a messenger from the city arrived. The Great King wanted a wife. "The Most Worthy and Beautiful Daughters in the Land are invited to appear before the King, and he will choose one to become Queen!" the messenger proclaimed.

Mufaro called Manyara and Nyasha to him. "It would be a great honor to have one of you chosen," he said. "Prepare yourselves to journey to the city. I will call together all our friends to make a wedding party. We will leave tomorrow as the sun rises."

"But, my father," Manyara said sweetly, "it would be painful for either of us to leave you, even to be wife to the king. I know Nyasha would grieve to death if she were parted from you. I am strong. Send me to the city, and let poor Nyasha be happy here with you."

Mufaro beamed with pride. "The king has asked for the most worthy and the most beautiful. No, Manyara, I cannot send you alone. Only a king can choose between two such worthy daughters. Both of you must go!"

That night, when everyone was asleep, Manyara stole quietly out of the village. She had never been in the forest at night before, and she was frightened, but her greed to be the first to appear before the king drove her on. In her hurry, she almost stumbled over a small boy who suddenly appeared, standing in the path.

"Please," said the boy. "I am hungry. Will you give me something to eat?"

"I have brought only enough for myself," Manyara replied.

"But, please!" said the boy. "I am so *very* hungry."

"Out of my way, boy! Tomorrow I will become your queen. How dare you stand in my path?"

After traveling for what seemed to be a great distance, Manyara came to a small clearing. There, silhouetted against the moonlight, was an old woman seated on a large stone.

The old woman spoke. "I will give you some advice, Manyara. Soon after you pass the place where two paths cross, you will see a grove of trees. They will laugh at you. You must not laugh in return. Later, you will meet a man with his head under his arm. You must be polite to him."

"How do you know my name? How dare you advise your future queen? Stand aside, you ugly old woman!" Manyara scolded, and then rushed on her way without looking back.

Just as the old woman had foretold, Manyara came to a grove of trees, and they did indeed seem to be laughing at her.

"I must be calm," Manyara thought. "I will *not* be frightened." She looked up at the trees and laughed out loud. "I laugh at you, trees!" she shouted, and she hurried on.

It was not yet dawn when Manyara heard the sound of rushing water. "The river must be up ahead," she thought. "The great city is just on the other side."

But there, on the rise, she saw a man with his head tucked under his arm. Manyara ran past him without speaking. "A queen acknowledges only those who please her," she said to herself. "I will be queen. I will be queen," she chanted, as she hurried on toward the city.

Nyasha woke at the first light of dawn. As she put on her finest garments, she thought how her life might be changed forever beyond this day. "I'd much prefer to live here," she admitted to herself. "I'd hate to leave this village and never see my father or sing to little Nyoka again."

Her thoughts were interrupted by loud shouts and a commotion from the wedding party assembled outside. Manyara was missing! Everyone bustled about, searching and calling for her. When they found her footprints on the path that led to the city, they decided to go on as planned.

As the wedding party moved through the forest, brightly plumed birds darted about in the cool green shadows beneath the trees. Though anxious about her sister, Nyasha was soon filled with excitement about all there was to see.

They were deep in the forest when she saw the small boy standing by the side of the path.

"You must be hungry," she said, and handed him a yam she had brought for her lunch. The boy smiled and disappeared as quietly as he had come.

Later, as they were approaching the place where the two paths crossed, the old woman appeared and silently pointed the way to the city. Nyasha thanked her and gave her a small pouch filled with sunflower seeds.

The sun was high in the sky when the party came to the grove of towering trees. Their uppermost branches seemed to bow down to Nyasha as she passed beneath them.

At last, someone announced that they were near their destination.

Nyasha ran ahead and topped the rise before the others could catch up with her. She stood transfixed at her first sight of the city. "Oh, my father," she called. "A great spirit must stand guard here! Just look at what lies before us. I never in all my life dreamed there could be anything so beautiful!"

Arm in arm, Nyasha and her father descended the hill, crossed the river, and approached the city gate. Just as they entered through the great doors, the air was rent by piercing cries, and Manyara ran wildly out of a chamber at the center of the enclosure. When she saw Nyasha, she fell upon her, sobbing.

"Do not go to the king, my sister. Oh, please, Father, do not let her go!" she cried hysterically. "There's a great monster there, a snake with five heads! He said that he knew all my faults and that I displeased him. He would have swallowed me alive if I had not run. Oh, my sister, please do not go inside that place."

It frightened Nyasha to see her sister so upset. But, leaving her father to comfort Manyara, she bravely made her way to the chamber and opened the door.

On the seat of the great chief's stool lay the little garden snake. Nyasha laughed with relief and joy.

"My little friend!" she exclaimed. "It's such a pleasure to see you, but why are you here?"

"I am the king," Nyoka replied.

And there, before Nyasha's eyes, the garden snake changed shape.

"I am the king. I am also the hungry boy with whom you shared a yam in the forest and the old woman to whom you made a gift of sunflower seeds. But you know me best as Nyoka. Because I have been all of these, I know you to be the Most Worthy and Most Beautiful Daughter in the Land. It would make me very happy if you would be my wife."

And so it was that, a long time ago, Nyasha agreed to be married. The king's mother and sisters took Nyasha to their house, and the wedding preparations began. The best weavers in the land laid out their finest cloth for her wedding garments. Villagers from all around were invited to the celebration, and a great feast was held. Nyasha prepared the bread for the wedding feast from millet that had been brought from her village.

Mufaro proclaimed to all who would hear him that he was the happiest father in all the land, for he was blessed with two beautiful and worthy daughters—Nyasha, the queen; and Manyara, a servant in the queen's household.

THINK IT OVER

1. *Do you think Mufaro's daughters were beautiful? Explain your answer.*

2. *Why was Manyara unhappy?*

3. *How did the king know to choose Nyasha for his queen?*

4. *When you are courteous or kind to others, do you expect a reward? Explain your answer.*

WRITE

Write a short folktale, using a classic tale like "Cinderella" as a model. Use your town or city for the setting.

Which did you enjoy more about *Mufaro's Beautiful Daughters*—the story or the illustrations? John Steptoe spent more than two and a half years writing and illustrating this book. He worked at writing stories that African American children could relate to and that would encourage them to follow their dreams. The Cinderella theme came to Steptoe's mind, and he found that almost every culture has its own version of the classic tale. *Mufaro's Beautiful Daughters* was based on an African Cinderella tale. The story and the art were inspired by the people living near Zimbabwe in southern Africa.

John Steptoe was already an award-winning author and artist before *Mufaro's Beautiful Daughters* was published. He began drawing as a child and attended the High School of Art and Design in New York City for three years. Steptoe wrote his first book, *Stevie*, at the age of sixteen.

John Steptoe illustrated not only his own books but also stories written by other authors, including *Mother Crocodile*, another African tale. He received many awards for both his illustrations and his writing. Steptoe died in 1989.

John Steptoe believed that there were many young people like himself who wanted to accomplish something important in their lives. It was Steptoe's hope that he could help encourage children to seek opportunities, take pride in themselves, and achieve their dreams.

Words About the Author and Illustrator:

John Steptoe

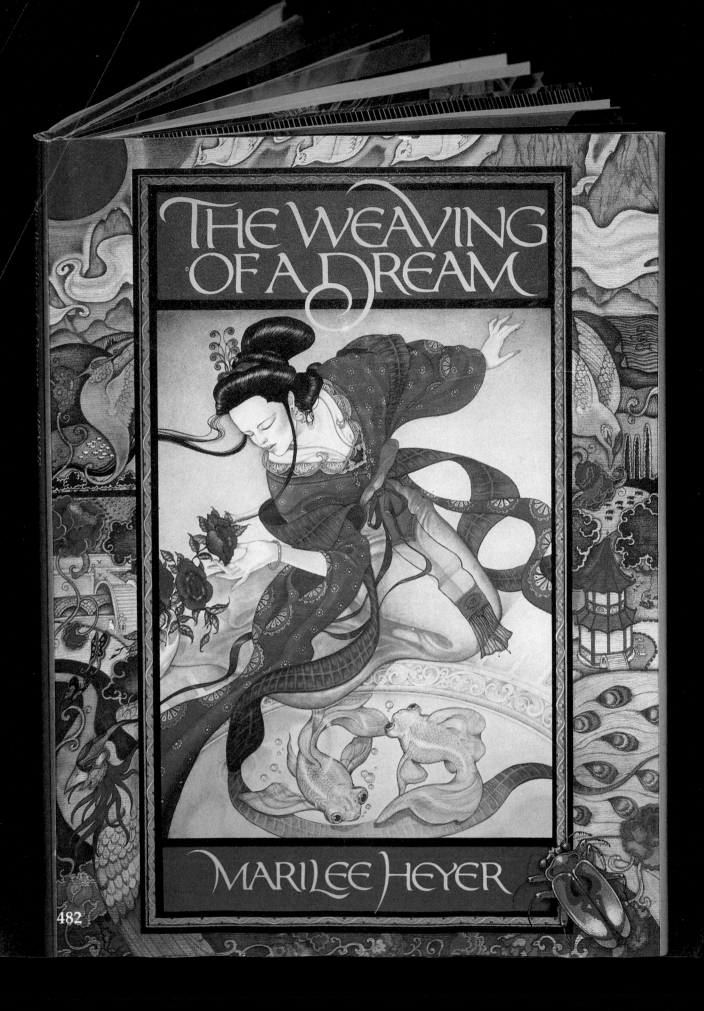

 Long ago, in a land far to the east, there lived an old widow who had three sons. The eldest was Leme, the second was Letuie, and the youngest was Leje. They lived in a small cottage in a mist-filled valley at the foot of a high mountain.

Everyone for hundreds of miles around knew the old widow, for she had a special gift. She could weave beautiful brocades that seemed to come alive under her fingers. The flowers, plants, birds, and animals she wove almost moved with the breeze. Her weaving was in constant demand at the marketplace in the village nearby. It was used to make dresses and jackets, curtains and coverlets. With the money she earned, the old widow supported her family, although the boys helped by chopping wood and selling it.

One day, while she was at the market selling some new weavings, she saw a most wondrous painting hanging in a stall nearby. It showed a large palace surrounded by beautiful flower gardens. There were vegetable gardens, too, fruit trees, pastures where cattle grazed, lovely birds, and even a fish pond. A river ran in front of the palace, and the whole painting was warmed by a great red sun. Everything she had always dreamed of was in the painting. She gazed at every detail, and her heart filled with happiness.

Although she knew she should not, she traded her brocades for the painting. I should be buying rice for my sons, she thought, but she could not help herself.

Three times on the way home she stopped to unroll the painting and gaze at it. "If only we could live in that palace," she whispered to herself.

When she got home she showed the painting to her sons and told them of her dream.

"It's lovely, Mother," said Leme and Letuie. "But where is the rice you went to buy?" They didn't understand her desire to live in the picture palace.

"It's a silly dream, Old Mother," they said.

She turned to Leje, her youngest son, with a sadness in her eyes he had never seen before.

"Leje, I know that *you* will understand. I feel I must live in this lovely place or I will die," she sighed.

"Don't be sad, Mother. I will think of something."

As he comforted her an idea came to him.

"Why don't you do a weaving of the painting? Your weavings are so lifelike that, as you work on it every day, it will be almost like living there."

"You are right, Leje," she said with a smile. "It is the closest I will ever come to this lovely place."

She set to work by candlelight that very evening.

Once she started weaving she didn't stop. For days and months she worked, her shuttle flashing through the threads.

Leme and Letuie became very upset with their mother. One evening they even pulled her hands away from the loom.

"You are no longer making brocades to sell, Old Mother. Now we must all live on the money we make chopping wood, and we are tired of working so hard."

Leje ran to stop them.

"Let Mother be. She must weave the beautiful palace, or die of grief. I will chop all the wood."

From then on, Leje chopped day and night, cutting wood to sell for food.

The old widow continued to weave every hour, on and on, never stopping. At night she worked by candlelight. The smoke burned her eyes and made them red and sore, but she didn't stop. After one year, tears began to drop from her eyes onto the threads, and they became part of the river and fish pond she was weaving. After two years, blood dripped from her eyes onto her hand. Down her hand onto the shuttle it ran, and the drops of blood were woven into the splendid red sun and glowing flowers.

On and on she worked. At last, during the third year, she was finished. What a beautiful brocade it was, the most magnificent ever seen. Mother and sons stared at it in wonder. Even Leme and Letuie couldn't take their eyes from it. The garden, the flowers, the beautiful palace, songbirds of every kind, luscious fruits and vegetables ready to pick, all in the most perfect detail. Behind the palace were pastures for the fat sheep and cattle, and fields of maize and rice. The river sparkled in front, and the marvelous sun warmed every thread.

"Oh, Mother, how proud we are of your wonderful work!" whispered her sons.

The old widow stretched her tired back and rubbed her bloodshot eyes. A smile creased her wrinkled cheeks and slowly grew into a joyous laugh.

Suddenly, a great wind blew the hut door open with a crash! It raced through the room, knocking everything over. Then taking the wondrous brocade with it, it blew out the window and up into the sky to the east.

They all ran after it, screaming and waving their arms, but the brocade was gone. Vanished! When the boys turned, they saw their mother lying unconscious on the doorstep.

They carried her inside and laid her on the bed. Slowly she opened her eyes.

"Please, Leme, my oldest son," she said. "Go east, follow the wind, and bring my brocade back to me. It means more to me than my life."

Leme nodded, put on his sandals, took a few supplies, and headed east. Within a month's time he came to a mountain. When he reached the very top he saw a strange house made all of stone, with a stone horse standing by the door. The horse's mouth was open, as if it were trying to eat some of the red berries that were growing at its feet. On the front doorstep sat a white-haired old crone.

"And where are you headed, young man?" she croaked in a little-used voice.

"I'm going east," said Leme, "where the wind has carried off a beautiful brocade my mother spent three years weaving."

"Ah, that brocade," cackled the fortune-teller, for that is what she was. "The fairies of Sun Mountain sent the wind to bring it to them. They wish to copy its beautiful design. You may never find it. The way is very difficult."

"Please tell me how to get there," pleaded Leme.

"First, you must knock out your two front teeth and put them into the mouth of my stone horse. Then it will be able to move and eat the berries it has wanted for so long. When it has eaten ten berries, it will let you on its back and will carry you to Sun Mountain, but on the way you must first pass over Flame Mountain, which is constantly on fire. When the horse goes through the flames, you must not cry out, even if the pain is unbearable. Keep your cries to yourself, or you will immediately be burned to ashes.

"Next, you will come to the Sea of Ice. When you go through the ice, you must not cry out, though your whole body will become numb with cold. If you do cry out, you will sink to the bottom of the sea. If you pass through these places as I have told you, you then will see Sun Mountain and will be given your mother's fine brocade to carry home."

Leme ran his tongue over his front teeth. He thought of the burning fire and freezing ice, and he grew very pale.

The old fortune-teller saw his face and laughed. "You will not be able to endure it, young man, and after all, you need not. I will give you a box of gold; go home and live happily."

From inside the house she brought the box. Leme took it quickly and turned toward home. He had gone about a mile before he realized how much better it would be if he spent all the gold on himself instead of sharing it with his family. So, instead of going home, he headed south toward the big city.

Waiting for Leme's return, the old widow grew thinner and thinner. After two months she could wait no longer.

"Letuie, you must go east and find my brocade. It means my life," she told her middle son.

Letuie agreed. He put on his sandals, took some supplies, and headed east. Within a month's time he was standing at the door of the stone house, listening to the old fortune-teller tell him he must knock out his teeth and go silently through fire and ice. Letuie also grew very pale. He, too, received a box of gold and went to the big city with it instead of returning home.

Again, the old widow waited. She grew as thin as a piece of old firewood. Every day she spent lying in her bed, staring at the door, waiting for Letuie's return. Every day when he didn't come, she wept. Her old tired eyes finally went blind from weeping.

Leje could stand it no longer.

"Old Mother, please let me go look for the brocade. Perhaps Leme and Letuie have been injured. I will search for them, too. I will ask the neighbors to care for you while I'm gone."

After thinking for a long time the old widow agreed, but she hated to let Leje leave, for she loved her youngest son the best.

Leje put on his sandals and took some supplies. He threw back his shoulders and proudly started on his mission to the east. In half the time it had taken his brothers, he reached the top of the mountain. Again there was the old fortune-teller with her stone horse. She repeated the instructions a third time and watched Leje's face closely. It didn't grow pale as his brothers' had, and when she offered him the gold that his brothers had accepted, he refused it.

"I must bring back the brocade for my mother or she will surely die."

Immediately he picked up a stone, knocked out his front two teeth, and fed them to the stone horse. After the horse had eaten the ten berries, Leje jumped on its back, and clinging to its mane, kicked the horse with his heels. High into the air the wonderful horse jumped, and away they flew, as fast as the wind they were following.

For three days and three nights they flew across the sky. At last they reached Flame Mountain. Into the fire they dashed without a pause. The red flames hissed around Leje and stabbed at his skin, but he didn't cry out. With teeth clenched tight, he endured the pain, and in half a day's time he came out of the flames and stood on the shore of the Sea of Ice. Again, without hesitation, he sped on. Steam rose from his burning-hot body as it hit the ice-cold water. He felt his legs and arms grow numb and bleed from the sharp edges of the ice, but he uttered no sound. In half a day's time he came out of the Sea of Ice, and before him, glowing in golden light, shone beautiful Sun Mountain. The warmth of it soothed his body and eased his pain.

The loveliest palace he had ever seen stood on the top of the mountain, and from its windows came the sound of women's voices singing and laughing.

Up the mountain the stone horse flew, and soon they stood before the palace door. There two very strange creatures, unlike anything Leje had ever seen before, stood guard, but not even they could stop him now. Down from the horse he jumped, and straight through the door he marched. The creatures didn't blink, nor did he.

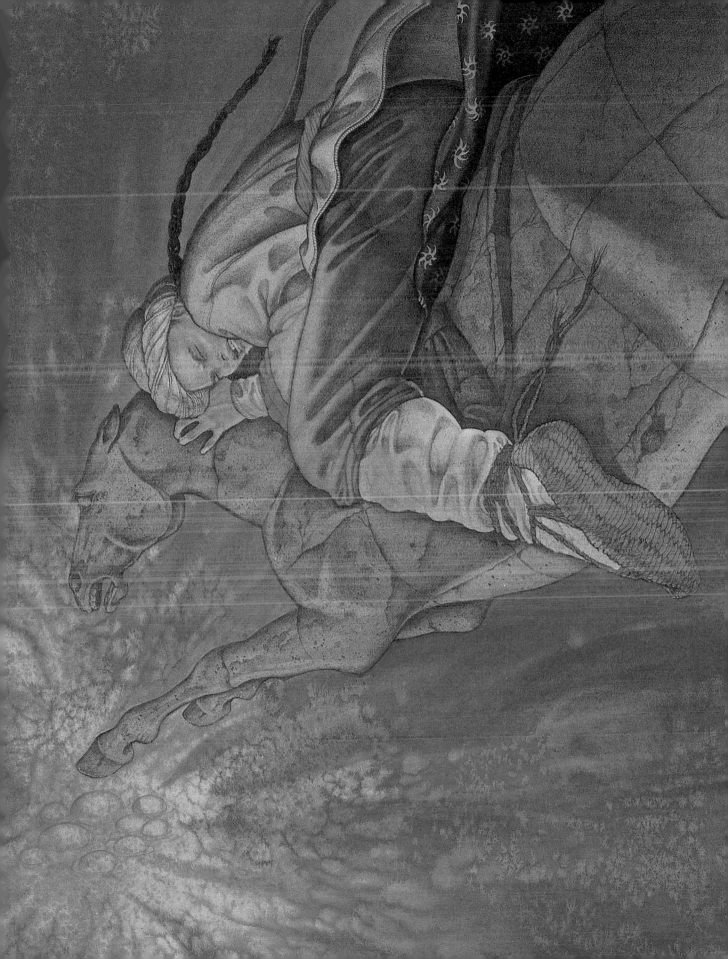

In front of him was a great hall filled with beautiful fairies, all weaving as fast as they could. In the very center of the hall, for them to copy, hung his mother's brocade.

Startled by the sight of Leje, the fairies stopped their weaving and sat as still as stones.

"Don't be afraid," he told them. "I have only come for my mother's brocade."

At the thought of losing the brocade, some of the fairies began to cry, but one fairy stood and said, "Very well, you may have the brocade in the morning. Just allow us one more night of weaving so that we can finish. You may stay here with us and rest for the night."

Leje agreed, and the fairies sent one of the creatures to prepare for him a most delicious dinner, after which Leje fell into a deep sleep.

When the sun set and the light in the hall began to grow dim, one fairy hung a shining pearl that filled the hall with light. They continued weaving through the night.

One beautiful fairy, dressed all in red, finished her weaving first. She had always been the finest and the quickest of the weavers, but when she held her weaving next to the old woman's, hers looked very poor by comparison, for the colors were not as bright nor the stitches so fine.

This brocade is so perfect, the fairy thought. Instead of trying to copy it, I wish I could become a part of it.

So while the other fairies worked on, the red fairy started to weave into the old widow's brocade a picture of herself sitting by the fish pond.

Late in the night Leje woke with a start.

Suppose the fairies will not give me the brocade in the morning, he thought. My poor mother has been ill so long. What will become of her?

As he looked around he saw that all the fairies had fallen asleep over their looms. There stood his mother's brocade, more lovely than ever by the light of the pearl. Quickly, Leje took down the brocade and ran to his waiting horse. Away into the moonlight they flew.

In three days and three nights they stood before the fortune-teller's house.

"Well done, my son," said the old woman. She took his teeth from the stone horse's mouth and put them back into Leje's mouth as if they had never been gone. The horse immediately froze into his old position.

"Quickly, my son, you must return home, for your mother is dying." From behind her back the old woman pulled a fine pair of embroidered boots and set them on the ground.

"Put these on; they will speed your way."

Hardly had Leje put the boots on than he was standing on his own doorstep. Inside, he saw his dear mother, now grown thinner than a splinter. At that very moment her heart was beating its last.

"No, Mother, don't die," cried Leje, running to her bedside. He pulled the brocade from his shirt and spread it over her. The warmth of its gleaming sun soothed her and pulled her back to life. She felt the delicate threads with her fingertips. Her eyes began to clear and her sight returned. She sat up in bed and gazed at the wonderful brocade that had taken three years from her and almost cost her her life.

"Oh, my most faithful son," she said, "help me take the brocade out of this dark hut into the sunlight, where we can see it better."

Outside they lovingly spread the brocade on the ground. Suddenly a soft, sweet-smelling breeze swept through the valley. It gently drew the brocade off the ground and spread it over the yard. Larger and larger and longer and wider it grew. Over the fence and over the house it spread, covering everything with its silken threads. The shabby hut disappeared, and in its place the brocade itself took on the very shape and form of the beautiful palace. Before their eyes the brocade was coming to life. The gardens, the fruit trees, the pasture—all became real. The colorful birds began to sing, the cattle grazed on the rich pasture grass, and there, sitting by the fish pond, was the red fairy, as bright as the sun overhead.

The old widow was greatly astonished, for she knew she had not woven a fairy into her brocade. But she welcomed her and brought her to live with them in the beautiful palace. She asked all her neighbors to live with them too, for there was more than enough room and they had all been kind to her while Leje was away. Leje and the red fairy were married, and so the weaving of the dream was completed.

One day as Leje, the fairy, and his mother sat in the garden making toys for the new baby that would be coming soon, two beggars crept up and stared at them through the garden fence. They were Leme and Letuie. They had gone to the big city and lost all their gold, squandering it on themselves. Now they had nothing left. When they saw the happy scene before them, they thought of the terrible thing they had done. They were filled with grief and remorse, and they turned silently, picked up their begging sticks, and crept away.

THINK IT OVER

1. *Why did the widow suffer as much as she did?*

2. *How did the widow's sons feel about the brocade while she was weaving it?*

3. *Why did the fairies of Sun Mountain take the widow's beautiful brocade?*

4. *Why was it difficult for the widow's sons to find the brocade?*

5. *Do you believe that dreams can come true? Explain why you think as you do.*

WRITE

Write a paragraph describing a beautiful painting or piece of art that you have admired.

ACHIEVERS

You read about characters who wanted to help others and, in doing so, they helped themselves. In what ways are Nyasha and Leje alike? Give examples of behavior that reveal what each is like.

How do you think Manyara and Leje's brothers would have acted differently if the stories were set in modern times? Explain why you think as you do.

WRITER'S WORKSHOP Suppose Nyasha's father and Leje's mother entered them in a contest for selecting the child who did the most good. Write a paragraph to persuade the judge to choose one of the children as the winner. Use convincing facts and examples from the selections.

1ST

504

YOUNG AT HEART

Think about a time when a grandparent or another relative helped you solve a problem or shared your secrets. The grandmothers and grandchildren in the following poem and selection have fun together and help each other through difficult times.

CONTENTS

505

GRANDMA'S
Bones

from *Nathaniel Talking* ·**by Eloise Greenfield**
illustrated by Jan Spivey Gilchrist

Grandma grew up
in the nineteen-forties
she can still do the jitterbug
a dance they used to do
to the music of Duke Ellington,
Benny Carter, Count Basie
and such

she can spin a yo-yo
much better than I
and sometimes she puts
two sticks called bones
between the knuckles
of one hand and goes

clack clack clackety
clackety clack
clackety clackety clackety
clack clack
uh clackety clack
uh clackety clack
clack clack clackety
clackety clack!

ALA
NOTABLE BOOK
CORETTA SCOTT
KING HONOR

A VERY SPECIAL GIFT

ALA NOTABLE BOOK

from *The Canada Geese Quilt*

by *Natalie Kinsey-Warnock*
illustrated by Donna Diamond

When Ariel's parents announced that they
were having a new baby, Ariel was confused. She went out to her favorite tree
to think about it, and her grandma followed
her. They walked to the hayloft and dis-
cussed all the babies that Grandma had
welcomed into her family and the wonderful friendships and memories that
Grandma shared with them.

Ariel began to look forward to the
arrival of the new baby. She wanted to
make a very special gift for her new
brother or sister, but she could not
decide what the gift would be.

Over the next few weeks, everyone's thoughts were on the baby. Papa whispered to Ariel that he was making a butternut cradle and asked if she wanted to help him build it. She said yes, but kept thinking about what she could do special for the baby. She could help Papa, but the cradle would still be his present, his idea.

Nothing I do will be good enough, she thought.

She went to talk to Grandma. She felt even closer to Grandma after their talk in the hayloft.

"I know what you mean," said Grandma. "I've been wondering what I could make, too."

"You?" Ariel asked, surprised. "You can make just about anything."

"Well," said Grandma, "I wanted to make a very special quilt for the baby. But I've only made quilts from patterns my mother taught me, handed down to her by her mother. I wish this quilt could be one that nobody's ever seen before. I hoped you'd draw it."

Ariel searched Grandma's face for hints of teasing, but saw none.

"Really?" she asked. "You think I could do it?"

Grandma stroked Ariel's hair.

"I know you could. You have so much talent. And it would mean so much to everyone."

"But, Grandma, don't you see?" Ariel cried. "It's the same thing as Papa's cradle. Even if I draw the design, you'll be the one making the quilt, so it'll be your present, not mine."

"Ariel," Grandma said, "I can sew, but I can't draw. I've always wished I could but I can't. But you can design a picture that's never been made into a quilt before."

Ariel had never thought of it like that. Her eyes sparkled.

Later, when Grandma went to the kitchen to start supper, she found Ariel sitting at the table, surrounded by crumpled paper.

"Looks like things aren't going so well," Grandma said.

"They're terrible," Ariel answered. "I don't know whether it's going to be a girl or boy, so I don't know what to draw."

Grandma sat thinking.

"This is going to be a special quilt because of you," she said, "so I think you should have the design show what's special to you. Why don't you think of it that way?"

Ariel worked on the drawing every afternoon when she got home from school. The geese were still migrating north, so she took her sketchbook to the wild apple tree and watched as the geese flew over. Out here, in the raw openness, she could feel what was important to her and the design came easily.

She took the rolled drawing to Grandma's room.

"I got it done, Grandma," she said softly. She unrolled it on the bed.

On the paper, three Canada geese flew over a stand of cattails and an apple tree just in bloom. The shape of Miles Hill rose behind the tree.

Grandma didn't say anything, and Ariel said, "You don't like it, do you?"

Grandma hugged her.

"Ariel, it's wonderful," she said. "I was just a little scared. I'm not sure I'll be able to make the quilt as beautiful as that drawing deserves. Come, help me decide on the colors."

Spring came with a rush of wildflowers and soft rain. Papa was busy in the fields. Ariel planted the garden for her mother who found bending difficult. Ariel would hate the weeding later, but she did enjoy the planting: opening the brightly colored packets and pushing the seeds into the warm tilled earth.

In the evenings, Ariel helped Grandma cut out the pieces of cloth and watched as Grandma sewed them together. The quilt began to take on a life of its own, as if the geese really were rising from the cloth.

School let out in June and haying began. The most Papa would let Mama do was drive the horses ("Really, Austin," she would say, "I'm not helpless."), so Ariel worked on the wagon while Papa tossed the hay up to her. She stomped the hay down with her feet as he had shown her, so that the load held together for the bumpy ride back to the barn.

It was hot, tiring work. Ariel rushed to keep pace with her father. Sweat trickled down her back, and chaff stuck to her face and arms. Just when it seemed that the itch of the chaff would drive her crazy, they'd have a load and be riding back to the barn, a slight breeze cooling her skin. Then she could relax for a few minutes and watch red-tailed hawks circle over Miles Hill.

They got one load in just before a storm hit. Black clouds had chased them, and Mama had backed the wagon into the barn just as the hailstones hit. While she ran to the house, Papa and Ariel unloaded the hay. The hail pelleted the roof like gunfire, so loud they couldn't speak above it. Everything seemed to glow in a strange green light.

Suddenly, Mama was standing in the doorway, her face unnaturally pale against the dark sky. There were red blotches on her arms where the hailstones had hit. Papa was beside her in an instant.

"Austin," she said, "it's Mother," and they both sprinted toward the house.

Ariel followed them, no longer aware of the storm. She'd heard the fear in Mama's voice; something was terribly wrong.

She stood on the porch, afraid to go into the house. The wind whipped at her clothes, and lightning tore jagged streaks through the sky. She shivered even though she wasn't cold.

Papa drove the car right up to the steps. He ran back into the house and, in a few minutes, he and Mama came back out, carrying Grandma. Grandma's eyes were closed, her face gray. Ariel shrank back against the porch railing. Papa lay Grandma in the back seat of the car.

Mama ducked back onto the porch and gripped Ariel's arms.

"Ariel, we have to get Grandma to the doctor. I'm counting on you to take care of yourself. Just go inside and stay there."

"Is Grandma going to die?" Ariel asked. Her voice sounded cracked and wavering.

Her mother was trying hard not to cry.

"I don't know, honey," she said. Her mouth trembled. She climbed into the back seat, cradling Grandma's head in her lap. Ariel watched the car go down the driveway and disappear over the hill. She was alone.

She wandered from room to room. Her footsteps echoed on the pine floors. The old house seemed to be holding its breath, waiting for someone to fill its emptiness.

Ariel took the Iris quilt from Mama's cedar chest. She wrapped it around herself and sat in the rocker. The picture of Grandma as she was carried to the car played over and over in her mind. She imagined Papa and Mama coming home, both of them crying and she'd know Grandma was dead without them telling her.

Papa didn't get home until dusk. Ariel met him at the door and he gathered her up in his arms.

"Where's Mama?" Ariel asked, afraid to ask about Grandma.

"She's staying at the hospital," he said. "Grandma's very sick, and Mama doesn't want to leave her."

"I'm scared, Papa," said Ariel.

"So am I," he said, "but worrying won't help. We need to keep busy."

The days blurred together. Ariel felt numb, as if her body belonged to someone else. Mama stayed with Grandma. Meals were a strange mixture of leftovers and the few things Papa could cook. Papa and Ariel did the milking, forked hay down for the cows, curried and fed the horses, collected eggs, and tried to keep the house tidy. Papa did his best to keep Ariel's spirits up, but nothing loosened the fear that gripped her heart.

Ariel had a dream. In it, Grandma was at the cookstove, making pancakes. There was a rolled-up quilt on the table behind her. The quilt unfolded and geese began to fly out, their dark bodies filling the kitchen. Grandma raised her arms in front of her face and pushed through their beating wings. Ariel called after her, but Grandma kept walking into the darkness of their wings until she disappeared.

Ariel sat up in bed, her heart thudding. The eastern sky was just beginning to lighten.

The smell of pancakes drifted up the stairs. Ariel was out of bed in an instant, running barefoot down the stairs.

Grandma? she thought.

Mama and Papa stood by the stove, talking softly as Mama flipped the pancakes. Mama turned and saw Ariel.

"Mother's out of the woods now," she declared, brushing back tendrils of hair. She had stayed at the hospital four days, but to Ariel it seemed like months since Mama had been home. Mama had grown thinner, but that only emphasized the growing roundness of the baby. Papa hugged her.

"Claire," he said, "you've got to get some rest. You've run yourself ragged. It's not good for the baby."

Mama was too tired to protest.

"I do need some sleep," she admitted. She handed the spatula to Papa, and walked to the bedroom. Ariel followed at a distance. She watched as Mama lay down.

Mama turned over in bed, and saw her standing in the doorway. She held out her arms and Ariel rushed into them.

"I'm sorry I've been gone so much," Mama said, stroking Ariel's hair.

"When is Grandma coming home?" Ariel asked.

"Not for a long time, honey," Mama said. "She's been very sick. And even when she does come home, she'll be different."

"What do you mean, Mama?"

"Grandma had a stroke. She can't walk very well and it's hard for her to pronounce words. She's going to need all of us to help her." Mama sounded so tired. Ariel had a dozen questions to ask, but Mama was already drifting off to sleep.

Grandma came home in August. Ariel was afraid of her. The frail, drooped-face woman in the bedroom couldn't be Grandma. Grandma had pink cheeks and busy hands; the woman in the bedroom was gray and shriveled.

Mama had said not to tire Grandma. Ariel told herself that that was the only reason she wasn't visiting with Grandma, but she knew it was more than that. She didn't like to look at Grandma. She didn't know what to say, or how to act. Ariel spent more and more time outside, helping Papa with his work. When she did come inside, if she didn't look at that closed door, she could almost forget how everything had changed.

It was almost a relief to start school. Then Ariel didn't need to make so many excuses. With school, chores, and homework, there just wasn't any time to visit with Grandma.

Then one evening, Mama came out of Grandma's bedroom, sat down heavily in the rocker and covered her face with her hands. Papa had just come in from doing the milking and saw her.

"What's wrong, Claire?" he asked. "Is it the baby?"

She shook her head.

"Oh, Austin," she said. "Mother's given up. I thought she'd get her strength back being home. She had therapy at the hospital, and the doctor said she was able to walk with a cane now. He thought she would do better at home, but she feels she's a burden, and she isn't even trying to get better. I just don't think I can take it anymore, watching her lie there like that."

Ariel hadn't realized before that this was as hard on Mama as it was on her. And even harder on Grandma. Grandma was lying in that room, feeling that the family would be better off without her.

If it was me who was sick, thought Ariel, Grandma would do everything she could to help me.

When she got home from school the next afternoon, she took a deep breath and walked into Grandma's room. She leaned against the door wondering what she would say.

Grandma looked pale and still, nothing like the determined, energetic woman Ariel remembered.

"We had a test at school today," Ariel said, hesitantly, "and I got an A. We've been studying mythology. You'd read me all those stories before, anyway, remember? And I told the teacher the legend about the stars being the sun's children. She liked it."

Grandma hadn't moved or said a word. Ariel felt very uncomfortable. She knew she was rambling on to fill the silence. She sighed.

"Well, I'll see you tomorrow, Grandma," she said.

Mama met her in the hall. She hugged Ariel.

"Thank you for visiting with Grandma," Mama said. "I know it's not easy."

"Mama, I felt like I might as well be talking to an empty bed."

"I know, honey," said Mama. "But we've just got to keep on trying. Something will break through that wall she's put up."

Ariel began bringing things from her walks: an apple from her special tree, a bunch of ripe wild grapes she'd picked from the fencerow. One afternoon, she walked over to the bed, her hands cupped.

"Grandma, look!" She opened her hands; an orange monarch butterfly rested lightly on them. "I was walking home through the pasture and hundreds of butterflies flew up. Papa says they're migrating. Oh, Grandma, they were so beautiful! They filled the air." And for the first time, Ariel saw a flicker of interest in Grandma's eyes.

She's listening! Ariel thought, excitedly.

"They're still in the pasture," she said. "Let's go out and see them."

Grandma shook her head. Ariel leaned closer.

"Please, Grandma. Why have you given up? We need you. Please don't give up," she pleaded, and saw tears in Grandma's eyes.

It was a short walk. Grandma held Ariel's arm and took slow, halting steps, but there was color in her cheeks where there had been none before.

They stopped to pick chicory and Queen Anne's lace. Grandma cradled the wildflowers lovingly and looked out over the valley. The hillsides were beginning to change color. The late afternoon sun slanted across the fields. Grandma breathed the fall air deeply. For the first time since she'd been home, she looked happy.

Grandma began to talk. Her tongue moved clumsily over the words, but Ariel heard and understood them.

"I forgot life is so good," Grandma said.

When they got back to the house, Ariel lifted the quilt from its drawer and laid it in Grandma's lap.

"Now we can finish the quilt together," Ariel said.

Grandma held up her crooked hand.

"It won't be as good as if you sewed it," Ariel admitted, "but you can teach me."

Grandma gave her a questioning look.

"I know," Ariel said, laughing, "I hate to sew. And don't expect me to do it again. But this is a special occasion. Besides, you've done most of the work."

Before her stroke, Grandma had appliquéd all of the design, added a border of deep blue cloth, and started the quilting. In the past, Grandma's quick, sure fingers would have flown through the rest. Now it was up to Ariel.

Papa was filling the barn with the summer's harvest, and Mama was so busy these days with canning and preserving the food from the garden and orchard that it was easy for Ariel to slip into Grandma's room to work on the quilt without getting questioned.

The quilting seemed agonizingly slow. Ariel made a lot of mistakes. She had to pull out stitches, and she pricked her fingers. Worst of all was sitting inside when the weather outside was so inviting.

As if to tease her, the days were especially lovely, the last warm days before the cold months of winter. The hills blazed with the scarlet and orange of maples, and the yellow of popples and birches. Apples and butternuts hung heavily from the trees along the fencerow, almost begging to be picked.

One afternoon, as Ariel walked home from school, one of the first great wedges of geese honked southward. Ariel watched them and her heart thrilled to their ancient song. She wished she was with them, sailing high and free on the wind. But Grandma was waiting.

Grandma's room seemed dark and airless compared to the deep ocean of sky and crystalline air. Ariel sat sulkily in her chair and picked up the quilt. She thought she could still hear the geese calling. She tugged at the knot in the thread until it broke, then threw the quilt to the floor.

"Oh, I'm so sick of sewing!" she cried. "A stupid quilt for a stupid baby. I'm never going to sew again. I hate it."

She jumped up and ran for the door.

"Ariel, wait," Grandma called.

Ariel spun around and before she could stop them, the words spilled out, "I want to be outside. I hate that quilt and I hate you!"

She froze in horror.

To her amazement, Grandma chuckled.

"Good for you," Grandma said in a slow, deliberate voice that was a result of her stroke. "Ever since I got home, you and your folks have been tiptoeing around here like you were on eggshells, afraid to say or do anything that might upset me. You're the first person to get mad, and I'm glad of it."

"But, Grandma, I didn't mean to say such a horrible thing. You must hate me."

"Oh, fiddlesticks, and I know you don't hate me. You're mad because I got sick and it made you scared. I get mad, too, because I can't do some of the things I used to."

Ariel ran to give Grandma a hug.

"I really love you, Grandma. And I think it's a beautiful quilt."

"But we'll both be glad when it's done, won't we?" Grandma said with a twinkle in her eye. "Run along and enjoy the afternoon. The quilt will still be here tomorrow."

After that, whenever Ariel got frustrated, she reminded herself of the battle Grandma faced. Grandma struggled with words, and with legs and hands that could no longer be trusted.

When the quilt was finally finished, Ariel was almost afraid to touch it. She'd never seen so beautiful a quilt.

THINK IT OVER

1. *How did Ariel and Grandma help each other?*

2. *Why couldn't Ariel decide what to make for the new baby?*

3. *Why do you think Grandma gave up after her stroke?*

4. *Do you think that the quilt in this story was important? Explain why you think as you do.*

WRITE

If you were Ariel, how would you have tried to help Grandma? Write a get-well message explaining why it's important to keep trying.

YOUNG AT HEART

We can learn a lot from our grandparents and other older adults. Think about why the grandmothers you read about are important to their families. What do they contribute to the lives of their children and grandchildren?

· ·

What special qualities do the grandmothers in the poem and selection share?

· ·

WRITER'S WORKSHOP Ask a grandparent or another older relative about what life was like when he or she was your age. Gather information about the time period when that person was young and the place where he or she lived. Write a report about that person's early life. You may want to include photographs with your report. Share your report with the person you wrote about.

STARGAZERS

Have you ever dreamed of what you would like to be in the future— maybe a great baseball player, a rancher, or an astronaut? Read about the goals that the people in the following selections and poems set for themselves.

C O N T E N T S

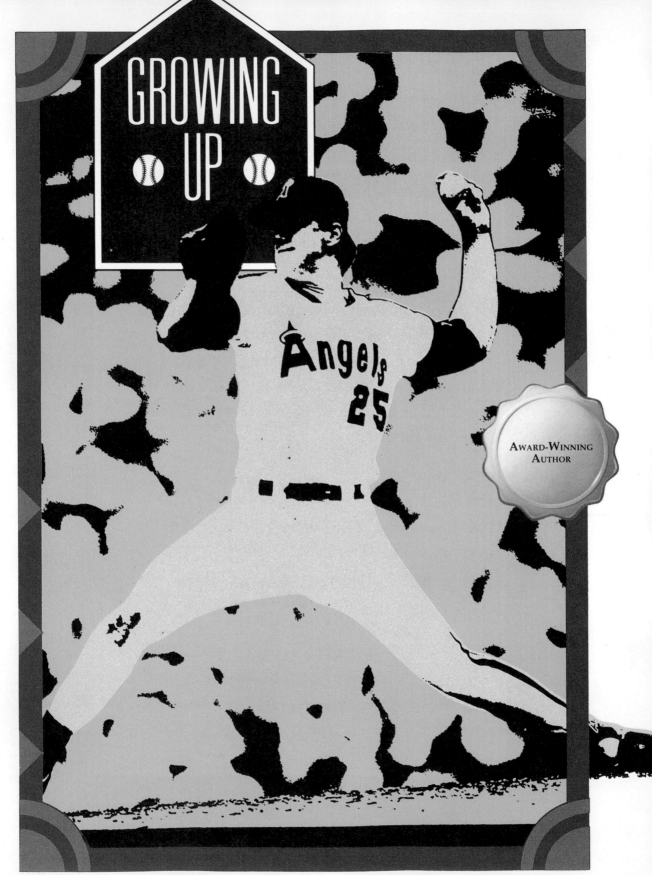

GROWING UP

from *Jim Abbott: Against All Odds* • by Ellen Emerson White • illustrated by Doug Suma

It is a clear summer night at famous Fenway Park in Boston, and a rookie has come to town. He is tall, and strong, and young.

The California Angels, his team, is in a hot pennant race and tonight they need a win from their rookie pitcher. But he is facing the Boston Red Sox, the best hitting team in the American League.

The old green stadium is overflowing with die-hard Red Sox fans as the rookie takes the mound. *Noisy* die-hard Red Sox fans. But the rookie knows that he has to ignore the crowd—that he has to concentrate on tonight's game.

The rookie has an easy first two innings, but then, the Red Sox load the bases in the third. There are two outs, and the cleanup hitter, Mike Greenwell, strides to the plate. The crowd claps and cheers, begging their slugger to get a big hit.

The rookie takes a deep breath. The hitter waits, his bat up and ready. And the rookie strikes him out with his best fastball.

As the game goes on, the rookie strikes out more Red Sox hitters. Star first baseman Nick Esasky. Future Hall-of-Famer Dwight Evans. Rising star Ellis Burks. In the end, the rookie strikes out seven batters. He gives up four harmless hits and, most importantly, no runs.

When the rookie gets the final out of the game, giving his team a 4–0 victory, he starts to walk off the mound. All over Fenway Park, the Red Sox fans stand and applaud, cheering the rookie off the field. Their team may have lost, but they know that they have seen someone very special. That *this* is a pitcher.

This is Jim Abbott.

James Anthony Abbott was born on September 19, 1967, and has already led an eventful life. While attending the University of Michigan, he pitched his team to two Big Ten championships and was selected to the All-America team. Then, while playing in the Pan-American Games, he helped Team USA win the silver medal. Later, as a pitcher for the 1988 Olympic team, Jim was on the mound when the United States won the gold medal. Finally, Jim was picked by the California Angels in the major league baseball draft, becoming only the fifteenth player in the history of the draft to go straight to the big leagues without ever spending a day in the minors.

What makes all of this even more remarkable is that Jim Abbott has only one hand.

Born with a normal left arm, Jim has a right arm that is normal, too—except that it stops at the wrist. But from the time he was a small child, no one ever told Jim that he was handicapped, and he never acted that way. In fact, Jim was always about as far from handicapped as it was possible to be.

Jim was born and grew up in Flint, Michigan. His parents, Mike and Kathy Abbott, married very young and had to work hard to make ends meet. Jim's father is now a sales manager, and his mother is an attorney. She works for a law firm that focuses on educational issues. Education was always very important to the Abbotts.

"My parents always stressed school," Jim says now. "They wanted me to do well. They always said that I thought of sports first, but they made me think not just about baseball, but about getting good grades."

When Jim first went to school, a doctor fitted him with an artificial right hand, which had metal hooks on the end that he could clamp together to pick things up. But Jim never liked this fake, mechanical hand. By the time he was six, he had stopped wearing it completely.

Jim's parents always told him that he could do anything he wanted to do. They knew that their son loved sports. They hoped that Jim would play soccer—one of the few sports where he wouldn't need two hands—but right from the very beginning, Jim loved baseball. So, Jim's parents bought him a baseball glove. As it turned out, Jim's brother Chad was the one who liked soccer.

Now that he had a baseball glove, Jim had to learn how to throw—and catch—with the same hand. With his father's help, Jim developed what is now known as his famous glove switch. What he does is very complicated, but *looks* very easy. In fact, people often watch him play without even noticing that he is doing it all with just one hand.

As Jim throws the ball, he bends his right arm up in front of him and balances his glove on the end of it. Then, after he releases the ball, he slides his left hand into his glove. By the time the ball is batted or thrown back at him, he is ready to catch it. To watch Jim, it seems so easy. But, as is true for every great athlete, he practiced for many hours to perfect this.

Jim would practice this glove switch by playing catch with his father and by throwing a ball against the side of his house and catching it as it bounced off. He would move closer and closer to the house, throwing the ball harder and harder, and getting better and faster with the glove switch. Today, he is able to pitch the ball and get the glove onto his hand before the ball even gets to home plate.

After Jim catches the ball, he moves his glove up under his right arm, pulls his left hand out, and grabs the ball to throw it—all in one quick motion. And he almost never makes an error.

The very first game Jim pitched in Little League was a no-hitter. His team, Lydia Simon Real Estate, scored so many runs that the game was stopped after only five innings. Word quickly got around that there was a pitcher in Flint, Michigan, who was better with one hand than most other pitchers were with two. For the first time, Jim was interviewed by reporters. He has had to deal with almost constant attention from reporters ever since.

Jim went on to pitch for Flint Central High School. He already had a very good fastball, but very few people believed that he would be able to field his position against more difficult competition. One high school team tested his fielding during his freshman year by having eight batters in a row bunt. The first hitter *did* get to first base safely, but Jim threw the next seven out. After that, teams didn't bunt against Jim very often.

"He was a tough kid, very competitive," Bob Holec, Jim's high school baseball coach, said. "You don't see too many like him. He was just a great kid. He was also very successful socially and academically. He had a lot of friends."

By the time Jim was a senior, he was pitching and playing first base. He also spent some time in the outfield and even played shortstop briefly. He pitched four no-hitters that year and had an incredible 179 strikeouts in only eighty innings. That averages out to *more* than 2 strikeouts per inning. Over the length of the season, he gave up fewer than two hits a game.

Jim was also a very good hitter. He would hold the bat in his left hand, bracing the handle against his right wrist. Using this technique, he batted .427 his senior year, with seven home runs and thirty-six RBIs.[1] He hit more home runs than anyone else on his team that year.

But there was more to Jim than just baseball. He was the top scorer in his school's intramural basketball league, and he played two years of varsity football. He was a punter, averaging thirty-seven-and-a-half yards per punt his senior year, and he was one of the team's quarterbacks.

Baseball coach Bob Holec is also one of the high school's football coaches. "I'll never forget this one game," he said, recalling one of the best punts Jim ever made. "Jim got a bad snap that went over his head, and he jumped up, snagged it with his one hand, and got the punt off. There were plenty of *oohs* and *aahs* from the crowd on *that* one." In fact, the whole time he played football, Jim never dropped a snap.

Then, late in the football season, when the starting quarterback became ineligible, Jim took over. He helped the Flint Central team get to the state play-offs, where they lost in the semifinals to the team that eventually won the state championship.

"He took a beating in that semifinal game," Coach Holec said, "but he still managed to get off four touchdown passes. He really came into his own at the end of the football season. You wish you had more like him."

---

[1]RBIs: runs batted in, runners in baseball that are driven to home plate by the batters

Jim's various athletic exploits resulted in more press attention than ever, and Coach Holec was particularly impressed by the way Jim handled the reporters.

"He's a very humble person," Coach Holec explained. "There was never any jealousy from his teammates. A lot of kids would get big-headed from all of the attention, but Jim never did. He always praised his teammates, never himself." Then Coach Holec paused. "I would give him the finest compliment of all—if I had a son, I'd like him to be like Jim Abbott."

THINK IT OVER

1. *Why is Jim Abbott an extraordinary athlete?*

2. *What position in baseball does Jim Abbott play?*

3. *Is playing baseball Jim Abbott's only great accomplishment? Explain your answer.*

4. *Would you like to play on a team with Jim Abbott? Explain your answer.*

WRITE

Write a letter to Jim Abbott explaining what you would like to do when you grow up.

ON THE PAMPAS

María Cristina Brusca

AWARD-WINNING
ILLUSTRATOR

I grew up in Argentina, in South America. I lived with my family in the big city of Buenos Aires, but we spent our summers in the country, at my grandparents' *estancia*. One summer my parents and brother stayed in the city, so I went without them.

My grandmother met me at the station in Buenos Aires, and we had breakfast as we rode through miles and miles of the flattest land in the world—the pampas. All around us, as far as we could see, were fences, windmills, and millions of cattle grazing.

537

Our station, San Enrique, was at the end of the line, where the train tracks stopped. My grandfather was there to meet us in his pickup truck and take us the five miles to the estancia.

The ranch was called La Carlota, and the gates were made of iron bars from a fort that had been on that very spot a hundred years before. As we drove up to the gates, we were greeted by a cloud of dust and a thundering of hooves—it was my cousin Susanita, on her horse.

Susanita lived at the estancia all year round. She knew everything about horses, cows, and all the other animals that live on the pampas. Even though she was three years younger than me, she had her own horse, La Baya. Susanita was so tiny, she had to shimmy up La Baya's leg to get on her back. But she rode so well that the gauchos called her La Gauchita—"The Little Gaucho."

I didn't have a horse of my own, but old Salguero, the ranch foreman, brought me Pampita, a sweet-tempered mare, to ride. She wasn't very fast, but she certainly was my friend.

Susanita and I did everything together that summer. She was the one who showed me how to take care of the horses. We would brush their coats, trim their hooves, and braid their manes and tails.

Susanita was always ready for an adventure, no matter how scary. She used to swim in the creek holding on to La Baya's mane. At first I was afraid to follow her, but when she finally convinced me, it was a lot of fun.

I wanted to learn all the things a gaucho has to know. I wanted to ride out on the pampas every day, as Salguero did, and to wear a belt like his, with silver coins from all over the world and a buckle with my initials on

it. Salguero said I'd have to begin at the beginning, and he spent hours showing Susanita and me how to use the lasso.

It was going to take a while for me to become a gaucho. The first time I lassoed a calf, it dragged me halfway across the corral. But Salguero told me that even he had been dragged plenty of times, so I kept trying, until I got pretty good at it.

Whenever the gauchos were working with the cattle, Susanita was there, and before long I was too. Sometimes the herd had to be rounded up and moved from one pasture to another. I loved galloping behind hundreds of cattle, yelling to make them run. I never got to yell like that in the city!

One day we separated the calves from the cows, to vaccinate them and brand them with "the scissors," La Carlota's mark. That was more difficult—and more exciting, too. I tried to do what Salguero told me to, but sometimes I got lost in the middle of that sea of cattle.

At noon, everybody would sit down around one big table and eat together. I was always hungry. Grandma, Susanita's mother, and Maria the cook had been working hard all morning too. They would make soup, salad, and lamb stew or pot roast, or my favorite, *carbonada,* a thick stew made of corn and peaches.

After lunch the grown-ups took a *siesta,* but not us. We liked to stay outdoors. Some afternoons, when it was too hot to do anything else, we rode out to a eucalyptus grove that was nice and cool, and stayed there until it got dark, reading comic books or cowboy stories.

Other times we would gallop for two hours to the general store and buy ourselves an orange soda. Then, while we drank it, we'd look at all the saddles and bridles we planned to have when we were grown up and rich. Sometimes the storekeeper would take down a wonderful gaucho belt like Salguero's, and we would admire the silver coins and wonder where each one came from.

One day we rode far away from the house, to a field where Susanita thought we might find *ñandú* eggs. They

are so huge, you can bake a whole cake with just one of them. After riding around all afternoon, we found a nest, well hidden in the tall grass, with about twenty pale-yellow eggs as big as coconuts.

Salguero had warned us to watch out for the ñandú, and he was right! The father ñandú, who protects the nest, saw us taking an egg. He was furious and chased us out of the field.

The next day we used the ñandú egg to bake a birthday cake for my grandmother. We snuck into the kitchen while she was taking her siesta, so it would be a surprise. The cake had three layers, and in between them we put whipped cream and peaches from the trees on the ranch.

We had a wonderful party for my grandmother's birthday. The gauchos started the fire for the *asado* early in the evening, and soon the smell of the slowly cooking meat filled the air.

There was music, and dancing, too. We stayed up almost all night, and I learned to dance the *zamba,* taking little steps and hops, and twirling my handkerchief.

Most evenings were much quieter. There was just the hum of the generator that made electricity for the house. We liked to go out to the *mate* house, where the gauchos spent their evenings.

We listened to them tell stories and tall tales while they sat around the fire, passing the gourd and sipping mate through the silver straw. We didn't like the hot, bitter tea, but we loved being frightened by their spooky stories.

The summer was drawing to a close, and soon I would be returning to Buenos Aires. The night before I was to leave, Salguero showed me how to find the Southern Cross. The generator had been turned off, and there was only the soft sound of the peepers. We could see the horses sleeping far off in the field.

The next morning, my last at the estancia, Susanita and I got up before dawn. Pampita and the other horses were still out in the field. Salguero handed me his own horse's reins. He told me he thought I was ready to bring

in the horses by myself. I wasn't sure I could do it, but
Susanita encouraged me to try.

I remembered what I'd seen Salguero do. I tried to get
the leading mare, with her bell, to go toward the corral,
and the others would follow her. It wasn't easy. The foals
were frisky and kept running away. But I stayed behind
them until finally the little herd was all together, trotting
in front of me.

I was so busy trying to keep the foals from running off that I didn't notice the whole household waiting in the corral with Salguero. Everyone cheered as I rode in, and before I knew it, my grandfather was helping me off the horse. "You've become quite a gaucho this summer," he said. My grandmother held out a wonderful gaucho belt like Salguero's, with silver coins from around the world—and my initials on the buckle!

"And," she added, "there's something else every gaucho needs. Next summer, when you come back, you'll have your very own horse waiting for you!" She pointed to the leading mare's foal, the friskiest and most beautiful of them all.

Before I could say a word, the foal pranced over to me, tossing his head. I would have the whole winter to decide what to name him, and to look forward to my next summer on the pampas.

THINK IT OVER

1. *Describe what life was like at La Carlota.*

2. *What object did Salguero have that María Cristina, the girl who tells the story, hoped to have someday?*

3. *How might María Cristina's summer have been different if her parents and brother had gone with her to the estancia?*

4. *Would you like to visit Susanita and her family for a whole summer? Explain your answer.*

WRITE

Pretend that you are María Cristina and you have returned home to Buenos Aires. Write a friendly letter to Susanita at La Carlota, thanking her for showing you how to be a gaucho.

ALA Notable Book
SLJ Best Books Of The Year

Last Laugh

by Lee Bennett Hopkins · from *Surprises*

They all laughed when I told them
I wanted to be

A woman in space
Floating so free.

But they won't laugh at me
When they finally see
My feet up on Mars
And my face on TV.

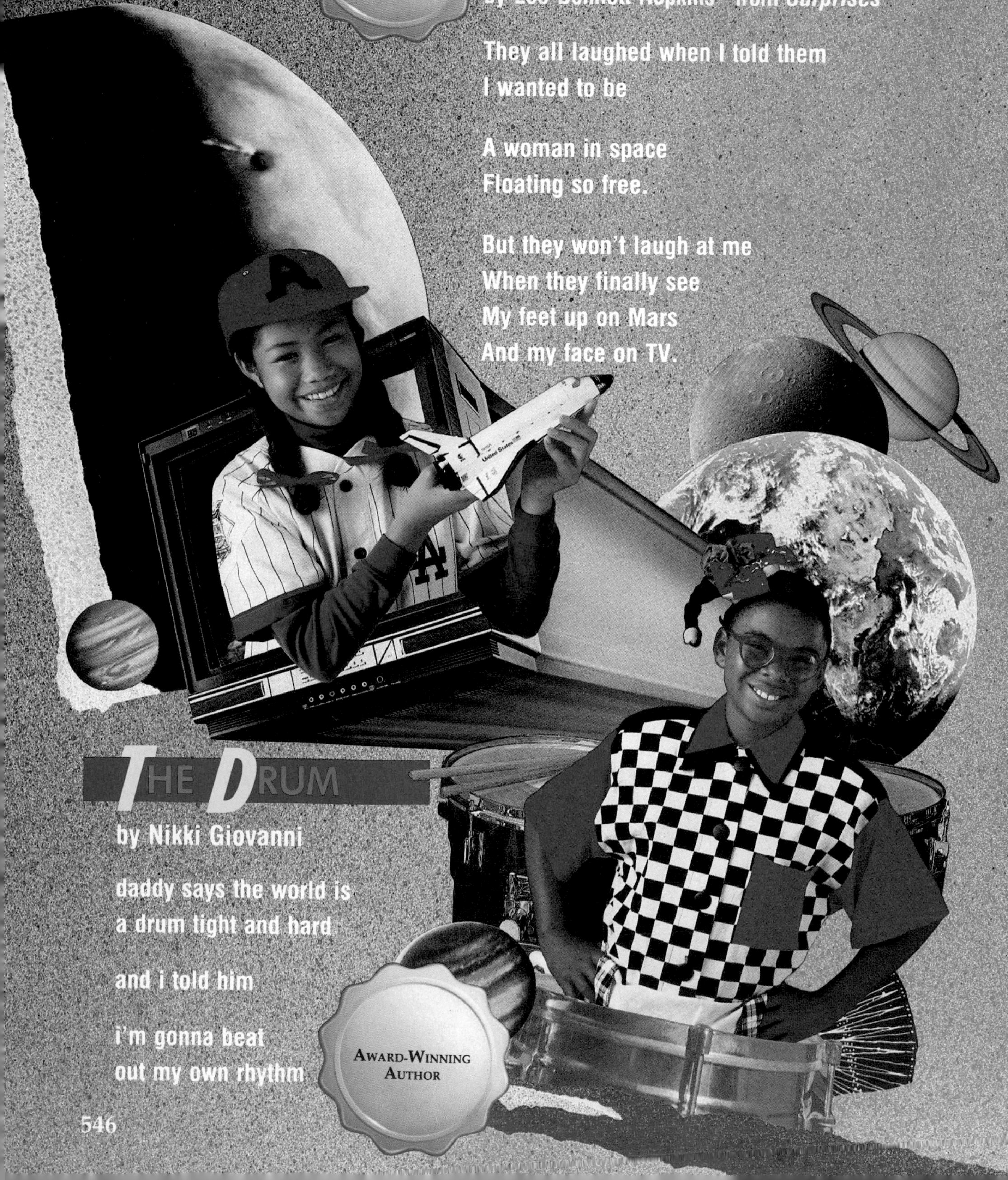

The Drum

by Nikki Giovanni

daddy says the world is
a drum tight and hard

and i told him

i'm gonna beat
out my own rhythm

Award-Winning Author

STARGAZERS

The selections and poems that you read told about people who had confidence in being able to reach their goals. Which character do you think showed the most determination? Share your reasons for thinking as you do.

• •

Think about the qualities that Jim Abbott and María Cristina share. How do their qualities make them special?

• •

WRITER'S WORKSHOP Would you rather meet Jim Abbott, María Cristina, or one of the speakers of the poems? Choose two of the characters, and write one or more paragraphs that compare and contrast how each one reaches for the stars in his or her own way. Make a diagram to list the information you gather.

DREAM OF A BETTER WORLD

"I have a dream," said Martin Luther King, Jr., while standing in front of the Lincoln Memorial in 1963. Thousands of people listened to his historical speech.

King's dream was to live in a nation with equal rights and freedom for all—no matter what color one's skin is. King did more than just dream. He spent his life fighting for what he believed in. Thanks to King's hard work and the example he set, the dream is being achieved.

■ *Many other African Americans, such as Rosa Parks and Thurgood Marshall, have taken part in the equal rights struggle. Find out more about the history of this struggle in America. Create a collage showing what you learned.*

AMERICAN DREAMERS

There have been many great dreamers like Martin Luther King, Jr., whose work has made our nation a better place. Read about other leaders, such as doctors, scientists, and soldiers, who improved the lives of others. Use what you learn to create a class bulletin board gallery of great Americans.

You can use a web like the one shown to help you organize your ideas.

ART CONNECTION

YOUR OWN DREAM

What is your own dream for a better world? With a small group, make a mural that shows some changes that you would like to see. Together, write a poem that tells how people can make a dream come true. Share your mural and poem with the rest of your classmates.

Handbook for Readers and Writers

ACTIVE READING STRATEGIES

A strategy is a specific plan for doing something successfully. Here are several strategies to use before, during, and after reading.

Lee knows that using reading strategies improves her understanding of what she is reading. Strategies also help her use her reading time more wisely.

Before reading, Lee

✓ **previews** what she is about to read. She reads the titles and the subtitles, looks at the pictures, and reads any captions. She may even read the first paragraph or two.

✓ **thinks about the topic** of the selection. She recalls what she already knows about the topic and anything she has heard or read about it.

✓ **predicts** what the selection will be about. She thinks about the clues she found while previewing the selection. Then she makes a guess about what she will learn from her reading.

✓ **sets a purpose** for reading. She decides whether she is reading to find out what happens, to learn information, or to study for a test.

✓ **chooses a reading rate.** She thinks about her purpose as she decides how quickly to read. If her purpose is to study for a test, she will read more slowly and carefully. She may even reread certain parts and take notes as she reads. She knows she can adjust her reading rate as she goes along.

During reading, Lee

✓ **remembers her predictions.** From time to time, she compares what she predicted to what she is reading. If she finds her predictions are not confirmed, she changes them.

✓ **relates what she is reading to what she knows,** to experiences she has had, or to other reading she has done. Sometimes she thinks of feelings she has had that are like those of a character she is reading about.

✓ **rereads** a paragraph or two when she realizes she didn't quite understand what she read the first time. Sometimes she rereads in order to figure out the meaning of an unfamiliar word.

After reading, Lee

✓ **reviews her purpose for reading and her predictions.** She compares her predictions to what she read. She may decide that she did not learn what she expected to. She may need to read something else to answer some questions she still has.

✓ **summarizes** the information she learned. She lists the main points that were new to her that she wants to remember.

READING FICTION

Fiction comes in different forms. **Realistic fiction** has characters and settings that are believable, although the story is made up. In **fantasy,** things happen that could not happen in real life. When you read fiction, you can use strategies to increase your enjoyment and understanding. Follow Alana as she uses strategies before and during her reading of "Election Day."

I wonder what kind of "Election Day" this is. The title of the book is Class President, *so it must be a school election. I wonder if this election day is anything like the one we had in our class.*

The introduction tells what happened earlier in the book. Now I know where I am in the story.

I think Cricket and Lucas will be important characters because they both are running for president.

Julio seems smart! What he says makes sense to me. I wonder if anyone will listen to him.

★ Election Day ★

from *Class President*

by Johanna Hurwitz

Julio's new teacher, Mr. Flores, has announced that there will be an election for class president. At first, it seems like a contest between Cricket Kaufman and Lucas Cott, two of the most popular students. But although Julio has promised to help Lucas campaign, he wonders what qualities a president should have besides popularity.

Before lunch, Mr. Flores read an announcement from the principal. "From now on, there is to be no more soccer playing in the schoolyard at lunchtime."

"No more soccer playing?" Julio called out. "Why not?"

Mr. Flores looked at Julio. "If you give me a moment, I'll explain. Mr. Herbertson is concerned about accidents. Last week, Arthur broke his glasses. Another time, someone might be injured more seriously."

Julio was about to call out again, but he remembered just in time and raised his hand.

"Yes, Julio," said Mr. Flores.

"It's not fair to make us stop playing soccer just because someone *might* get hurt. Someone might fall down walking to school, but we still have to come to school every day."

I don't understand why Cricket is saying this. I think I'd better reread the last few paragraphs to see what's going on.

Julio didn't mean to be funny, but everyone started to laugh. Even Mr. Flores smiled.

"There must be other activities to keep you fellows busy at lunchtime," he said. "Is soccer the only thing you can do?"

Lucas raised his hand. "I don't like jumping rope," he said when the teacher called on him.

All the girls giggled at that.

"You could play jacks," suggested Cricket. Everyone knew it wasn't a serious possibility, though.

"Couldn't we tell Mr. Herbertson that we want to play soccer?" asked Julio.

"You could make an appointment to speak to him, if you'd like," said Mr. Flores. "He might change his decision if you convince him that you are right."

"Lucas and I will talk to him," said Julio. "Right, Lucas?"

"Uh, sure," said Lucas, but he didn't look too sure.

The principal, Mr. Herbertson, spoke in a loud voice and had eyes that seemed to bore right into your head when he looked at you. Julio had been a little bit afraid of Mr. Herbertson since the very first day of kindergarten. Why had he offered to go to his office and talk to him?

Mr. Flores sent Julio and Lucas down to the principal's office with a note, but the principal was out of the office at a meeting.

"You can talk to him at one o'clock," the secretary said.

Julio is really determined. But this hasn't told me anything about the class election yet. I'll keep reading to see what I can find out.

Going to the principal can be scary! I wonder if Julio and Lucas will talk to the principal later and if this will help Lucas win the election.

(See pages 22–37 for the entire story of "Election Day.")

READING NONFICTION

Nonfiction contains facts, or information that is true. Often illustrations and diagrams present facts or make them clearer. Headings and subheadings that show how the information is organized may also be included. A strategy that can help when you are reading nonfiction is **K-W-L**.

- **K** stands for "What I **K**now." As you preview the selection, think about what you already know about the topic. Read the headings and subheadings to see how the information is organized. Look at the illustrations and read the captions.
- **W** stands for "What I **W**ant to Know." After you preview, think of questions that you want to find the answers to as you read.
- **L** stands for "What I **L**earned." After you have read, review your questions to see whether you learned what you expected to.

Lance makes a chart before he reads "Running With the Pack." He goes through the **K** and **W** steps and makes notes in the first two columns. He keeps his questions in mind as he reads.

What I **K**now	What I **W**ant to Know	What I **L**earned
The selection must be about wolves because I see wolves in the picture. Wolves are like wild dogs. They have some way to talk to each other.	What does the word _pack_ in the title mean? How do wolves talk to each other? Why do wolves attack people?	

Those stories about wolves eating people aren't true at all!

It says that a pack is a group of wolves that live together.

I was right. Wolves are like dogs.

Well, wolves don't really talk, but they do have ways of telling each other things.

Running With the Pack

In a well-known fairy tale, the Big Bad Wolf tries to eat up Little Red Riding Hood. This story is one of many that have caused people to mis-understand and fear wolves. The truth is that healthy wolves do not attack people. Scientists say wolves tend to be intelligent and shy. They live in groups called packs, and cooperate to survive.

Wolves are the largest wild members of the dog family. Gray wolves, shown on these pages, live in parts of North America, Europe, and Asia—usually in packs with no more than eight members. A pack includes a head male and female, their young, and sometimes other adults. The head male usually decides when and what to hunt, and he settles fights. The head female leads the other females, the young, and sometimes the weaker males. The leaders and other pack members communicate by using facial expressions, body postures, and sounds. For example, by standing tall with its ears erect and tail held high, a leader says: "I'm boss." By crouching and lowering its ears and tail, a follower replies: "I know."

After Lance finishes reading, he thinks for a few minutes about what he has learned. Then he writes down the main points in the last column of his chart. Here is part of his list.

What I Learned

1. A pack is a group of about eight wolves that live together so they can survive.

2. Wolves use their faces, bodies, and sounds to communicate.

3. Healthy wolves don't attack people.

4. Wolves live in North America, Europe, and Asia.

(See pages 186–190 for the entire selection of "Running With the Pack.")

VOCABULARY STRATEGIES

When you're reading and you meet an unfamiliar word, you may decide you don't need to know its exact meaning. The sentence or paragraph may become clear if you continue reading. When you do need to know the meaning of the word, there are several strategies to help you.

The following letter includes some words you may not know. On the next page you will see how you could use **context** and **structural clues** to figure out the meanings of the underlined words.

Dear Classmates,

As <u>director</u> of Jamal Turner's campaign, I ask you to vote for him. He is the best candidate for class president. Besides being hardworking, Jamal is <u>smart</u> and <u>enthusiastic</u>.

Because Jamal is quiet, people sometimes <u>misjudge</u> him. But he is just careful when he speaks. He wants to <u>clarify</u> issues, not confuse them.

Jamal gets things done. He met with the principal and her assistants — the school <u>administration</u> — about the mess in the cafeteria. Today our school is a cleaner place because of him. Vote for Jamal!

Sincerely,

Maria Vilan

The **context,** or words and sentences that surround the unfamiliar word, will often lead you to discover its meaning.

clarify The word *not* tells you that *clarify* is the opposite, or **antonym,** of *confuse.* Sometimes a **synonym,** a word with a similar meaning, may help you.

administration The **definition** of a word may appear close by it. The definition of *administration* comes right before the word.

The **structure** of a word may provide clues to its meaning also. When you understand the parts, you can often combine them to decode the whole word, as in these examples.

director The suffix *-or,* meaning "one who," tells you that *director* means "one who directs."

misjudge If you know that the prefix *mis-* means "incorrectly," you can figure out that *misjudge* means "judge incorrectly."

A glossary or dictionary will give definitions. Sometimes a word's dictionary meaning, or **denotation,** doesn't fit the way it is used. Words often suggest ideas, called **connotations,** that go beyond the dictionary definition.

smart, enthusiastic The words *smart* and *enthusiastic* make you think well of Jamal. They have good **connotations.** His opponents might use the words *tricky* and *excitable.* The **denotations** would make you think Jamal is sneaky and acts without thinking. These words have negative connotations.

Keep a vocabulary notebook to record each word, its meaning, and a sentence that includes the word.

SPEAKING

Speaking in front of a group can be fun if you feel sure of yourself. Some strategies can help you feel more confident.

- Think carefully about your **purpose.** Decide what you want to say and why you think it's important. Do you want to share an idea or experience that you think others will appreciate?
- **Prepare** by writing down your ideas. This will help keep your thoughts organized. If you forget where you are or feel nervous, your notes will help you get back on track.
- **Practice** speaking. Concentrate on speaking clearly and loudly enough to be understood. Explain your ideas thoroughly and use examples when you can.

Dena wants to run for class president. She is nervous about speaking in front of her classmates. Her teacher suggests that she write out the speech and practice it.

When Dena gives her speech, she feels prepared and sure of herself. She knows what she wants to say so well that she only glances at her notes a couple of times.

During a class discussion about South America, Enrico's teacher asks him to tell about living in Colombia. At first Enrico is shy. But as he starts talking he becomes enthusiastic. His classmates ask him lots of questions. Enrico finds that he enjoys participating in discussions.

LISTENING

Being a good listener is as important as being a good speaker. Here are some helpful strategies you can use the next time you are listening.

- Think about the topic ahead of time. What do you know about it and what do you want to learn? What is your **purpose** for listening?
- Give your complete **attention** to the speaker. Save your reactions or questions until the speaker is finished.
- Decide which of the speaker's points are **facts** and which are the speaker's personal **opinions.**
- Think about whether you agree with the speaker's points.

Dena's classmates were interested in hearing her plans for running for the class presidency. They listened carefully and thought about whether they agreed with her ideas. This helped them decide who to vote for in the class election.

Enrico's classmates enjoyed hearing about what it's like to live in a different country. They were interested in hearing him talk. At first they were very quiet because he spoke softly. When Enrico told a funny story, his classmates enjoyed it and asked him more questions.

THE WRITING PROCESS

The writing process is a plan that writers use. The steps involve choosing a **task,** or the kind of writing, choosing the **audience,** and deciding on the **purpose.** You might choose a personal narrative as your task. If your audience is your classmates, your purpose might be to entertain them. At any point during the writing process you can decide to move ahead or start again.

PREWRITING

Begin by choosing a topic. You might find ideas for a personal narrative in your personal journal—perhaps a time when you entered a contest or you helped an animal. Make a list of possible topics and choose one to write about.

After you have chosen your topic, organize your thoughts. List the details and then use a time line, an outline, or a chart to put the details in order. Now you are ready to go on to the next stage.

DRAFTING

Remember these strategies as you write your first draft.

- Write a strong first sentence to catch your audience's interest.
- Use your organizer to be sure the details are in order.
- Write your ideas quickly. You can revise your writing later.

RESPONDING AND REVISING

Good writers often ask other people to read their writing and tell them how it could be improved. The reader might recommend any or all of the following changes.

- Make the first sentence more interesting.
- Use more colorful words to make your writing come alive.
- Add dialogue to make your narrative seem more real.
- Take out unnecessary details.

If your partner did not understand your writing, reread your draft and decide whether to continue with it.

Imagine that you wrote about a time when you played a musical instrument in front of an audience. You might use Editor's Marks to make revisions like these on the first part of your draft.

EDITOR'S MARKS	
∧ Add something.	↻ Move something.
✄ Cut something.	⌒ Replace something.

Every time I thought about playing in front of an audience, my fingers ~~became tight~~ froze. There was no way that I ~~am~~ was going to play the piano at the school recital. My friend Kelly said it would be exciting. I shook my head and said ~~that~~ I ~~knew~~ know I ~~would~~ will mess up and ~~they~~ everyone will laugh at me. ~~I didn't want to play.~~

"You'll never know unless you try," ~~she~~ Kelly said.

PROOFREADING

After you have decided what to revise, you are ready to correct your errors. Here are more Editor's Marks to use.

EDITOR'S MARKS	
≡ Capitalize.	∿ Transpose.
⊙ Add a period.	◯ Spell correctly.
⋏ Add a comma.	⁋ Indent paragraph.
⩔⩔ Add quotation marks.	/ Make a lowercase letter.

Use the following checklist as you proofread.

✓ Did you indent your paragraphs? Use this mark to show where to indent: ⁋ .

✓ Did you capitalize correctly? Mark a letter to be capitalized with three underlines: ≡ . Mark a letter to be made lowercase like this: / .

✓ Did you circle misspelled words and write the correct spelling above? Write correctly in your spelling notebook any words you misspelled. This way you can help yourself remember them.

✓ Did you check and correct your grammar? Use this symbol: ⟋‾ .

✓ Did you check punctuation? Add quotation marks like this: ⩔⩔ . Add a period with this mark: ⊙ . Add a comma with this mark: ⋏ .

I practiced for hours every day. then the day
of the recital was finally here. I felt as if I
had (butterflys) butterflies in my stomach. My knees ~~shook~~ trembled,
and my hands were sweaty. "I just can't do it," I
thought.
Kelly ~~tells~~ told me not to be a coward. "The show
must go on!" she said After I played the first
line of notes, I was surprised to find that my
fingers weren't (num) numb and I wasn't messing up. I
actually felt very calm. The audience clapped,
which made me feel good. I can't wait until our
next recital!

PUBLISHING

When you have corrected your writing and made a clean
copy in your best handwriting, you can publish it by giving it
to your classmates to read. Here are some other publishing
ideas.

- Dramatize your narrative as if it were a television
  program. Choose classmates to play the parts. You be
  the director.
- Use your narrative as the introduction to a class book of
  experiences of your class. You may want to include artwork
  drawn by members of the class and musical compositions
  written by classmates.

RESEARCHING INFORMATION

The first step in doing research is to **define your topic.** Are you writing a biography about the famous aviator Amelia Earhart, making a class presentation about the settling of the American West, or writing a research report about wolves? After you have defined your topic, you need to **gather information** about it. Look for **reference sources** that are likely to have information about the topic. Then you can begin to **search for facts.** Helpful strategies include **skimming, scanning,** and **taking notes.**

SKIMMING: Skimming means looking over a book or reference source quickly to find out what it is about and how it is organized. When you skim, look mainly at the headings and subheadings.

SCANNING: Scanning means looking quickly through a passage to find certain key words or facts.

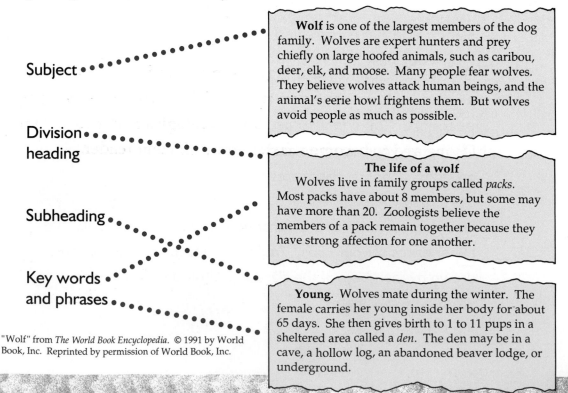

Subject

Division heading

Subheading

Key words and phrases

Wolf is one of the largest members of the dog family. Wolves are expert hunters and prey chiefly on large hoofed animals, such as caribou, deer, elk, and moose. Many people fear wolves. They believe wolves attack human beings, and the animal's eerie howl frightens them. But wolves avoid people as much as possible.

The life of a wolf
Wolves live in family groups called *packs.* Most packs have about 8 members, but some may have more than 20. Zoologists believe the members of a pack remain together because they have strong affection for one another.

Young. Wolves mate during the winter. The female carries her young inside her body for about 65 days. She then gives birth to 1 to 11 pups in a sheltered area called a *den.* The den may be in a cave, a hollow log, an abandoned beaver lodge, or underground.

"Wolf" from *The World Book Encyclopedia.* © 1991 by World Book, Inc. Reprinted by permission of World Book, Inc.

TAKING NOTES: Take notes on the information you find as you skim and scan. Notes are important because you will use them when you write your report.

Write the topic at the top of your page. · · · · · · · · · · · · · · · · · ·

Write in short phrases instead of sentences. ·

Use your own words. · · · ·

Write only what you need to · remember.

Write the name of the source, including the author's name if it · · · · · · · · · · is given.

Wolves

among largest members of dog family

expert hunters

avoid humans

live in packs of 8–20

pack members like a family

litters 1–11 pups

live in dens

World Book Encyclopedia, 1991

Remember that skimming, scanning, and taking notes are strategies that can save you time and help you when writing your report. You can also use these strategies to improve your studying and to become a faster, more efficient reader.

THE LIBRARY

A library contains information in books, magazines and newspapers, reference materials, and video and audio materials.

CARD CATALOG

The library is organized so that it is easy to locate information. The **card catalog** is the first place to look for books. The card catalog is a set of cards that lists every book in the library in alphabetical order by the first word on the card. The three kinds of cards are **title card, author card,** and **subject card.** The cards are usually filed in drawers. However, today many libraries keep the information on a computer data base or on microfilm.

The subject card lists the subject of the book first.

The author card lists the author's last name first.

The title card lists the title of the book first.

WOLVES
J   R. D. Lawrence
599.74

J   Lawrence, R. D.
599.74 Wolves / R. D. Lawrence;

Wolves.
J   R. D. Lawrence
599.74 Wolves / R.D. Lawrence;
        Boston: Little, Brown, c1990.

COMPUTERIZED CATALOG

The computerized card catalog contains the same information as the card catalog that is found in drawers. There are three ways to find a book in the computerized catalog: by title, by author, or by subject. Suppose you want to use the computerized catalog to find information on wolves. First, you type the subject command and the word *wolves* on the computer keyboard, according to the instructions in the printed guide. The printed guide explains on the screen the options and steps as you go along. For example, the instructions on the screen may tell you to type a command such as *S = wolves*. The computer then gives you a list of titles and call numbers of books on the subject *Wolves*. The call numbers help you find the books on the library shelves.

CALL NUMBERS

Each nonfiction book has a **call number** that appears on its three cards or on the computer screen. This call number is also on the book itself. Each fiction book is identified by the first letters of the author's last name instead of by a call number. The library shelves are labeled with the call letters or call numbers of the books they contain.

GLOSSARY

The **pronunciation** of each word in this glossary is shown by a phonetic respelling in brackets; for example, [ad'vər·tīz'mənt]. An accent mark (') follows the syllable with the most stress: [ik·splōd']. A secondary, or lighter, accent mark (') follows a syllable with less stress: [ek'splə·nā'shən]. The key to other pronunciation symbols is below. You will find a shortened version of this key on alternate pages of the glossary.

Pronunciation Key*

a	add, map	m	move, seem	u	up, done
ā	ace, rate	n	nice, tin	û(r)	burn, term
â(r)	care, air	ng	ring, song	yōo	fuse, few
ä	palm, father	o	odd, hot	v	vain, eve
b	bat, rub	ō	open, so	w	win, away
ch	check, catch	ô	order, jaw	y	yet, yearn
d	dog, rod	oi	oil, boy	z	zest, muse
e	end, pet	ou	pout, now	zh	vision, pleasure
ē	equal, tree	ŏŏ	took, full	ə	the schwa,
f	fit, half	ōō	pool, food		an unstressed
g	go, log	p	pit, stop		vowel representing
h	hope, hate	r	run, poor		the sound spelled
i	it, give	s	see, pass		a in *above*
ī	ice, write	sh	sure, rush		e in *sicken*
j	joy, ledge	t	talk, sit		i in *possible*
k	cool, take	th	thin, both		o in *melon*
l	look, rule	th	this, bathe		u in *circus*

A

accordion

ac·cor·di·on [ə·kôr′dē·ən] *n.* A musical instrument that is played by fingering keys and squeezing the instrument at the same time.

ac·cus·ing·ly [ə·kyo͞oz′ing·lē] *adv.* In a way that blames someone for something.

a·chieve·ment [ə·chēv′mənt] *n.* Something that a person has done very well: **Learning to ride a horse was a special *achievement* for Felipe.**

ac·knowl·edge [ak·nol′ij] *v.* To look at someone and speak to him or her.

a·cre [ā′kər] *n.* A large amount of land.

ad lib [ad′lib′] *v.* To make up words or actions at the moment, not before.

ad·ver·tise·ment [ad′vər·tīz′mənt *or* ad·vûr′tis·mənt] *n.* A printed or spoken statement whose purpose is to sell something. *syn.* notice

ad·vise [ad·vīz′] *v.* To tell someone what to do. *syn.* recommend

ag·ile [aj′əl] *adj.* Able to move easily.

a·light [ə·līt′] *v.* To land: **Vern saw a robin *alight* on a tree branch.**

ad lib *Ad lib* is a shortened form of the Latin phrase *ad libitum*, which means "at pleasure." So speakers and comedians who *ad lib* say whatever gives them pleasure instead of following a set script.

appliqué

an·ces·tor [an′ses·tər] *n.* A family member who lived a long time ago.

an·ni·ver·sa·ry [an′ə·vûr′sə·rē] *n.* The day of the year when people remember something of importance from the past.

anx·ious [angk′shəs] *adj.* Worried or nervous: **Tom felt *anxious* and concerned about his sick uncle in the hospital.** *syn.* uneasy

ap·pli·qué [ap′li·kā′] *v.* **ap·pli·quéd, ap·pli·qué·ing** To decorate by sewing one piece of cloth onto another.

ar·gu·ment [är′gyə·mənt] *n.* A strong reason for or against something: **One of Jerome's *arguments* for getting a bike was that he could use it to run errands for the family.**

ar·ti·fi·cial [är′tə·fish′əl] *adj.* False; not natural or real: **The colored leaves in the store window were *artificial*, but the pumpkins were real.**

as·sem·bly [ə·sem′blē] *n.* A gathering or meeting of people; in school, a gathering of all students and teachers for entertainment or educational programs.

at·ten·tive [ə·ten′tiv] *adj.* Careful to notice things and pay attention. *syn.* aware

au·thor·i·ty [ə·thôr′ə·tē] *n.* Someone who is in charge of doing things the right way: **The city *authorities* decide who will march in the front of the parade.**

av·a·lanche [av′ə·lanch′] *n.* The falling of objects suddenly in a heap.

a·void [ə·void′] *v.* **a·void·ed, a·void·ing** To stay away from something.

B

baf·fle [baf′əl] *v.* **baf·fled, baf·fling** To mix up. *syn.* confuse

bal·ance [bal′əns] *n.* The ability to move without leaning or falling.

be·have [bi·hāv′] *v.* To act.

be·wil·der·ment [bi·wil′dər·mənt] *n.* The feeling of not understanding something: **Oscar looked with *bewilderment* at the math problem because it did not make sense to him.** *syn.* confusion

board [bôrd] *n.* A colorful, flat piece of heavy paper or wood on which a game is played: **The *board* for checkers has squares of two colors.**

bored [bôrd] *adj.* Without interest or excitement: **The children were *bored* after the clown left the party.**

boun·ti·ful [boun′tə·fəl] *adj.* Plentiful; generous in size: **The crop was so *bountiful* that the farmer gave apples away.**

brand [brand] *v.* To make a permanent mark on an animal to identify it.

bro·cade [brō·kad′] *n.* A rich cloth that is embroidered with raised designs.

bur·den [bûr′dən] *n.* Something that causes people to worry or have extra work.

C

cam·paign [kam·pān′] *n.* Activities organized to gain or win something.

can·di·date [kan′də·dāt′] *n.* A person being considered for a certain position.

can·vas [kan′vəs] *n.* A piece of heavy cloth stretched over a frame on which pictures are painted: **For his art project, Randy bought oil paints, special brushes, and a *canvas* to paint on.**

car·bon di·ox·ide [kär′bən dī·ok′sīd′] *n.* A gas that has no color or smell and that plants need.

balance

candidate A candidate was originally someone dressed in white. To the ancient Romans, white symbolized purity and honesty. Our words *candid*, "honest," and *candor*, "honesty," go back to the same root, meaning "white."

canvas

a	add	o͞o	took
ā	ace	o͞o	pool
â	care	u	up
ä	palm	û	burn
e	end	y͞oo	fuse
ē	equal	oi	oil
i	it	ou	pout
ī	ice	ng	ring
o	odd	th	thin
ō	open	th	this
ô	order	zh	vision

ə = { a in *above*   e in *sicken*
i in *possible*
o in *melon*   u in *circus* }

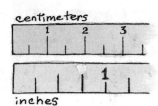

centimeter

chemical In the Middle Ages, the Arabs who invaded Europe brought with them practices they called *al-kimia*. The Europeans changed the Arab word to *alchemy*. From the name for the practices of working with metals and medicines came our scientific words *chemical*, *chemistry*, and *chemist*.

collection

car·ni·val [kär′nə·vəl] *n.* **1** A festival with parades and dancing. **2** (*written* **Carnival**) A special holiday that comes a few weeks before Easter: **Maria is happy about the beautiful costume she will wear during** *Carnival.*

cau·tious·ly [kô′shəs·lē] *adv.* Carefully: **Always cross a busy street** *cautiously.*

cel·e·brate [sel′ə·brāt′] *v.* To take part in special activities in honor of a holiday or special day: **Our town** *celebrates* **the Fourth of July with a parade, a huge picnic, and fireworks displays.**

cen·ti·me·ter [sen′tə·mē′tər] *n.* A measure of length somewhat less than half an inch: **Luis learned that one** *centimeter* **equals almost half an inch.**

cer·e·mo·ny [ser′ə·mō′nē] *n.* Actions done for the purpose of celebrating something.

char·coal [chär′kōl′] *n.* A black substance that is made from wood burned in a special way; often used in drawing.

chem·i·cal [kem′i·kəl] *n.* One of many basic materials or elements found in nature and often combined by scientists to make medicines.

cit·i·zen [sit′ə·zən] *n.* A person born in a country or legally made a member of it: **Mr. Kwan took tests to become an American** *citizen* **after he moved here from Korea.**

claim [klām] *n.* Something a person demands that rightfully belongs to him or her: **Pioneers established their** *claim* **to land by living on it.**

clam·or [klam′ər] *n.* A loud and constant noise.

clan [klan] *n.* A group of families who are all related to the same ancestor.

clum·sy [klum′zē] *adj.* Without much control or grace of movement.

col·lard greens [kol′ərd grēnz] *n.* The green leaves of a cabbagelike plant: **Our family's Thanksgiving dinner includes my two favorite vegetables, corn and** *collard greens.*

col·lec·tion [kə·lek′shən] *n.* A group of the same kind of things kept together: **Angela is proud of her** *collection* **of seashells.**

com·mon [kom′ən] *adj.* Usual; widely available or found: **Chickens, pigs, and cows are** *common* **farm animals.**

com·pete [kəm·pēt′] *v.*
com·pet·ed, com·pet·ing
To work at winning a contest: **The teams were *competing* for the first prize in the storytelling contest.**

com·pet·i·tive
[kəm·pet′ə·tiv] *adj.* Fond of being in contests for the purpose of winning.

com·pli·ment
[kom′plə·mənt] *n.* A nice thing that someone says about another person: **Carmen received a *compliment* when her teacher said that she was a very good painter.** *syn.* praise

con·cen·trate [kon′sən·trāt′] *v.* To think about one thing very hard.

con·clude [kən·klo͞od′]
v. **con·clud·ed, con·clud·ing** To form an idea or opinion after thinking about something: **Nora saw the dark clouds and *concluded* that it was going to rain.**

con·fi·dence [kon′fə·dəns] *n.* Trust; the feeling that everything will turn out all right: **Ellen had *confidence* that she would do well on the spelling test.**

con·sid·er·ate [kən·sid′ər·it] *adj.* Caring about another person's feelings. *syns.* kind, polite

con·so·la·tion
[kon′sə·lā′shən] *n.* Something given to someone to cheer him or her up: **Phil lost the drawing contest, but he felt better when he was given a small prize as a *consolation.*** *syn.* comfort

con·tra·dict [kon′trə·dikt′] *v.* **con·tra·dict·ed, con·tra·dict·ing** To disagree or say the opposite. *syns.* deny, oppose

con·verse [kən·vûrs′] *v.* **con·versed, con·vers·ing** To talk: **Sometimes my mother and Mrs. Potter *converse* on the phone for an hour.** *syn.* speak

con·vince [kən·vins′] *v.* To cause someone to believe something. *syns.* persuade, prove

cor·ral [kə·ral′] *n.* A fenced area where animals are kept: **All the cattle were driven into the *corral* so that they could be kept together.**

cow·er [kou′ər] *v.* **cow·ered, cow·er·ing** To curl up with fear. *syns.* tremble, cringe

crys·tal·line [kris′tə·lin] *adj.* Clear and sparkling.

cus·tom [kus′təm] *n.* A practice followed by most people in a group, often for many years.

converse

corral This word was added to the English language by the Spanish explorers, who brought horses and cattle to the southwestern part of the United States. They kept their animals in pens called *corrals*, where animals had room to run. The word can be traced all the way back to the Latin word *currere*, meaning "to run."

a	add	o͞o	took
ā	ace	o͞o	pool
â	care	u	up
ä	palm	û	burn
e	end	yo͞o	fuse
ē	equal	oi	oil
i	it	ou	pout
ī	ice	ng	ring
o	odd	th	thin
ō	open	th	this
ô	order	zh	vision

ə = { a in *above*   e in *sicken*
     i in *possible*
     o in *melon*   u in *circus* }

design

disguise

dugout

dilemma A *dilemma* is a choice between two things. The word part *di-* is related to *dwo*, an ancient word for *two*.

D

dead·line [ded'līn'] *n.* The time that something must be finished.

deed [dēd] *n.* A written note proving that someone owns a piece of land.

del·i·cate [del'ə·kit] *adj.* Very fine and not heavy: **The old curtains were made of very delicate lace.**

de·sign [di·zīn'] *n.* The shapes and colors that are on something, such as a piece of cloth. *syn.* pattern

des·ti·ny [des'tə·nē] *n.* Something that seems certain to happen to someone. *syn.* fate

de·vice [di·vīs'] *n.* Something designed for a certain purpose. *syn.* tool

di·lem·ma [di·lem'ə] *n.* The need to choose between two unpleasant things.

dis·ap·point·ment [dis'ə·point'mənt] *n.* A feeling of sadness because things did not happen as expected: **Regina's disappointment showed in her face when she wasn't allowed to go to the zoo.**

dis·cour·aged [dis·kûr'ijd] *adj.* Feeling bad about the way things happened. *syn.* disappointed

dis·guise [dis·gīz'] *n.* Something that changes the way someone usually looks. *syn.* costume

dis·qual·i·fy [dis·kwol'ə·fī'] *v.* **dis·qual·i·fied, dis·qual·i·fy·ing** To take someone out of a contest for some reason.

dis·solve [di·zolv'] *v.* **dis·solved, dis·solv·ing** To become a liquid or to melt: **The grease on the dirty frying pans will dissolve when Raymond washes them with detergent.**

dis·tinct [dis·tingkt'] *adj.* Very clear: **The distinct smell of cookies filled the bakery.** *syn.* sharp

dou·ble [dub'əl] *n.* A two-base hit in baseball.

dug·out [dug'out'] *n.* A home built by digging out a living space in the side of a hill or river bank.

E

ech·o [ek'ō] *n.* Sound reflected or bounced back: **The echoes in the empty room made it sound as if more than two people were talking.**

e·lec·tion [i·lek'shən] *n.* The choosing of a person for a position by voting.

em·bar·rassed [im·bar′əst] *adj.* Ashamed: **Craig felt** *embarrassed* **because he made a mistake in front of his classmates.**

em·broi·dered [im·broi′dərd] *adj.* Decorated with fancy stitching: **The** *embroidered* **purse was covered with gold stitching.**

e·merge [i·mûrj′] *v.* To come out or become visible.

emp·ty [emp′tē] *adj.* Holding nothing; unfilled. *syn.* vacant

en·dan·gered [in·dān′jərd] *adj.* In danger of no longer existing.

en·dur·ance [in·d(y)oor′əns] *n.* The ability to work hard for a long time.

en·vi·ron·ment [in·vī′rən·mənt] *n.* The place where something lives, or its surroundings: **Peaches grow best in a warm, sunny** *environment.*

er·rand [er′ənd] *n.* A short trip for the purpose of doing something, usually for someone else.

e·rupt [i·rupt′] *v.* To suddenly burst out.

e·vap·o·rate [i·vap′ə·rāt′] *v.* **e·vap·o·rat·ed, e·vap·o·rat·ing** To dry up: **The hot sun had** *evaporated* **the puddles on the sidewalk, so we didn't get wet feet.**

e·vent·ful [i·vent′fəl] *adj.* Filled with important happenings: **Martin Luther King, Jr., was given many awards during his** *eventful* **life.** *syns.* noteworthy, significant

ex·er·tion [ig·zûr′shən] *n.* Hard work.

ex·haus·tion [ig·zôs′chən] *n.* The feeling of being very tired.

ex·ot·ic [ig·zot′ik] *adj.* Strange and interesting.

ex·pen·sive [ik·spen′siv] *adj.* Costing a lot of money: **Even with a loan from his father, Luis decided the bicycle was too** *expensive* **to buy.**

ex·pe·ri·ence [ik·spir′ē·əns] *n.* What someone knows by watching or doing something.

ex·pla·na·tion [ek′splə·nā′shən] *n.* A reason given that makes something easier to understand: **The students learned from the teacher's** *explanation* **of the story.**

ex·plode [ik·splōd′] *v.* **ex·plod·ed, ex·plod·ing** To suddenly burst with great force.

ex·qui·site [eks′kwi·zit *or* ik·skwiz′it] *adj.* Very beautiful: **Bright yellow, blue, and green feathers made the bird look** *exquisite.*

empty

explode

explode When we say that something exploded, we are describing a destructive blowup. The origins of *explode* are much less violent. *Explode* comes from two Latin words — *ex,* "out," and *plaudo,* "clap." If the ancient Romans disliked a theatrical performance, they would "explode," or clap the actors off the stage.

a	add	o͞o	took
ā	ace	o͞o	pool
â	care	u	up
ä	palm	û	burn
e	end	yo͞o	fuse
ē	equal	oi	oil
i	it	ou	pout
ī	ice	ng	ring
o	odd	th	thin
ō	open	th	this
ô	order	zh	vision

ə = { a in *above* e in *sicken*
       i in *possible*
       o in *melon* u in *circus* }

F

G

furrow

gaucho

greenhorn You wouldn't want anyone to call you a greenhorn. It would mean that you are a beginner and lack the experience to do a good job. This word was first used in the days when people used oxen to do farm work. If a farmer had a beast whose horns were still *green* ("young" or "new"), it probably wouldn't have been trained to pull a plow.

fas·ci·nate [fas′ə·nāt′] *v.* **fas·ci·nat·ed, fas·ci·nat·ing** To interest or attract.

field [fēld] *v.* **field·ed, field·ing** To catch or pick up a batted baseball and throw it to the proper player.

file [fīl] *v.* To register or record formally.

flu·ent [flōō′ənt] *adj.* Spoken smoothly and easily: **Maria spoke such *fluent* Spanish that no one believed she grew up in Chicago.**

fore·close [fôr·klōz′] *v.* **fore·closed, fore·clos·ing** To take away land from a person who owes money on it.

fra·grant [frā′grənt] *adj.* Having a sweet smell: **Aurora's perfume smelled like *fragrant* roses.**

frail [frāl] *adj.* Very weak. *syn.* feeble

frame [frām] *v.* **framed, fram·ing** To trick someone into the appearance of being involved in a crime.

fur·row [fûr′ō] *n.* A groove in the ground where seeds are planted: **Andrew made a *furrow* for the flower seeds.**

fu·ry [fyŏŏr′ē] *n.* Great anger.

gar·ment [gär′mənt] *n.* A piece of clothing: **Mr. Sawado sells shirts, jackets, suits, and other *garments*.**

gau·cho [gou′chō] *n.* A South American cowhand: ***Gauchos* are workers who ride horses and take care of cattle.**

gen·er·a·tion [jen′ə·rā′shən] *n.* A group of people born around the same time.

gen·er·ous [jen′ər·əs] *adj.* Eager to share: **Alma's *generous* grandparents bought new books for the school library.** *syns.* unselfish, giving

gin·ger ale [jin′jər āl] *n.* A bubbly drink flavored by the ginger plant: **Bradley liked *ginger ale* better than any other soda pop.**

glis·ten [glis′(ə)n] *v.* **glis·tened, glis·ten·ing** To shine. *syns.* sparkle, shimmer

green·horn [grēn′hôrn′] *n.* A person who is new at doing something: **I felt like a *greenhorn* as I tried without success to get on my horse.** *syn.* beginner

grieve [grēv] *v.* To be very upset and sorry about something lost: **Tony will *grieve* when his cousin Alonso moves to a faraway city.** *syn.* mourn

H

herb [(h)ûrb] *n.* A plant used for medicine or adding flavor to food.

hes·i·tant·ly [hez′ə·tənt·lē] *adv.* Doubtfully; undecidedly: **The princess wasn't sure whether to kiss the frog, so she did it** *hesitantly.* *syn.* uncertainly

hes·i·tate [hez′ə·tāt′] *v.* **hes·i·tat·ed, hes·i·tat·ing** To act slowly, as if in doubt. *syn.* pause

hon·ored [on′ərd] *adj.* Feeling loved and admired: **Grandfather felt** *honored* **on his birthday when his grandchildren spent the whole day with him.**

hoof [hŏŏf *or* hōŏf] *n.; pl.* **hoofs** or **hooves** The hard cover on the foot of an animal, such as a horse: **You can hear the** *hooves* **of a running horse beat the ground.**

ho·ri·zon [hə·rī′zən] *n.* The line where the sky and the earth seem to meet.

I

id·i·o·syn·cra·sy [id′ē·ō·sing′krə·sē] *n.* A way of acting that is odd or different.

im·me·di·ate·ly [i·mē′dē·it·lē] *adv.* Right away; without waiting; now.

im·mer·sion heat·er [i·mûr′shən hē′tər *or* i·mûr′zhən hē′tər] *n.* A tool heated electrically and put into liquid to warm it.

im·mi·grant [im′ə·grənt] *n.* A person who comes to live in a new country.

im·pa·tient [im·pā′shənt] *adj.* Not wanting to wait: **Tim was** *impatient* **for his favorite television show to begin.**

in·de·scrib·a·ble [in′di·skrī′bə·bəl] *adj.* Impossible to describe or tell about.

in·no·cent [in′ə·sənt] *adj.* Not to blame.

in·spec·tion [in·spek′shən] *n.* A careful look at something.

in·stinct [in′stingkt] *n.* A natural force that makes people or animals act in certain ways: **The mother duck's** *instincts* **were to provide food for and protect her babies.**

in·su·lat·ed [in′sə·lāt′əd] *adj.* Designed to keep contents hot or cold: **I have an** *insulated* **container in my lunch box that keeps my soup hot all day.**

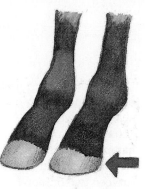

hoof

instinct *Instinct* comes from the Latin word *instinguere,* meaning "to prod or force." Instincts are inner forces that cause animals to behave in certain ways. *Instinct* is also related to our word *stick.* Think of an instinct as something that sticks or prods a rabbit, forcing it to run away from danger.

insulated

a	add	ŏŏ	took
ā	ace	ōō	pool
â	care	u	up
ä	palm	û	burn
e	end	yōō	fuse
ē	equal	oi	oil
i	it	ou	pout
ī	ice	ng	ring
o	odd	th	thin
ō	open	th	this
ô	order	zh	vision

ə = { a in *above*   e in *sicken*
      i in *possible*
      o in *melon*   u in *circus* }

international *Inter-* means "between or among." An airplane that makes an *international* flight travels between two or more nations, such as the United States and France.

journalist

lasso

in·tel·li·gence [in·tel′ə·jəns] *n.* The ability to learn and to solve problems: **The clever monkey showed its** *intelligence* **by putting a puzzle together.**

in·ten·si·ty [in·ten′sə·tē] *n.* Great force in feelings or actions.

in·ten·tion [in·ten′shən] *n.* Plan or purpose: **Carla had no** *intention* **of going to the party because she was too busy.** *syn.* motive

in·tent·ly [in·tent′lē] *adv.* With full attention: **The children listened** *intently* **to the interesting story about dinosaurs.**

in·ter·na·tion·al [in′tər·nash′ən·əl] *adj.* In nations all over the world. *syn.* worldwide

in·ter·pret·er [in·tûr′prit·ər] *n.* Someone who understands several languages and helps people who speak different languages to understand each other: **The** *interpreter* **told the Russian visitor that the French woman wanted to thank him.** *syn.* translator

in·ter·rupt [in′tə·rupt′] *v.* **in·ter·rupt·ed, in·ter·rupt·ing** To start talking before someone else has finished.

jour·nal·ist [jûr′nəl·ist] *n.* Someone who writes or edits articles for newspapers or magazines: **The** *journalist* **wrote an article about recycling for the magazine.** *syn.* reporter

kin·ship [kin′ship′] *n.* A relationship or connection like that between family members.

L

lan·tern [lan′tərn] *n.* A kind of lamp used outdoors.

las·so [las′ō] *n.* A rope with a loop at the end, used for catching cattle.

laun·dry [lôn′drē] *n.* Clothes that need washing: **Donnie piled the family's** *laundry* **next to the washing machine.**

la·va [lä′və *or* lav′ə] *n.* Very hot melted rock that bursts out of a volcano.

league [lēg] *n.* A group of sports teams that usually play each other.

log·i·cal [loj'ə·kəl] *adj.* In a way that is orderly and makes sense: **The plan was so *logical* that it was easy to carry out.**

loom [lo͞om] *n.* A machine used for weaving cloth.

loop·hole [lo͞op'hōl'] *n.* A way of getting around a law or legal agreement.

lum·ber [lum'bər] *v.* **lum·bered, lum·ber·ing** To move along slowly and heavily. *syn.* plod

lu·nar [lo͞o'nər] *adj.* Having to do with the moon: **In the *lunar* calendar, one month equals the number of days from one full moon to another.**

M

mag·nif·i·cent [mag·nif'ə·sənt] *adj.* Wonderful; impressive: **The king wore a *magnificent* jeweled crown that we all admired.** *syn.* splendid

mane [mān] *n.* The long hair on the neck of an animal such as a horse.

mem·o·ry [mem'ər·ē] *n.* Something a person remembers: **Mr. White has happy *memories* of the times he went fishing with his sons.**

me·nag·er·ie [mə·naj'ər·ē] *n.* A group of different animals: **There was a *menagerie* of stuffed animals in the toy store.**

mi·grate [mī'grāt'] *v.* **mi·grat·ed, mi·grat·ing** To move from one place to another when the season changes: **The birds are *migrating* south to spend winter in a warmer part of the country.**

mis·chief [mis'chif] *n.* Harmful or tricky acts.

mon·o·tone [mon'ə·tōn'] *n.* A voice that never changes in highness or lowness.

mound [mound] *n.* In baseball, the small hill that the pitcher stands on when throwing the ball to the batter: **Derrick stood still on the *mound* before throwing the pitch.**

muf·fled [muf'əld] *adj.* Sounding as if wrapped or covered up. *syns.* quieted, deadened

N

nec·tar [nek'tər] *n.* A sweet liquid made by flowers.

nom·i·nate [nom'ə·nāt'] *v.* To name someone to run in an election.

loom The word *loom* comes from Old and Middle English words that mean "tool." Native Americans began weaving beautiful blankets and clothing, often using looms made of tree branches, as early as in the 700s.

mane

menagerie

a	add	o͞o	took
ā	ace	o͞o	pool
â	care	u	up
ä	palm	û	burn
e	end	yo͞o	fuse
ē	equal	oi	oil
i	it	ou	pout
ī	ice	ng	ring
o	odd	th	thin
ō	open	th	this
ô	order	zh	vision

ə = { a in *above*   e in *sicken*
      i in *possible*
      o in *melon*   u in *circus* }

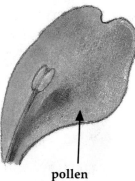

pollen

principle Homophones are pairs of words that sound alike but have different spellings and meanings, such as *principle* and *principal*. Both are related to the Latin word *primus*, which means "first." A *principle* is a basic ("first") belief or idea, while *principal* means "major or first in importance."

property

oc·ca·sion [ə·kā′zhən] *n.* Event or situation: **We had a party for Enrico because his return home from Mexico was a special** *occasion.*

oc·cu·py [ok′yə·pī′] *v.* **oc·cu·pied, oc·cu·py·ing** To live in a place.

op·por·tu·ni·ty [op′ər·t(y)ōō′nə·tē] *n.* A chance to do something.

or·di·nar·y [ôr′də·ner′ē] *n.* Something usual.

ox·y·gen [ok′sə·jin] *n.* The part of air that animals and people need to stay alive.

pol·len [pol′ən] *n.* A powder made by flowers from which new seeds grow.

pos·ses·sion [pə·zesh′ən] *n.* Something that belongs to a person: **Almost all of Uncle Diego's** *possessions* **were saved before the fire burned the house down.**

prac·ti·cal [prak′ti·kəl] *adj.* Full of common sense. *syn.* sensible

praise [prāz] *v.* To say nice things about someone or something. *syn.* compliment

pre·cious [presh′əs] *adj.* Very special or valuable.

pre·serve [pri·zûrv′] *v.* To keep from harm. *syn.* save

pre·tend [pri·tend′] *v.* **pre·tend·ed, pre·tend·ing** To fake or make believe: **Steve knew his sister was only** *pretending* **to be asleep so she could listen to him talk to his friends.**

prey [prā] *n.* An animal used by another animal as food.

prin·ci·ple [prin′sə·pəl] *n.* An important idea or rule on which people's behavior is based: **One of the** *principles* **of American democracy is that all people are equal in the eyes of the law.**

probe [prōb] *v.* **probed, prob·ing** To explore with a pointed object or tool.

prop·er·ty [prop′ər·tē] *n.* Land belonging to someone: **Mr. Teng built a fence around his** *property* **to keep the neighbor's dog out.**

pros·per·i·ty [pros·per′ə·tē] *n.* Success that includes wealth.

pro·test [prə·test′] *v.* **pro·test·ed, pro·test·ing** To object: **Some people** *protested* **that a new airport would make their neighborhood too noisy.**

R

ran·sacked [ran'sakt'] *adj.* Torn apart during a search.

rare [râr] *adj.* Very uncommon; found in very few places.

re·cite [ri·sīt'] *v.* **re·cit·ed, re·cit·ing** To say something that has been memorized in front of an audience.

re·cov·er·y [ri·kuv'ər·ē] *n.* A return to good health: **Everyone hoped Alana would make a quick *recovery* from the flu and return to school soon.**

re·flec·tion [ri·flek'shən] *n.* Something seen because its image is bounced back from a shiny surface: **Robert looked at his *reflection* in the mirror.**

re·lief [ri·lēf'] *n.* A feeling of freedom from pain, discomfort, or worry.

re·morse [ri·môrs'] *n.* Sorrow for having done something: **After Rachel yelled at her little brother, she felt such *remorse* that she made him a card.** *syn.* regret

res·er·va·tion [rez'ər·vā'shən] *n.* An area of land set aside by the government for a certain group of people to live on.

res·i·dent [rez'ə·dənt] *n.* A person living in a certain place.

re·spon·si·bil·i·ty [ri·spon'sə·bil'ə·tē] *n.* Something someone must do or take care of; duty.

ri·dic·u·lous [ri·dik'yə·ləs] *adj.* Funny: **The puppet's green, fuzzy hair looked *ridiculous* and made us laugh.** *syns.* laughable, silly

roam [rōm] *v.* To wander around.

rook·ie [rŏŏk'ē] *n.* A person who is playing his or her first year in a professional sport.

reflection

S

sci·en·tist [sī'ən·tist] *n.* A person who learns by studying and experimenting with things in nature.

scrunch [skrunch] *v.* **scrunched, scrunch·ing** To sit with arms and legs pulled in close to the body. *syn.* crouch

se·nhor [si·nyō(ə)r'] *n.* Portuguese title for a man, the same as *Mr.* or *Sir:* **In Brazil, where they speak Portuguese, the people Mr. Mason met called him *senhor*.**

senhor This Portuguese word for "Mr." traces its origins to the Latin word *senior*, which means "older." Only an adult man was considered worthy of this formal title. The Spanish word *señor* and the Italian *signor* have the same origin and meaning. Even our English word *sir* can be traced to *senior*.

a	add	ŏŏ	took
ā	ace	ōō	pool
â	care	u	up
ä	palm	û	burn
e	end	yōō	fuse
ē	equal	oi	oil
i	it	ou	pout
ī	ice	ng	ring
o	odd	th	thin
ō	open	th	this
ô	order	zh	vision

ə = { a in *above*   e in *sicken*
       i in *possible*
       o in *melon*   u in *circus* }

shield

silhouette This word comes from the name of Etienne de Silhouette, who was in charge of the treasury of France during the 1700s. We aren't exactly sure why his name was given to this kind of picture, which shows only an outline filled in with a solid color. Perhaps he was such a bad treasurer that his name seemed to fit these pictures that appeared so simple and unfinished.

stamen

sen·si·ble [sen′sə·bəl] *adj.* Smart; reasonable: **Mike knew that eating all that candy was not** *sensible* **because too many sweets are not healthy.** *syn.* wise

sheep·ish·ly [shē′pish·lē] *adv.* With a feeling of shame.

shel·ter [shel′tər] *v.* To provide a safe, covered place.

shield [shēld] *n.* Something held up in front of a person for protection: **The soldier held up his** *shield* **as he marched into battle.**

shriv·eled [shriv′əld] *adj.* Small and dried up. *syn.* shrunken

shut·tle [shut′(ə)l] *n.* In weaving, an object used to carry a thread over and under other threads.

si·es·ta [sē·es′tə] *n.* A nap in the afternoon.

sil·hou·ette [sil′oo·et′] *v.* **sil·hou·et·ted, sil·hou·et·ting** To make a dark outline of a person or thing against a light background.

sliv·er [sliv′ər] *n.* A thin and sometimes sharp piece broken, split, or cut off from something: **When Alan slid down the pole, he got** *slivers* **in his hands from the rough wood.** *syn.* splinter

splen·did [splen′did] *adj.* Wonderful. *syn.* glorious

squan·der [skwon′dər] *v.* **squan·dered, squan·der·ing** To spend money in a wasteful way. *syn.* waste

sta·men [stā′mən] *n.* The part of the flower that sticks out from the center.

stam·pede [stam·pēd′] *v.* To rush wildly in a group.

star·tling [stär′tling] *adj.* Surprising; shocking. *syn.* amazing

sta·tion·er·y [stā′shən·er′ē] *n.* Paper used for writing letters: **Carmela wrote a letter on yellow** *stationery* **to send to her aunt.**

steer·age [stir′ij] *n.* The crowded area of a ship for passengers with the cheapest tickets.

stunned [stund] *adj.* Very surprised.

sub·stance [sub′stəns] *n.* Material that something is made of.

sur·vive [sər·vīv′] *v.* To stay alive.

sus·pend [sə·spend′] *v.* **sus·pend·ed, sus·pend·ing** To hang: **The swing was** *suspended* **from a tree branch.**

sus·pi·cious [sə·spish′əs] *adj.* Having a feeling that something is wrong. *syn.* untrusting

sym·pa·thy [sim′pə·thē] *n.* The understanding of another person's feelings: **Because Kendra was crying, Gloria hugged her in *sympathy*.**

T

tech·nique [tek·nēk′] *n.* A way of doing something. *syns.* method, procedure, strategy

tem·per [tem′pər] *n.* Mood.

ter·ri·to·ry [ter′ə·tôr′ē] *n.* An open area of land that has not been settled or claimed by anyone.

tes·ti·fy [tes′tə·fī] *v.* To speak under oath in a court of law.

ther·a·py [ther′ə·pē] *n.* Treatment to help a person do something better.

thick·et [thik′it] *n.* A group of trees growing very close together. *syn.* grove

tra·di·tion [trə·dish′ən] *n.* An idea or way of doing things that is passed down among people over many years.

trans·late [trans·lāt′] *v.* **trans·lat·ed, trans·lat·ing** To explain the meaning of words or actions. *syn.* interpret

trans·par·ent [trans·pâr′ənt] *adj.* Able to be seen through: **We could see the cat sleeping behind the *transparent* curtains.**

trim [trim] *v.* **trimmed, trim·ming** To decorate something: **We *trimmed* the tree with lights.**

tri·um·phant·ly [trī·um′fənt·lē] *adv.* With joy and pride

tu·ber [t(y)oo′bər] *n.* A thick part of the stem of some plants that grows underground.

tur·moil [tûr′moil] *n.* Loud fussing: **The crowd at the baseball game was in a *turmoil* because of the shortstop's error.**

twi·light [twī′līt′] *n.* The light as the sun sets.

transparent

tuber *Tuber* and *thumb* are both related to the same ancient root word. They both refer to something swollen or fat. A *tuber* such as a potato or peanut is a swelling on a plant. Compared to your other fingers, your *thumb* is fat.

U

UFO [yoo′ef·ō′] *n.* *U*nidentified *F*lying *O*bject; something seen in the sky that seems too strange to be real.

un·doubt·ed·ly [un·dou′tid·lē] *adv.* Certainly: **The sun is *undoubtedly* important to growing plants.** *syn.* surely

a	add	oo	took
ā	ace	oo	pool
â	care	u	up
ä	palm	û	burn
e	end	yoo	fuse
ē	equal	oi	oil
i	it	ou	pout
ī	ice	ng	ring
o	odd	th	thin
ō	open	th	this
ô	order	zh	vision

ə = { a in *above* e in *sicken* i in *possible* o in *melon* u in *circus* }

585

violinist

u·ni·ty [yoo′ni·tē] *n.* The quality of being together and sharing: **The *unity* among the people of the village helped them choose and work together on their goals.**

ur·gent·ly [ûr′jənt·lē] *adv.* In a way calling for quick action.

V

vain [vān] *adj.* Too proud of the way one looks: **The *vain* beauty queen thought she was the prettiest woman in the world.**

vig·or·ous·ly [vig′ər·əs·lē] *adv.* With strength and energy: **The girls played basketball so *vigorously* that they were worn out after the game.**

vi·o·lin·ist [vī′ə·lin′ist] *n.* A person who plays a musical instrument called a violin: **The *violinist* broke a string on her instrument as she was playing it.**

vol·ca·no [vol·kā′nō] *n.* A kind of mountain from which melted rock, stones, and ashes sometimes explode.

volcano *Volcano* comes from the name Vulcan, the Roman god of fire and metalworking. The Romans believed that Vulcan's workshop and fiery furnace were buried under Mt. Etna, a volcano on the island of Sicily near Italy. When Vulcan and his helpers were heating and hammering, the mountain rumbled and shook, and sometimes fire and smoke came from the top.

yoke

W

weird [wird] *adj.* Very strange.

wil·der·ness [wil′dər·nis] *n.* Land where people do not usually live.

wound [woond] *v.* **wound·ed, wound·ing** To injure or hurt. *syn.* harm

Y

yoke [yōk] *v.* **yoked, yok·ing** To join together by a wooden frame.

INDEX OF
TITLES AND AUTHORS

Page numbers in light print refer to biographical information.

Acknowledgments continued

HarperCollins Publishers: "Pearls" from *Hey World, Here I Am!* by Jean Little. Text copyright © 1986 by Jean Little. "Is It Waiting Just for Me" from *Flower Moon Snow: A Book of Haiku* (Retitled: "Wildflower") by Kazue Mizumura. Text copyright © 1977 by Kazue Mizumura. Cover illustration by Pat Cummings from *Go Fish* by Mary Stolz. Illustration copyright © 1991 by Pat Cummings. From *Charlotte's Web* by E. B. White, illustrated by Garth Williams. Copyright 1952 by E. B. White. Text copyright renewed © 1980 by E. B. White; illustrations copyright renewed © 1980 by Garth Williams. "Runaway" from *On the Banks of Plum Creek* by Laura Ingalls Wilder, illustrated by Garth Williams. Text copyright 1937 by Laura Ingalls Wilder, renewed © 1963 by Roger L. MacBride; illustrations copyright 1953 by Garth Williams, renewed © 1981 by Garth Williams.

Holiday House: From *Totem Pole* by Diane Hoyt-Goldsmith. Text copyright © 1990 by Diane Hoyt-Goldsmith. Cover photograph by Lawrence Migdale from *Pueblo Storyteller* by Diane Hoyt-Goldsmith. Photograph copyright © 1991 by Lawrence Migdale.

Henry Holt and Company, Inc.: *On the Pampas* by María Cristina Brusca. Copyright © 1991 by María Cristina Brusca.

Houghton Mifflin Company: *Jumanji* by Chris Van Allsburg. Copyright © 1981 by Chris Van Allsburg.

Georgeanne Irvine: Cover photograph by Ron Garrison from *Raising Gordy Gorilla at the San Diego Zoo* by Georgeanne Irvine. Copyright © 1990 by Zoological Society of San Diego and Georgeanne Irvine.

Lerner Publications Company, 241 First Avenue, Minneapolis, MN 55401: From *Carnivorous Plants* by Cynthia Overbeck. Text copyright © 1982 by Lerner Publications Company.

Little, Brown and Company: "Philippe and the Blue Parrot" from *Light: Stories of a Small Kindness* by Nancy White Carlstrom. Text copyright © 1990 by Nancy White Carlstrom.

Little, Brown and Company, in conjunction with Sierra Club Books: Cover illustration from *Urban Roosts: Where Birds Nest in the City* by Barbara Bash. Copyright © 1990 by Barbara Bash.

Lodestar Books, an affiliate of Dutton Children's Books, a division of Penguin USA Inc.: Cover photograph by Richard Hewett from *Getting Elected: The Diary of a Campaign* by Joan Hewett. Photograph copyright © 1989 by Richard Hewett. "The Case of the Million Pesos" from *Encyclopedia Brown Gets His Man* by Donald J. Sobol. Text copyright © 1967 by Donald J. Sobol.

Lothrop, Lee and Shepard Books, a division of William Morrow & Company, Inc.: Cover illustration from *The Discovery of the Americas* by Betsy and Giulio Maestro. Illustration copyright © 1991 by Giulio Maestro. Cover photographs by George Ancona from *Making a New Home in America* by Maxine B. Rosenberg. Photographs copyright © 1986 by George Ancona. *Mufaro's Beautiful Daughters* by John Steptoe. Copyright © 1987 by John Steptoe. Used with the approval of the Estate of John Steptoe.

Macmillan Publishing Company: Cover illustration by Diane deGroat from *Jace the Ace* by Joanne Rocklin. Illustration copyright © 1990 by Diane deGroat. Cover illustration by Karl Swanson from *Carver* by Ruth Yaffe Radin. Illustration copyright © 1990 by Karl Swanson. Cover illustration by Jerry Pinkney from *Turtle in July* by Marilyn Singer. Illustration copyright © 1989 by Jerry Pinkney. From pp. 67-77 in *Grasshopper Summer* (Retitled: "Sailing") by Ann Turner. Text copyright © 1989 by Ann Turner.

Margaret K. McElderry Books, an imprint of Macmillan Publishing Company: "Apple Tree" from *Remembering and Other Poems* by Myra Cohn Livingston. Text copyright © 1989 by Myra Cohn Livingston. *Chin Chiang and the Dragon's Dance* by Ian Wallace. Copyright © 1984 by Ian Wallace.

McIntosh and Otis, Inc.: "The Case of the Locked Room" from *Two-Minute Mysteries* by Donald J. Sobol. Text copyright © 1967 by Donald J. Sobol. Published by Scholastic Book Services.

Morrow Junior Books, a division of William Morrow & Company, Inc.: Cover illustration by Sheila Hamanaka from *School's Out* by Johanna Hurwitz. Illustration copyright © 1991 by Sheila Hamanaka.

William Morrow & Company, Inc.: From *Aldo Ice Cream* (Retitled: "Muddy Sneakers") by Johanna Hurwitz. Text copyright © 1981 by Johanna Hurwitz. From *Class President* (Retitled: "Election Day") by Johanna Hurwitz, cover illustration by Sheila Hamanaka. Text copyright © 1990 by Johanna Hurwitz; cover illustration copyright © 1990 by Sheila Hamanaka. Cover illustration by Gail Owens from *Encyclopedia Brown and the Case of the Treasure Hunt* by Donald J. Sobol. Illustration copyright © 1988 by William Morrow & Company, Inc. and Bantam Books, Inc.

National Geographic Society: "Running With the Pack" from *National Geographic World* Magazine, February 1987. Text copyright © 1987 by National Geographic Society.

Philomel Books: "Far, Far Will I Go" from *Beyond the High Hills* by Knud Rasmussen. Text copyright © 1961 by The World Publishing Company; copyright renewed © 1989 by Guy Mary Rousseliere. Cover illustration by Ed Young from *Yeh-Shen: A Cinderella Story from China*, retold by Ai-Ling Louie. Illustration © 1982 by Ed Young.

Plays, Inc.: "Close Encounter of a Weird Kind" by A. F. Bauman from *Space and Science Fiction Plays for Young People*, edited by Sylvia E. Kamerman. Text copyright © 1981 by Plays, Inc.

Pleasant Company: Cover illustration by Renée Graef from *Meet Kirsten: An American Girl* by Janet Shaw. Illustration copyright © 1986 by Pleasant Company.

Prentice Hall, a division of Simon & Schuster, Inc.: From *Alexander the Grape: Fruit and Vegetable Jokes* (Retitled: "Fruit and Vegetable Stew") by Charles Keller. Text © 1982 by Charles Keller.

Random House Inc.: Cover illustration by Sheila Hamanaka from *The Skates of Uncle Richard* by Carol Fenner. Illustration copyright © 1990 by Sheila Hamanaka.

Roberts Rinehart Publishers, Post Office Box 666, Niwot, CO 80544: Cover illustration by Birgitta Säflund from *The People Who Hugged the Trees* by Deborah Lee Rose. Illustration copyright © 1990 by Birgitta Säflund.

Scholastic, Inc.: Cover illustration by Deborah Haeffele from *The Ring and the Window Seat* by Amy Hest. Illustration copyright © 1990 by Deborah Haeffele. "How Many Spots Does A Leopard Have?" from *How Many Spots Does A Leopard Have? and Other Tales* by Julius Lester, illustrated by David Shannon. Text copyright © 1989 by Julius Lester; illustration copyright © 1989 by David Shannon. *With Love From Koko* by Faith McNulty. Text copyright © 1990 by Faith McNulty. From *Jim Abbott: Against All Odds* (Retitled: "Growing Up") by Ellen Emerson White. Text copyright © 1990 by Ellen Emerson White.

Charles Scribner's Sons, an imprint of Macmillan Publishing Company: From pp. 45-66 in *The Cat Who Escaped from Steerage* (Retitled: "Chanah's Journey") by Evelyn Wilde Mayerson, cover illustration by Ronald Himler. Text copyright © 1990 by Evelyn Wilde Mayerson; cover illustration copyright © 1990 by Ronald Himler.

Viking Penguin, a division of Penguin Books USA Inc.: From *The Midnight Fox* (Retitled: "The Stormy Rescue") by Betsy Byars. Text copyright © 1968 by Betsy Byars. From *The Weaving of a Dream* by Marilee Heyer. Copyright © 1986 by Marilee Heyer.

Walker and Company: Cover illustration by Barbara Lavallee from *This Place Is Wet* by Vicki Cobb. Illustration © 1989 by Barbara Lavallee. Text and illustrations from *Tiger Lilies and Other Beastly Plants* by Elizabeth Ring, illustrated by Barbara Bash. Text copyright © 1984 by Elizabeth Ring; illustrations copyright © 1984 by Barbara Bash.

Sharon Wooding: Cover illustration by Sharon Wooding from *I'll Meet You at the Cucumbers* by Lilian Moore. Illustration copyright © 1988 by Sharon Wooding.

Handwriting models in this program have been used with permission of the publisher, Zaner-Bloser, Inc., Columbus, OH.

Photograph Credits

KEY: (t) top, (b) bottom, (l) left, (r) right, (c) center.

UNIT 1
20, HBJ/Britt Runion; 38(t), HBJ/Lisa Quinones for Black Star; 38–39(background), HBJ Photo; 74–75, HBJ/Britt Runion; 76, HBJ Photo; 89(t), Karl Bissinger; 96(t), The Granger Collection; 96(bl), Mark E. Gibson; 96(br), Chip & Rosa Maria Peterson.